WALK ON

WALK ON

The Spiritual Journey of

U2

STEVE STOCKMAN

Published by Relevant Books, a division of Relevant Media Group, Inc.
www.relevantbooks.com
www.relevantmediagroup.com

by Relevant Solutions (www.relevant-solutions.com)
Cover design by Mark Arnold
Interior design by Jeremy Kennedy, Joshua Smith

Printed in the United States of America

Library of Congress Control Number: 2005902180
International Standard Book Number: 0-9760357-5-8

For information or bulk orders:
RELEVANT MEDIA GROUP, INC.
100 SOUTH LAKE DESTINY DRIVE, SUITE 200
ORLANDO, FL 32810
407-660-1411

05 06 07 08 9 8 7 6 5 4 3 2 1

Printed in the United States of America

CONTENTS

ACKNOWLEDGMENTS

Let me acknowledge first of all the genius of U2's members—Bono, The Edge, Adam Clayton, and Larry Mullen Jr.—who have thrilled me with their rhythms and touched me deep in my soul, and the journalists and authors whose books and articles I have mined for background and quotations and whose work on U2 is much more insightful than mine—especially Bill Flanagan, Neil McCormick, Joe Jackson, the late Bill Graham, Liam Mackey, Robert Hilburn, Steve Turner, Niall Stokes, Sean O'Hagan, and John Waters.

Thanks also to my friends who have given me enthusiasm, little hints of insight, or resources along the way: Tim Flaherty, Tina Murphy, William Mackay, Derek Poole, Paul Bowman, Jude Adam, Graeme Thompson, Bernie Joyce, Ian Scott, Geoff Bailie, Gordon Ashbridge, Brian Houston, Mark Houston, Chris Fry, David Dark, Rick Johnston, Stephen Orr, Lorna McMahon, Gareth Dunlop, Juliet Turner, and Adrian Stewart.

More thanks than words can say to Cameron Strang and all at Relevant Media Group for taking a chance with an Irish novice they had never met. It has been an honor that I often have felt unworthy of. Thank you to Cara Davis and Tia Stauffer for patience and speed beyond the call ... we cut it mighty fine ...

Special thanks to Kyle Minor, whose fault this book is and whose patience, enthusiasm, and insightful editing shaped it and made it possible. Thanks to Melissa Bogdany, who needed much patience during the final editing.

Thank you to my students who live with me in Derryvolgie Hall in Belfast; you keep me having to sharpen my faith to meet the needs of our culture.

Thank you to all who helped with the revised edition: Cathleen Fulsani; John Cheek; Declan McConville; Bob Flayhart; Jay Swartzendruber; Kristie Franck; Martin and Heather Baxter, Beth Maynard, Ralston Bowles, Tim Bogertman, and the crew at Messiah College; Ken Heffner and the crew at Calvin College and The Festival of Faith and Music; Dal Shindell, Bob Derrenbacker, Lorene Baxter, and all at Regent College, Vancouver; Lisa Ho and the Chaplaincy at Ohio Wesleyan University; Steve Austin and the guys at Taylor University; Alex and Karoline Bettenhausen; @u2 and U2.com. Also to Rosalind Dunlop, who got unforgivably overlooked the last time.

I would like to send love to my family: to my Mum and Dad, to my in-laws and, most of all, to my long-suffering and wonderful wife, Janice, and my two incredible daughters, Caitlin and Jasmine Grace. It is over ... "come, come away, my love ..."

Steve Stockman – Belfast City

FOREWORD

BY STEVE BEARD

As a devout Los Angeles Lakers fan, I was tuned into the first game of the 2001 NBA Championships when it was announced that U2 would be performing live during the halftime show. U2's concert was in Boston while the game was being played in Los Angeles. When the cameras switched from one venue to the other, television viewers saw Bono praying on his knees.

"What can I give back to God for the blessings He poured out on me?" he said. "I lift high the cup of salvation as a toast to our Father. To follow through on the promise I made to you." The lead singer of arguably the most popular rock band on the planet was loosely reciting a prayer from Psalm 116 on national television.

In describing U2's 2001 Elevation tour to *Rolling Stone* magazine, Bono said fans had told him they sensed "good vibrations" at the concerts. "God is in the room," he reported, paused, and added, "more than Elvis. It feels like there's a blessing on the band right now. People are saying they're feeling shivers—well, the band is as well. And I don't know what that is, but it feels like God walking through the room, and it feels like a blessing, and in the end, music is a kind of sacrament; it's not just about airplay or chart positions."

Are rock 'n' roll bands supposed to talk to *Rolling Stone* about blessings? Sacraments? God walking in the room? Why would this all sound so incredibly cliché coming from a well-scrubbed contemporary Christian rocker created by Nashville, yet actually sound sincere and authentic coming from a theatrical rock star?

Bono has the reputation as rock 'n' roll's most effective and enigmatic spiritual provocateur—rattling the souls of fans all over the globe. "I sometimes think I have a kind of Tourette's Syndrome where if you're not supposed to say something, it becomes very attractive to do so," he once confessed. "You're in a rock band—what can't you talk about? God? OK, here we go. You're supposed to write songs about sex and drugs. Well, no, I won't."

Most of the world is tired of being berated and tutored about social issues by spoiled and overpaid rock stars, yet we still give an audience to Bono, whose heart bleeds with the best of them. Pope John Paul II wanted to wear his sunglasses when they met. Arch-conservative senator Jesse Helms cried when he heard Bono describe the plight of hungry children in Africa. Bono has done more single-handedly to relieve Third World debt than all the Armani-clad finance ministers that could be packed into a United Nation's conference room. He has a mysterious charisma, an unpretentious grace that affords him the ability to be the only one wearing sunglasses indoors without coming off as a megalomaniac. Would one dare to say he had an anointing to be a rock star?

It seems as though there is a riddle to unwrapping the significance, relevance, and longevity of U2. Very little is ever predictable about their next sound. They never seem to follow rock 'n' roll's party line. They seem to be in the MTV world, but not of it. There is an underground river of depth that rolls through the tracks of U2's recordings. They make you think and invite you to imagine.

For more than twenty years, U2 has done their part to puncture the power of nihilism and hopelessness by pointing listeners to a transcendent reality of heaven, hell, angels, demons, deliverance, redemption, grace, and peace. Their lyrics unfold a world beyond the things that can be merely seen and rationally grasped. The music is not a simplistic mish-mash of yummy lyrics about skipping with Jesus through fields of daisies. Instead, their songs wrestle with pain and frustration without catering to hopelessness.

In this book, Steve Stockman has been a faithful interpreter of the spiritual trek of the members of U2. There is very little garden-variety evangelicalism (in the North American sense of the word) found in the members of the band. They drink, smoke, swear, and wear leather pants. But there is a hefty and poetic theological substance that I think would startle Saint Paul and would bring a smile to the psalmist. This rock 'n' roll band is committed to social justice and eternal truth. In this day and age, that is no small luxury.

For those willing to take the time to look, popular music is brimming with songs of spiritually energized quests—some worth avoiding, but many worth engaging. Artists and fans alike have seen what is on the world's buffet table and are still growling with hunger pangs. Stockman does a tremendous service to those who follow Jesus, as well as those who aren't traveling that path. To those who count themselves among the faithful, Stockman will help you open the eyes of your soul to intellectually and spiritually engage the music that touches the deepest part of what it means to be human. To those who do not consider themselves believers, this book will go a long way in helping explain why U2's music seems to scratch an unidentifiable itch.

When I saw U2 during their Elevation tour, I was amazed at how often I felt the presence of God in the arena. Granted, I am a U2 fan and not a terribly objective rock critic. Nevertheless, God used the opportunity to speak to me throughout the night. Not being a well-attuned mystic, I was rather surprised. The culmination of the evening was the final encore. After thanking "the Almighty" numerous times, Bono began singing "hallelujah" over and over and over again. This rather contagious melody and message rang throughout the audience's soul. Soon, it seemed as though all sixteen-thousand fans in the arena were singing the song with Bono. This one word: *hallelujah*—praise ye the Lord. With that, they walked off the stage.

The great theologian George Eldon Ladd used to press the point that the kingdom of God was both already and not yet; some of the ramifications of the kingdom are realized now, while some will not be manifest until the Second Coming. As I sang "hallelujah" over and over with the audience, I felt as though, just for a moment, I had been caught up in the rapturous not yet.

As the band was just starting off many years ago, Bono wrote the following words to his father, who has now passed away:

> [God] gives us our strength and a joy that does not depend on drink or drugs. This strength will, I believe, be the quality that will take us to the top of the music business. I hope our lives will be a testament to the people who follow us, and to the music business where never before have so many lost and sorrowful people gathered in one place pretending they're having a good time. It is our ambition to make more than good music.

It seems as though that ambition continues to be fulfilled.

Steve Beard is the editor of *Good News* magazine and is the founder of *thunderstruck.org*.

chapter 01

THREE QUESTIONS FOR BONO

If I could ask Bono three questions, what would they be? I was asked that question while speaking at the Greenbelt Arts Festival in England. The first response that came to mind was a question my friend David Dark has had ready for the moment he might find himself in a lift with Bono: "How much Flannery O'Connor have you read?" Cool. Intellectual engagement.

I also would be intrigued to know how long it took to come up with the live extravaganza that was the Zoo TV tour. I would love to be talked through its development from the initial inspiration to the opening night and the tweaking thereafter.

The main question, though, is one that has been like a dog at my heels for the last couple of years. During that time I have watched the passion with which Bono has involved himself in the Jubilee 2000 campaign to get rid of Third World debt; I have listened to the spiritual depth of the *All That You Can't Leave Behind* album; I have seen the band reconquer the world on its Elevation tour, ending with thanks to the Almighty and a chorus of "hallelujahs." The question: "How have you kept the vitality of your Christian faith so vibrant in the world of rock music and in the absence of regular Christian fellowship?" It is for me one of the most fascinating questions of the amazing story of U2, perhaps still the biggest rock band in the world almost twenty-five years after being formed.

Within the Christian community of which three of U2's four members were once a part, however, my question is more likely to receive much cynicism and be bypassed by more basic questions.

"Somebody told me that the members of U2 were once Christians. Is that true?"

"Where do you think they stand on their faith now?"

"I saw Bono dressed up as the devil. How can a Christian do that?"

"They seem ashamed of the Gospel, and that is no way for Christians to be! How can they be that way if they're Christians?"

"They drink and smoke and swear. How can you believe that they are still Christians?"

"If they say that they haven't found what they are looking for, they cannot possibly still be believers in Christ, can they?"

No matter where I go, when people know I am a Presbyterian minister from Ireland, once I throw in the name U2, there is a reaction. I have found myself in heated discussions in the United States, South Africa, The Philippines, and many, many times back home in Ireland. The axis of the discussion has more recently moved to cyberspace. Judging by reaction to articles on my website, I have what can be described as red rags to a bull dangled in my feedback section. Are they Christians?

The vast majority of U2 interviews and reviews over the past twenty years touch or often concentrate on the Christian faith that is so much a part of what the band is. Their faith isn't ridiculed. It has never been questioned, though how they keep it with the rock lifestyle has often been a fascination. The Christian press and Christians in general have been the doubters. There seems to have been a keen enthusiasm to denounce the band's Christian members as lost. There has been confusion as to what they have tried to do in the nineties and condemnation on their lifestyles, which include smoking cigars, drinking Jack Daniels, and using language that is not common currency at Southern Baptist conventions. The Christian community seems to have confined its definitions of faith to various precise behavioral patterns and clichéd statements of faith. In getting caught up in the minutia of behavioral codes that have had more to do with respectable middle-class behavior than biblical guidelines, many have been so obsessed with the cigar hanging out of Bono's mouth that they are missing the radical biblical agenda that has fired his life and work.

MANY HAVE BEEN SO OBSESSED WITH THE CIGAR HANGING OUT OF BONO'S MOUTH THAT THEY ARE MISSING THE RADICAL BIBLICAL AGENDA THAT HAS FIRED HIS LIFE AND WORK.

That the band members have distanced themselves from the Church for various reasons over the years has, of course, added fuel to the fire for doubters. That the band has been adamant in not speaking to the Christian press has not helped. But in the very early days when the band did speak to Christian magazines, they were often misquoted and felt used and abused. The evangelical Christian world seemed to claim U2 as its property, and, therefore, U2's members found their faith defined and explained by magazines rather than by the members themselves. Aligning themselves with the Christian press would have pigeonholed their faith and their art, squeezed them into the mold of other peoples' expectations, and narrowed the focus of the band's influence and scope. In their work, however—whether on records, on stage, on video, or in interviews—they have never denied their faith, even if at times they have questioned how that faith fits with the events of their generation. They have constantly kept spiritual issues at the heart of all they have done, whether looking at the light or the darkness around them.

U2 inhabits that dangerous and exhilarating space that connects spiritual and physical, mortal and divine. The band's music stretches every sinew of our imaginations in a most courageous attempt to take us as far as a rock 'n' roll band can. The members of U2 have filled every millimeter of the gap with the most profound social commentaries, exposing the nonsense of postmodern life. Inside and outside the lines of their art, they have campaigned for a spiritual kingdom that they believe in but still haven't found.

U2 INHABITS THAT DANGEROUS AND EXHILARATING SPACE THAT CONNECTS SPIRITUAL AND PHYSICAL, MORTAL AND DIVINE.

Bruce Springsteen once wrote that he learned more from a three-minute record than he ever learned in school. U2 has been my lecture hall of learning for twenty years. These guys have lifted my spirit to dance on higher plains, taught me about American injustice in Central America and apartheid in South Africa, and personified how faith and the world continually caress and collide. They have led me into an understanding of what the postmodern technological world looks like and the shallow and fickle nature of the madness in which we live. A madness that is no more frenetic or bright or loud than the Zoo TV or Popmart tours.

This book is not a new exposé of U2 or a comprehensive biography of the members' lives. It is a spiritual companion to their career. It is an attempt at telling the story of the band members' journeys of faith and exposing the underlying spiritual themes in U2's music. In examining these issues, it is also essential to take a look at evangelical Christianity—the stream of faith that has both undergirded the band's work and caused them to react in anger and disillusionment when people of faith have seemed more concerned with appearances than with just responses to human suffering.

It is impossible to understand U2's perspectives toward the world, especially in the band's early work, without also understanding the unique political, religious, and social climate of Northern Ireland in the late seventies and early eighties. It was a country torn by civil unrest and barbaric inhumanity in the name of God and country. The country's troubles have had a significant impact on U2 over the years because they hit close to home: Northern Ireland is located only seventy miles from the band members' boyhood homes in Dublin.

To fully understand someone, you must first understand where they come from. Aside from the restlessness of Northern Ireland, you must also understand the makeup of the band's homeland in the Republic. You must understand the spiritual and musical climate of Dublin. It is an unlikely setting for this story, but probably the only one that could give birth to one of the greatest rock bands the world would ever know.

chapter 02

DUBLIN CITY, IRELAND

Dublin City, Ireland, might have been the last place that such a thing would be expected to happen, but it was conceivably the only place in the English-speaking Western world that the U2 phenomenon of conundrum could have been minted. Some people joke that if you ask an Irishman for directions, he might be quick to answer, "Well if I were going there, I would not start here." At the end of the seventies, if you wanted to audition for the job of biggest rock band on the planet, you would not have started in music-starved Dublin.

Yet when *Hot Press* journalist Bill Graham began championing U2 seventeen months before it released its first single, there was something about the band that suggested, or near prophesied, that they were destined to go places. Even in that first article, while the band members were still at school, Graham used words such as "contenders," "professional," and "vocation." The band members, too, had an almost arrogant belief in their destiny. In their first mention in *Rolling Stone* magazine in February 1981, lead singer Bono said, "I don't mean to sound arrogant, but at this stage, I do feel we were meant to be one of the great groups. There's a certain spark, a certain chemistry, that was special about the Stones, The Who, the Beatles and I think is also special about U2."[1]

U2 WAS NOT THE RESULT OF SUCH A HEALTHY MUSIC SCENE. IT WAS THE CAUSE OF IT.

Ten years later, in 1991, Dublin had become one of the coolest cities in Europe and was chosen the European City of Culture. As a result of a government scheme encouraging the rich and famous to spend their money there and granting tax-exemption to artists, many rock stars were happy to make it their home. Dublin was dubbed the city of a thousand bands. On every street corner, somebody was trying to make it in the music business. The Hot House Flowers, Emotional Fish, Fat Lady Sings and Engine Alley were just a few of the bands signed to major international deals as the city on the banks of the Liffey became what Liverpool had been in the early sixties. Of course, few of these bands broke out from their parochial popularity, but at the beginning of the third millennium you will find Irish acts dominating U.K. music charts. Names like Ronan Keating and his old band Boyzone, Westlife, and Bewitched have the teen market sown up. And, of course, The Corrs, The Cranberries and the infamous Sinead O'Connor have achieved worldwide success.

U2 was not the result of such a healthy music scene. It was the cause of it. When CBS released U2's first vinyl record, an EP titled *U2-3* in Ireland in September 1979, there was little happening in the way of Irish rock. In the Republic, Rory Gallagher and Thin Lizzy had reached beyond the shores but could hardly have been said to be on a world stage. A year earlier, The Boomtown Rats' song "Rat Trap" reached number one on U.K. single charts—the first Irish band to achieve this. The Rats' breakthrough raised the hopes of Dublin bands, but to have ideas of grandeur was still to fantasize against the odds rather than be an inheritor of any kind of birthright.

Yet Dublin's punk scene was burgeoning, giving many young wannabes the energy to make noise and dream big. And though it never could have been labeled as such, U2 arrived on the slipstream of New Wave adrenaline. Through the band's passionate live shows and the charismatic antics of its frontman, the band got noticed. Their manager, Paul McGuinness, discovered them playing The Project and later said it was not their competence, but their raw energy that drew him. By the time Bono, The Edge, Adam Clayton, and Larry Mullen Jr. released their debut album, *Boy*, in October 1980, there was no limit to people's predictions for the group.

The reason? *Boy* shone with originality. Producer Steve Lillywhite had harnessed the promise of the band's early singles. Everything was built around a ringing guitar sound that The Edge conjured through a cheap Memory Man echo unit that Bono had bought him. It was with that sound that they began to build an album and, some would say, a career. *Boy* was vibrant, passionate, lively. It had a sense of searching restlessness that would best describe the adolescence that the lyrics attempted to tackle and would be a trait that followed these guys into manhood.

Bono said the album's song "Twilight" was "about the gray area of adolescence, that twilight zone where the boy that was confronts the man to be in the shadows. It is about the confusion, pain and occasional exhilaration that results from that confrontation."[2] If ever a guitarist could take that sentiment and put it through an amplifier, it was The Edge. That's what *Boy* is all about.

When it comes to songwriting, Bono would admit that he didn't discover the art until the group's 1987 release, *The Joshua Tree*. But in U2's early albums, he was able to reach deep within himself and find lyrics that expressed what his peers were feeling. It was his honesty more than his literary ability that made *Boy* so endearing. Whether it was dealing with suicide on "A Day Without Me" and seeing his own ego being surrendered (a recurring theme for U2), or youthful dreaming of stardom and changing the world in "The Ocean," or confronting his mother's death on "I Will

Follow," a young man was dealing with his world eye to eye. Looking at life in the eye would become a trademark of Bono's lyric-writing.

At the time, U2 would always dismiss the band's punk influence. At their early gigs, they would make it a point to cover songs by the likes of Peter Frampton, the Rolling Stones and even the Bay City Rollers—and nothing by The Undertones, Stiff Little Fingers or the Sex Pistols. It would be more than twenty years before U2 would turn to the punk catalog, when in 2000 the band name-checked the New York scene of the late seventies and played "I Remember You" by the Ramones at The Irving Plaza in New York City. Joey Ramone passed away a few months later during the first leg of the Elevation tour, and there would be much eulogizing. The Edge told the *Chicago Tribune*: "We didn't sound like the Ramones, but what we got from The Ramones was more fundamental and central: They were the reason we became a band. Having seen the Ramones play, and then The Clash soon after, it was like, 'Whoa! We can be part of this. These guys have done it their way, and we will find our way.' There was sense that the door of possibility had swung wide open."[3]

Punk may have been the musical motivation behind *Boy*, but there was another significant dimension to the band members' work—their Christian faith. During Bill Graham's first full-length interview with Bono, he stunned Graham by announcing abruptly, "One other thing you should know ... we're all Christians."[4] U2's bass player, Adam, was not a Christian, but he was an exception to the rule in that group. Graham expressed concern about this revelation in his book *Another Time, Another Place*: "I, a typically Irish ex-Catholic agnostic, feared for their reputation. Born-again Christianity could hinder their career—a view which, the more I pondered it, was riven with illogicalities."[5] Those fears were well-founded, but had the band been from anywhere but Dublin, there would have been less chance of overcoming such hindrances.

Many other young Christians have tried to make it in the world of rock music and failed for many reasons. But it is not necessarily the worldview of

Christianity that is the obstacle so much as it is the isolated subculture that the Church has created. Dublin was a city where U2's new, young, zealous believers were not going to get drawn into any Church subculture.

Since its start, U2 has lived its art in the eye of a storm that has been kicking up dust since the days Jesus walked the streets of earth. In Jesus' day, the Pharisees strictly differentiated between what was sacred and what was profane. Today in the United States and Northern Ireland—two places of particular reference to U2—there is a similar dualism at work, and it has put bands like U2 under pressure regarding where they perform and what they say.

If U2 had been in fellowship in the United States or even just sixty miles north of Dublin, in Northern Ireland, it would have been easy to get sucked into a Christian subculture. Many bands in similar situations are discouraged from playing in secular venues like bars or clubs because Christians shouldn't be in these places. The theory is that you shouldn't take Jesus into what are often called "dens of iniquity." The only acceptable reason for attending these places would be to evangelize the lost who go there.

As a result of this mindset, many talented musicians are steered into a gospel band scenario, going from church to church singing cliché-driven songs with limited content. The audience members are almost exclusively Christian, and, as the majority of them already have assented to the beliefs being preached from the stage, the clichés are wasted. A safe Christian industry ghetto is created with pop stars and record companies. There is a magazine, *Contemporary Christian Music*, which has become the label for the entire industry—an industry that is always in danger of ending up culturally irrelevant. When Jesus told His disciples they were the light of the world, where did He want them to shine (Matt. 5:14)? As more beams of light that make the light shine blindingly bright upon itself, or as strobes of illumination flashing radical alternative lifestyles across the darkness? Do you blame the dark for being dark, or the light for not shining?

In the early eighties, Os Guinness, one of the most intellectual Christian writers of our time, wrote a book titled *The Gravedigger File*. Based on C.S. Lewis' *The Screwtape Letters*, a book that would sneak its way into the U2 story, it was written from the viewpoint of a senior devil outlining the strategy of subverting the Church from within. One of the most powerful schemes for doing this would be to make Christianity "privately engaging but socially irrelevant."[6] Christians can have all the energy and resources that the Church can muster, which can be enormous, but if they spend all their time looking in at themselves rather than looking out, the devil will be pleased. It's why Christian singer Rich Mullins signed all his autographs "Be God's." He was aware that people could "be good" and still make the devil smile with their ineffectualness.

U.K.'s Delirious? is an example of a band that has suffered from the constraints of the Christian industry ghetto. Emerging out of a community church scene on the south coast of England, Delirious? has been trying to crack the U.K. mainstream for years. Originally experimenting in their local youth group, the members of Delirious? discovered a worship sound that drew a following far beyond that group. Soon they began filling major venues across Britain and entered the U.K. Top Twenty with "Deeper," as radio-friendly a pop rock tune as any.

However, even though their future single "See a Star" reached number sixteen and their *Mezzamorphis* album reached number thirteen, they seem to have been shunned by Top of the Pops, Radio 1, and the other major media support that could propel them into the higher plains of rock stardom and influence. There could be various reasons for the stumbling block. Their first album that attempted to break new ground, *King of Fools*, might have had too many references rooted in the ghetto, dealing with spiritual issues that critics and secular music fans might not have been able to understand. Maybe they had a rabid little bunch of paranoid fans who believed their favorites were being prejudiced against because of their faith and made nuisances of themselves to editors and programmers. Or maybe those fans were right; maybe it is easier to be accepted in the mainstream if you are Buddhist or Muslim than if you are followers of Jesus.

Whatever the reason, U2 did not face such difficulties because in Dublin there was no such Christian ghetto and, therefore, no such exclusively Christian fan base. They were not in any need to break out of one thing to crack the other.

The Republic of Ireland is 96 percent Roman Catholic, and the evangelical subculture is predominantly Protestant. The fact that U2, looking at the members' parents, was five-eighths Protestant is a phenomenon in itself, but that they formed a band and discovered a fervent evangelicalism at the same time without getting caught up in some kind of dualism was only possible because of their location. With Irish evangelicals so small in number, integration of faith and daily living is vital. There are no Christian venues for budding Christians trying to do something in rock. If you do not make it in the real world, you do not make it.

"ONE OTHER THING YOU SHOULD KNOW ... WE'RE ALL CHRISTIANS." —BONO

So while the three teenage Christian members of U2—Bono, The Edge, and Larry—were immersing themselves in Bible studies and beginning to make efforts to create an impression in the local music scene, Bono and The Edge were also running around with a motley group of eccentric, young, wild boys called Lypton Village. It was the Village that gave Bono and The Edge their names. The other band in the musical fraternity, the Virgin Prunes, wore eye makeup and dresses and had a wild performance art-type set. Some of these guys, too, were passionate about a newfound Christian faith, and in these early days, there seems to have been no contradictions in that.

At the earliest point in U2's formative years, spirituality and music were allowed to run together. Few bands with three such impassioned and fervent new believers would have had the freedom from within and without to record an album like *Boy* on their time off from Bible studies. *Boy* is about adolescence and the benefits of being unshackled by missionary expectations, which would try to weigh them down without success, as they pushed out from Dublin to conquer the world.

On *Boy*, "I Will Follow" is the song that perhaps best touches on the faith within the band. Bono uses a phrase from Jesus' parable of the prodigal son, whose father told him he was lost and is now found. As he would do seventeen years later on "Mofo" from the group's *Pop* album, Bono was interweaving the loss of his mother and finding God. "I Will Follow" would be their most enduring song. It's a song about adolescent tragedy as well as discipleship, skillfully disguised but just as powerful. This type of skillful disguise would become another trademark of U2's work.

In Howard Sounes' biography of Bob Dylan, *Down the Highway*, band member T-Bone Burnett spoke of Dylan's conversion to Christ: "Beginning in 1976, something happened all across the world. It happened to Bono and The Edge and Larry Mullens (of U2) in Ireland. It happened to Michael Hutchence (of INXS) in Australia, and it happened here in Los Angeles: There was spiritual movement."[7] Burnett himself was converted to Christianity, along with fellow band members Steven Soles and David Mansfield on Bob Dylan's Rolling Thunder Review tour. INXS did play the Australian Christian circuit for a short time, though how spiritual their reasons for doing so is a little blurred. Dylan himself would confess faith in Christ, too. There is little doubt that something unique and out of the blue was happening in Dublin. Bono was the first to find God, and it seems he was the one who led the others into charismatic and evangelical Christianity by way of the Shalom fellowship.

Bono had a few encounters with Christianity. As a child, he regularly visited his neighbors, the Rowans. Robbie Rowan was a member of the Brethren. His son Derek, nicknamed Guggi, was one of Bono's early accomplices. Guggi later became one of the Virgin Prunes, along with Bono's soul brother, Gavin Friday. Trevor "Strongman" Rowan was also a Prune, and his younger brother Peter was later the cover face of *Boy* and *War*. Bono would go to Bible studies and revival meetings with the Rowans and attend a Boys Club at the YMCA.

If what was happening on his street nudged Bono God-ward, what was happening in his school gave him a shove. Mount Temple was a liberally minded seat of learning that was experimental in being the first nondenominational school in a country that was still in the grips of the Roman Catholic Church. The school attracted progressive and creative teachers, most of whom had a more open view of Church things and some of whom had a free and serious commitment to Christian faith. One such teacher was Sophie Shirley, whom Bono once described as someone who "really showed us what God can do in someone's life, and although we fought against her and threw bricks at her and stoned her in the name of adolescent freedom, we all inwardly respected her, and she had a deep effect on us."[8]

In the late seventies, something spectacular was happening in Mount Temple. The school had just changed its name and ethos from the traditional gown-wearing Rugby school Mountjoy and Marine to this new progressive experiment. Change was in the air. Prayer meetings were taking place every morning, and at lunchtime, upward of one hundred students would meet for praise. There were barbecues on the beach at Rush, north county Dublin, at which Bono was known to do a campfire version of the popular Christian chorus "Light Up the Fire." Many of the prefects were Christians, and the prefects' room became another location for God chat and fellowship. Everywhere you turned, it seemed people were becoming Christians.

A respected teacher at the school, Jack Heaslip, offered support and sympathy to Bono. Being a believer in Christ in any way other than having been baptized and confirmed and going to Mass once a week would have been a bit weird in late seventies Dublin. Heaslip seemed to have great empathy with Bono and would be an encouragement to the spiritual happenings at that time. Heaslip later became a Church of Ireland minister and performed the marriage ceremony of Bono and his childhood sweetheart, Alison Stewart, whom he met at Mount Temple in 1982. Bono continues to thank him on album sleeves, and he continued to go on the road with the band even to the start of its 2001 Elevation tour.

Don Moxham, a history teacher at the school who also developed relationships with his students, struck up a friendship with the boys in U2. They had many long "talk sessions." Moxham believed teaching was as important in the informal interconnections as in the classroom. Moxham was a positive influence on his students—especially these fledgling musicians. He was no charismatic, but he had a deep faith and would touch U2 for years to come. Musically, Albert Bradshaw, like Moxham, went beyond his duties to inspire especially The Edge to develop his love of music, technical ability, and exploration of melodies and chords.

FOR MANY YEARS THE BAND MEMBERS SAID THAT THEIR FAITH—NOT THEIR ROCK 'N' ROLL LIFESTYLE—WAS THE REAL REBELLION.

Bill Graham suggests that the spiritually liberal Mount Temple reinforced U2's faith in God. He suggests that had the guys gone to a traditional Catholic school instead, they would have turned to the anti-Catholic agnostic ways of himself, their manager Paul McGuinness, or Boomtown Rats' Bob Geldof.

One incident led to a few of the U2 members becoming Christians, according to The Edge. While some in their teenage gang, Lypton Village, were in McDonald's one afternoon, a Hare Krishna began abusing a man who was reading the Bible. When the boys joined the man, Denis

Sheedy, partly out of curiosity and maybe to support him, they struck up a friendship. It was because of this that they started to attend the Shalom community.

Bono had been searching in that direction for a while before Larry and The Edge. Soon after meeting Sheedy, they were going to Bible studies and prayer group gatherings. The Edge said: "There was sort of a move in Dublin in those early days. Bono was the only real Christian then. He started sharing his feelings and thoughts about God. And it seemed a natural progression from what was happening in school to go along to the meetings outside school. I realized that that was where it was at, and about the same time, Larry and I became Christians."[9]

Writer John Waters asked Bono in 1993 if he had always been a believer. Bono replied, "No. I knew." He explained the great attraction that liberating faith was to him. "I suppose it's the idea," Bono replied. "Judeo Christianity is about the idea that God is interested in you—as opposed to a god is interested in you. This was a radical thought: that God who created the universe might be interested in me ... It is the most extraordinary thought."[10]

The idea of it being radical attracted U2. In any other city in the Western world, this kind of Christian behavior would have been seen as old-fashioned and almost nerdish. In any other city, Bono would have laughed at such middle-class, respectable, religious behavior. But in Dublin, this was radical stuff. To take Jesus seriously was far out. In some ways, Shalom was an out-there kind of gang on parallel lines with the Lypton Village gang. It wasn't as if one of them was dangerous and the other one safe.

For many years the band members said that their faith—not their rock 'n' roll lifestyle—was the real rebellion. In 1983, Bono told *Rolling Stone*: "I think that, ultimately, the group is totally rebellious because of our stance against what people accept as rebellion. The whole thing about rock stars driving cars into swimming pools—that's not rebellion ... Rebellion starts at home, in your heart, in your refusal to compromise your beliefs and your values. I'm not interested in politics like people fighting back with sticks and stones, but in the politics of love."[11] For this band, it was more rebellious to be reading Bibles in the back of the tour bus than it was to be doing drugs—a perspective on Christianity that was not a cultural norm. But being from a place where those with intense spiritual faith were the minority helped the band members grab hold of the radical edge of following Jesus.

Over the last twenty years, U2's music and discussion of its own Christian freedoms have made an impression on the spiritual landscape of modern Dublin. There have been huge changes in how young Dubliners look at God and faith. In what is a traditionally Roman Catholic country, young people have increasingly voiced a strong belief in Jesus even though they rarely go to Mass. Belief has become much more personal and not restricted to the voice of traditional church hierarchy.

The guys in U2 have made their faith in Jesus Christ known. They have made it clear that though they had feet in both camps of Ireland's denominational divide, they found a personal relationship with God outside of both. For two decades, U2 has seemed suspicious of any organized religion. The band members have believed their faith lived and thrived outside the narrow gates of religion. Bono once said, "I have this hunger in me ... everywhere I look, I see the evidence of a Creator. But I don't see it as religion, which has cut my people in two. I don't see Jesus Christ as being any part of a religion. Religion to me is almost like when God leaves—and people devise a set of rules to fill the space."[12]

chapter 03

OCTOBER

U2's second album, *October*, landed on critics' desks "with a shout"—as one of its songs is titled—in August 1981. The shout was a cry of strong spiritual confession—so strong, in fact, that Neil McCormick's review in *Hot Press* called *October* "a Christian LP."[1] With titles like "Gloria" and "Rejoice" and mentions of the cross in "Tomorrow" and "With a Shout (Jerusalem)," the songs dig deep with a passionate searching and reach out to the heavens in a way that is highly intoxicating. Rarely has Christianity collided with rock music in such force or with such rich reward. *October* was the first declaration to the outside world of the spiritual twist in the U2 story.

U2 had been garnering a rabid little following from its extensive live gigging, but *Boy* had not exactly broken any sales records. This second album surely would have to capture the kind of response their charismatic performances were receiving. Could the spiritual preoccupations of *October* be accepted? The unveiling of these new Christian anthems came when U2 was the supporting act to Thin Lizzy in a concert at Slane Castle, on the banks of the Boyne River north of Dublin. The band members hurled themselves into their set, singing about Jerusalem crosses on hills and blood being spilled. It was bold and zealous. There was uncertainty in the crowd—perhaps more than new material typically draws. But by the time they got to "Gloria" and "Rejoice," the audience seemed to get past the band's evangelical zeal. They seemed to realize that even though they were not sure about this subject matter, they were going to get on board the great ride of celebratory rock music that made this band the most exciting around.

It could not have been seen as a cunning plan or a shrewd marketing ploy to bring such a Christian-focused album into a rock world that was usually dismissive of such things. There were few artists who had ever been able to effectively hold their Christian faith before a rock music audience. Cliff Richard, Britain's equivalent of Elvis Presley, cashed in his rebellious sneering lip for a laughed-at, respectable smile when he went public about his conversion in the mid-sixties. Bob Dylan won a Grammy Award for the song "Gonna Serve Somebody" from his Christian album, *Slow Train Coming*, two years earlier, but his more recent albums *Saved* and *Shot of Love* did not meet with a sympathetic press. Many saw it as a nail in the coffin of his career.

Hot Press, the Irish music paper that has followed U2's career through journalists Bill Graham, Niall Stokes, Neil McCormick, and Joe Jackson, has defined the band's history. *Hot Press* discovered U2 and was the champion of the cause, even though it has not given much good press to anything related to Christianity. The paper constantly takes cheap swipes at the Roman Catholic Church, the predominant religion in the Republic of Ireland. The scandals within that religion and its conservative approach to birth control, abortion, and divorce have made it an antithesis of the progressive rock culture that has developed in Ireland in the *Hot Press* years. That this paper took the crusading Christian U2 to its heart is an exception to its rule.

The exuberance and vitality of the sound U2 cast across Dublin was enough to see the band through any misunderstandings of its faith-infused music. That the band was local and seemed destined for megastardom may have helped. That U2 had been discovered by the fledgling music paper perhaps gave the band a whole lot of grace. That the band's school friend Neil McCormick reviewed it may have added to the sympathetic coverage of *October*. But whatever the reasons, the music press chose to deal with the incongruity of the band's blatant faith on a quality rock album rather than simply dismissing it. It might be a lesson to Christians who feel the music press is prejudiced against them: if you make great music, the content will not hinder it.

Behind the scenes, the band members themselves were trying to come to terms with whether they would deal with it or dismiss it. Bono, Larry, and The Edge had become more involved in the Shalom fellowship. They were just twenty years old and had discovered their faith amid an enflamed charismatic revival. Questions of ego and fame and the seemingly trivial pursuit of rock music were beginning to arise. There seemed to be a wind of change within the Shalom community and its leadership. Remember, the Lypton Villagers had lived parallel to and relatively comfortably with Shalom. But somewhere along the way, there was a closing in of behavioral patterns. It may have been that the great evangelical movement on the cusp of which the Villagers joined the fellowship was more sympathetic to their weaknesses and quirks in order to draw them in. Once involved, when things again returned to normal and regular fellowship numbers, then the legalists began to turn the screw.

While the band was on tour between *Boy* and the recording of *October*, a member of the north Dublin satellite of the community claimed to have a prophecy that God wanted the band to give up. When the band members returned to the fellowship, which at that time they craved and thrived upon, they were looking forward to the support of their spiritual family. Instead, they entered a tense situation where the fellowship was split over whether God wanted U2 to carry on or pack up their instruments.

In his book *Faraway So Close* about the exploits around the Zoo TV tour, B.P. Fallon recalls a morning when after recording and without a key to his own hotel room in Dublin, Bono, Gavin Friday, and he had a fry up in a café off Capel Street. Upon their return to Bono's car, the singer showed them a place where, he said, "I used to go to revival meetings there ... the place would be on fire! Studying the Bible, that kind of stuff. I miss it ... "[2] Given that Bono, The Edge, and Larry were young kids caught up in such a fire, it is little wonder that their souls were in turmoil as they attempted to untangle their future. The miracle is probably that they came out of it and decided to go on. The pressure could have easily deafened out the music. They saw it as a pull between the world and the Lord, but it seems that it may have been a pull between the devil and the deep blue sea. The question of the usefulness of rock music and art in general has been a huge debate within Christendom for some time. If The Edge, Bono, and Larry had been coming under the influence of such preaching, it would be understandable that when the same young exuberance that was rocking the world at that time was channeled into thinking about Christ, there would be an intense focus on the dilemma.

QUESTIONS OF EGO AND FAME AND THE SEEMINGLY TRIVIAL PURSUIT OF ROCK MUSIC WERE BEGINNING TO ARISE.

This is where the downside of their isolation kicked in. Though the lack of Christian industry ghetto in Dublin helped them from having their art curtailed, it hurt when they needed advice from other Christians in the arts. They made an unannounced appearance at the Greenbelt Arts Festival in England in August 1981. Greenbelt has long been the biggest Christian arts festival in Europe and has been a pioneer in encouraging Christians to take their art out of the ghetto. The band made some lifelong connections at Greenbelt, and the event, though Bono would only make one more appearance there as a steward, would ease their sense of spiritual loneliness.

Andy McCarroll, the top Christian singer in Belfast, was someone whom the band respected and listened to at the time. He had made two Dylan-inspired solo albums in the late seventies before becoming excited by New Wave and forming Moral Support. With some of the rawness left over from punk and McCarroll's snarling voice, the group performed some intelligent Christian songs. It seems The Edge was especially taken with McCarroll's magnetic stage presence, natural songwriting ability, and the spiritual intensity of the production. The Edge would eventually invite McCarroll to Dublin for a weekend just to shoot the breeze about the purpose of what they were trying to achieve.

In a twist, McCarroll's spiritual support base decided that Moral Support should come off the road in early 1982. The group's first album, *Zionic Bonds*, had sold well. The band was filling any venue in Northern Ireland. The members had been high up the bill at the Greenbelt that U2 attended and were on the verge of opening up all kinds of possibilities worldwide. Then there was a change in attitude with the leadership of their fellowship. In Ireland in the early eighties, there were many fellowship groups like Shalom that had started outside of any accountability of established churches. One of the trends was to set in place pastoral care that became much too strict and controlling. The pastor told people what decisions to make in their everyday lives. Some even had a shepherding system where everyone was designated someone to whom to be accountable.

The leaders in Moral Support's Belfast fellowship felt, maybe as a result of difficulties, that the band was not able to cope spiritually with the life of a rock band on the road. Like a car needing an overhaul, the band was asked "to come off the road for a time" until everything was put right. There was an errant but fashionable Christian virtue then that suggested that "laying it down for the Lord," especially while so successful, would be the righteous thing to do. The fame and the danger of getting caught up in the adulation could lead to compromise. There was also a strange slant on discipleship, which called people to surrender what they were good at or enjoyed. McCarroll was a gifted songwriter with a natural flare for pop melodies and a gripping live presence. He didn't perform another song for more than a decade and, in the end, had personal and spiritual crises that may be attributed to a church's decision to take him away from his vocation. The same thing happened to another charismatic Belfast performer, Brian Houston, a few years later. Houston, however, after a few years of frustration and dissatisfaction with his post-musical life, went against his church leader's advice and returned to the stage, pioneered a booming Belfast club scene as well as later becoming an internationally known worship leader. U2 would have lived with that kind of news and peer pressure filtering through the Irish charismatic fellowships.

It would be wrong to suggest that these are not serious issues that need to be dealt with. To be a Christian and to find that you are a gifted musician with a contemporary slant brings with it certain questions and responsibilities. It is a field fraught with temptations in drugs and sex and materialism, and it is an easy place to lose your head with the intoxication of fame or even lose your very soul in trying to gain the world. It is the place where the members of U2 found themselves around the time of *October*.

Jesus told a parable about a master who gave his servants money and went off to another country (Matt. 25:14-30). On his return he asked the servants what they had done with the money. Some had put it to work to make more money, but one servant simply gave it back to the master saying that he simply kept it safe. The master was angry with that servant. The lesson from the parable is that when you are given a gift, you have to use it. You have to deal with the responsibility and dilemmas of it. You cannot run from it. You cannot hide your light under some bushel of safety and hope that it just goes away. You've got to face the consequences of who you are and what your vocation is.

In 1981, U2 could have given in to someone's prophecy that was based on good intentions of trying to give good Christian advice. But where would they be now? What would it have done to their spirits and their souls to be taken away from this avenue of creativity that obviously burned within them? Who might have they become? For sure, the rock world would have missed one of the most influential bands of the latter part of the twentieth century. Imagine a world without *The Joshua Tree* and *Achtung Baby*. Imagine no Zoo TV or Popmart tour. Imagine the biblical imagery and spiritual provocation that would have been absent from the world's record stores, pop charts, MTV programming, and music press.

October was recorded in the dilemma of deliberation over these issues. The Edge would later tell Bill Flanagan: "October was a struggle from beginning to end. It was an incredibly hard record for us to make because we had major problems at the time. And I had been through this thing of really not knowing if I should be in the band or not ... It was reconciling two things that seemed for us to be mutually exclusive. We never did resolve the contradiction. That's the truth. And probably never will."[3]

There was another problem that the three band members' faith had brought. There was a danger at this time of division within their very ranks. Adam was into the whole rock 'n' roll lifestyle, and even though the others were Christians, they still had great chemistry at making vibrant rock 'n' roll. But during the recording of *October* something changed. There was a new soapbox fervor in the proselytizing lyrics, maybe even written to appease the doubters in the fellowship. The recording sessions of *October* were peppered with praise and prayer times, as the band's friends who shared their faith and their belief that they were doing God's will by keeping at the music came to support them in seeking God's blessing on the songs. Windmill Lane was constantly switching roles from being a church to being a recording studio. Adam was aware of all that had been going on around Mount Temple and seemed to accept not only that it was part of who the guys were, but also that whatever this Christian thing was, it added something special to the band. Still, he and Paul McGuinness felt out in the cold as Bible studies took place on the tour bus and other places. Time resolved this uneasiness, and Bono asking Adam—not The Edge, Larry, or another member of Shalom—to be his best man in 1982 was a huge gesture of acceptance.

This feeling of acceptance continued twenty years later. In 2001, Adam was not necessarily comfortable with the way the band's spirituality was portrayed, but he admitted that something special happens at U2 gigs: "I don't know what it is ... but I definitely know when it's there. It doesn't happen every night, but some nights, there's a sense of community and fellowship. And people have said there's a spiritual aspect to what's happening in the house."[4] The one in the band who has never made any public confession of a Christian faith or ever spoken on things spiritual seems to have come to terms with that vital part of the band's makeup. Likewise, during interviews for John Waters' book *Race of Angels*, The Edge recognized that Adam's presence in the band was a positive friction to its early zealous spiritual focus.[5] Having a skeptic so close to their sense of vocation forced the band members to apply their faith to wider issues than if they had been a naive, homogeneous bunch of believers.

"THE CENTRAL FAITH AND SPIRIT OF THE BAND IS THE SAME. BUT I HAVE LESS AND LESS TIME FOR LEGALISM NOW. I JUST SEE THAT YOU LIVE A LIFE OF FAITH." —THE EDGE

Besides the spiritual upheaval and uncertainty, the band encountered another problem during the days of *October*. Bono had all of his lyrics stolen on the U.S. tour prior to recording. When it came time to hit the studio, the guys were running short of time, and Bono was struggling on every front. Considering these circumstances, *October* was a powerful piece of work. The best word to describe it may be celebration. It was uplifting and joyful. It was worship music like no one had ever attempted to achieve—maybe because it hadn't been written as such. "Gloria" is nothing short of a thumping rock hymn. "Tomorrow," again showing Bono's penchant for weaving his mother and God into the same song, has you looking to the skies in expectation that they will rip in two and the Messiah will return to change the whole world order. "Rejoice" and "Scarlet," which simply repeated "rejoice," were reclaiming words that had been lost as archaic in the minds of most young people.

Besides the bombastic rejoicing and the looking up to see God, the album also had the honest soul searching that marked *Boy*. There was still the need to throw bricks through windows. Hints of the questioning about what they should be doing also were audible. In "Gloria," Bono tells God that if he does have anything to offer, he is going to give it back to Him. Would that mean giving up the music? In the same song, he realizes it is not in fame or music, but his sense of completeness is only found in God. That reflection that he is keen to throw a brick through is realizing that he is going nowhere, which wasn't exactly a description of their career potential then. Was there another way? Was the music meaningless? On "With a Shout," that omnipresent question about what they should do and where should they go starts the song. The album ends with a limp and trivial lyric, unless you are writing from such a cauldron of confusion. Bono goes on about singing songs and ends up asking if that is all that is expected of him. Is there more, or is that indeed what these guys were created for?

Bono would say a few years later,

> Yeah, we were a bit uptight at one stage, though you must remember that with Lypton Village and so on, we weren't coming from an at all pious or monk-like existence. But at the same time when we first started exploring the teachings of Christ and studying the Scriptures, we got involved in something that on one level was opening our minds to a wider reality but which on another just closed us off to certain experiences. But you know you go through things.[6]

The Edge would say something similar: "I suppose we've changed our attitudes a lot since then. The central faith and spirit of the band is the same. But I have less and less time for legalism now. I just see that you live a life of faith."[7]

Somehow, as Bono says, they got through it. How close it was, only the band knew. What saved them from it, maybe only God knows. Perhaps Friday and Guggi becoming a little suspicious of the Shalom goings-on sent alarm bells to their fellow Lypton Villagers. The two Virgin Prunes had left the fellowship for various reasons, and maybe the band members were more committed to their fellow Villagers than to Shalom. Certainly the fact that the fellowship was only one of the voices of peer pressure, influence, and accountability was a blessing. Guggi and Friday are still in-house confidants of U2's life and art to this day. Even in the interviews that followed the release of *All That You Can't Leave Behind* in 2000, Bono would say of them: "We've released experimental records, or whatever, but we've never released a crap record. That's because we have people around us. The band first of all. And then people like Gavin and Guggi."[8]

In living ever since in the contradiction that The Edge says they have never resolved, the members of U2 have lived on the edge of a cliff dividing the sacred and the profane. No one would say they have lived on that thin line between heaven and hell without at times dipping their feet into the fires and getting burned in the process. But surely they have lived out the balances in as successful a way as most other Christians in the arts. They have dealt with it better than the ghetto called Christian music.

At a Christian youth leaders conference in the United States, Steve Taylor, founder of Squint Entertainment (label of crossover hit Sixpence None the Richer) and a successful crossover Christian artist in his own right, spoke to thousands of youth leaders about how Christian artists could best serve God. He showed with simple logic how the music industry was the most influential factor on the development of young people and that as a Christian, he felt this influence was not good. It was far from it. He then made it clear that the problem lay with the Church: "You reap what you sow, and we have reaped nothing because we have sown nothing in that world."[9] Taylor touched on an issue that the Christians in U2 must have been dealing with during the days they spent wondering where to turn. The Christian Church has put a spiritual hierarchy on jobs. Ministers and missionaries are on top, then perhaps doctors and nurses come next, and so on to the bottom, where artists appear. Artists of whatever kind have to compromise everything to entertain. Art is fluffy froth that is no good in the kingdom of God. What nonsense. The place Christians need to be to make an impact is at the forefront of the music industry, where the most influence is exerted.

U2 has shown the way. These guys have made mistakes along the way, but maybe the Church should take some of the blame. As Taylor said, "You reap what you sow," and the Church has been slow to support the life and art of U2. Maybe the times they have stumbled and admitted their imperfections have been worth the risk to be boundary-pushers in a world the Church has neglected. Jesus always seemed happier with followers who would chop people's ears off with swords (Matt. 26:51) than He was with people who claimed to have kept all the commandments.

chapter 04

SUNDAY BLOODY SUNDAY

Bono interrupted the euphoria of U2's pre-Christmas Maysfield Hall gig in Belfast. It was December 1982, and the band's third album, *War*, was slated to release the following March. The three-thousand-person, sell-out crowd was enraptured by Bono climbing on top of anything he could, giving every ounce of his being to that which he was made for. But in the introduction to a new song, the mood changed. When Bono told the crowd the next song was about Northern Ireland, things got a little tense. He was careful to point out that it was not a rebel song, and if they didn't like it, the band would never play it in Belfast again. But by the end of "Sunday Bloody Sunday," the crowd had a new U2 live favorite and understood the true intentions of its message. There was an affirming, relief-releasing cheer.

To be from Dublin and title a song "Sunday Bloody Sunday" was asking for misinterpretation. Bloody Sunday was the name given to two of the darkest dates in Ireland's bloody history. One is January 30, 1972, the day British troops shot and killed thirteen people during a civil rights march in nationalist Derry in Northern Ireland. The army has said it was shot at first. The civil rights marchers and the families of the dead have always disputed this, saying the victims were innocent. It fanned the flames of the area's troubles. In 2000, a fresh inquiry began to look again at the evidence of what happened. This memorable and controversial event even caused John Lennon to release a song of the same name on 1972's *Some Time in New York City* album along with another anti-British anthem "The Luck of the Irish."

Bloody Sunday was also the name of another tragic day in Dublin. On November 21, 1921, the British—in the form of the Regular Royal Irish Constabulary and the ruthless auxiliary the Black and Tans—entered Croke Park, the headquarters for the Gaelic Athletic Association. The association often was accused of being affiliated with Republicans, and the British shot and killed twelve people. The operation was carried out in retaliation for the IRA murdering fourteen British undercover agents in their beds. In recent years, this event became a crucial part of the film *Michael Collins*, starring Liam Neeson.

Bono has always said that though Dublin was removed from the epicenter of the bombing and killing in the 1969–1994 troubles, it was where most of the bombs were made, and therefore he was unable to ignore it and had a right to speak out. He has made it clear that he had hopes for a united Ireland, something most evangelical Christians in Northern Ireland would oppose. But he has always made his stand against the violence.

There were, of course, those who misunderstood "Sunday Bloody Sunday." The band got into trouble on both sides of the political divide. The Protestants were displeased with the seeming glorification of Bloody Sunday, which the Nationalists had been using as propaganda against the British troops. The Republicans were unhappy that the band was condemning the violence and therefore taking an anti-IRA stance.

Even amidst its political overtones, "Sunday Bloody Sunday" is one of the more Christian statements on *War*. The band members bring in the prophet Isaiah and the psalmist when they ask, "How long must we sing this song?" This line is reprised in their version of Psalm 40 at the end of the album. They also take the idea of blood and war back to Jesus' victory on the cross and in the resurrection (John 20:1-9). Connecting these acts of bloody violence across the centuries to that first Palestinian Easter was in some sense pointing to their Christian faith as an answer to the problems of the North.

PERHAPS IT WAS TOURING THE WORLD AND GETTING AWAY FROM THE IDEALISTIC WALL OF THE SHALOM FELLOWSHIP THAT CAUSED THE BAND TO BEGIN LOOKING OUT.

"Sunday Bloody Sunday" was the most successful moment on *War*. It is an inflammatory title, which is why Bono had to clarify that it isn't a rebel song. "Rebel" had Republican connotations in the Irish conflict. Instead, "Sunday Bloody Sunday" is an antiwar song, an ideal opening track for an album called *War*. It was a big first step into confrontational politics for the band and was a sign of the hard-edged political commentary to come.

If the eighties would be looked back upon as the flag-waving, stance-shouting, political activist phase of U2, the fact is there was little social activism in the band until this album. Prior to *War*, U2 concentrated on the soul, the spirit, and the heart. Apart from perhaps "Stranger in a Strange Land" on *October*, there was nothing outward-looking until *War*, when it seems the band began dabbling in world events. Perhaps it was touring the world and getting away from the idealistic walls of the Shalom fellowship that caused the band to begin looking out. A couple of years later, Bono would tell *Hot Press*: "We grew up in an odd way as people ... We were completely occupied with spiritual things ... We weren't even sure we wanted to be in a band. So we were interested in growing on spiritual levels but quite retarded on other levels."[1]

The title track of *October* was probably the border checkpoint into *War*. There was a cold and bleak peering out to the kingdoms rising and falling in a world that was by no means kind or tender. On the cover of *War*, Peter Rowan's face looks fearfully aware. This was a change from the naiveté portrayed on *Boy*. The band shots were set in snow that seemed to be nudging toward the harsh chill of Siberia rather than the pleasures of Colorado. These were all signs that these formerly parochial Dublin boys had begun to notice all was not well with the world.

"I WANT IT ALL, AND I WANT IT NOW. HEAVEN ON EARTH—NOW—LET'S HAVE A BIT OF THAT." —BONO

As a first foray into such issues, it could be said that *War* was a naive realization and that the album suffers in depth of content. But "Sunday Bloody Sunday" still stands as one of U2's best. The song was a constant in the band's live set and probably had its definitive rendering on a night that marked another dark day in the North's history. On Remembrance Sunday, November 8, 1987, the IRA exploded a bomb at the War Memorial in Enniskillen, Co. Fermanagh. Whether it was meant for the British forces or not, it killed thirteen innocent people and is probably best remembered for one of the better stories to come out of such murderous brutality. A man named Gordon Wilson was standing with his daughter, Marie, when the bomb went off. She was buried beneath the rubble and died holding his hand and telling him she loved him. The poignancy of those dying moments touched the world. His courageous and radical response to the loss of his daughter—forgiving the killers immediately—made him a symbol of new possibilities in Ireland. He campaigned for peace and reconciliation and even gained a place in the Republic of Ireland's senate.

On the night of the bombing, U2 was giving a concert in Denver, Colorado. In the middle of "Sunday Bloody Sunday," Bono, emotional from the day, ranted about how brave it was to kill children and old men who had just cleaned up their medals for the day. "F--- the revolution" was Bono's conclusion. Never before had the song's opening lines about not believing the headlines and the inability to get rid of them been more apt. The band didn't play the song again until the end of the Popmart tour almost ten years later because it could never really escape that day in 1987.

U2 has always had a glimpse north in its political activism. IRA leader Gerry Adams and Rev. Ian Paisley, a fundamentalist born-again anti-Catholic preacher, joined David Trimble of the predominantly Protestant Unionist Party (Ulster Unionist Party) and John Hume from the predominantly Catholic Nationalist Party (Social, Democratic, and Labor Party) on the cover of the "Please" single. This sent a message to all the people of the North to please give us peace. The marching bands on "Wake Up Dead Man" on *Pop* also pointed to the nonsense that divides and costs lives. Every July, the traditionally Protestant marching season (a cultural parallel to Morris Dancing in England) enflames the country. The Orange Order, a supposedly Christian order, wants to march the routes it has marched for hundreds of years. These roads, through demographic change, have become predominantly Roman Catholic—the people the Orange Order is celebrating victory over in the march. The trenches dug within our hearts that U2 sang about on "Sunday Bloody Sunday" have caused bitter, irreconcilable stand-offs, violence, and civil disorder.

Of course, Ireland has continued to be on U2's agenda right up to the present, when "Peace on Earth" on *All That You Can't Leave Behind* was written as an angry exorcism to another all too similar event—the Omagh bombing. On Saturday afternoon, August 15, 1998, in the little market town of Omagh, Tyrone County, twenty-nine shoppers were blown to pieces and scores more were maimed for life. This happened not far up the road from Enniskillen. A renegade terrorist organization called the Real IRA, which was opposed to the IRA's ceasefire and involvement in the peace process, claimed responsibility. It was Northern Ireland's darkest day and garnered the highest death toll in the four decades of such bombings. And it happened during what was supposedly peace time.

The Omagh bombing impacted Bono, as it did the whole country, more than most of the horrendous things that have been done on the little island that Bono's father used to tell him was just sod to keep his feet from getting wet. The story goes that Bono wrote the words of "Peace on Earth" the night after it occurred. The fact that the bomb exploded in August and the title of the song is taken from the biblical Christmas story makes little difference to its impact.

Perhaps what made the Omagh bombing even more painful to Bono was that he and the band had been part of the peace process that seemed to have been shattered that day. Since Bloody Sunday and Enniskillen, something miraculous had been happening in Northern Ireland. The Republican and Loyalist terrorists had declared ceasefires at the end of August 1994, and though a bombing in London in March 1996 interrupted the peace progress, another ceasefire led the way to a momentous Good Friday agreement in 1998. Almost all of the political parties signed an agreement that would look at local government reforms—from the police service to the decommissioning of weapons and more—that would build a platform to a lasting solution to hundreds of years of hostility.

There was to be a referendum in May 1998. The people of both the Republic of Ireland and Northern Ireland would vote on the agreement. Leading up to the vote, some of the anti-agreement parties had been trying to convince the people that this was a sellout to terrorism and to vote "no." Some of the strongest arguments came from evangelical Christians who supposedly followed a Bible that teaches them "to make every effort to live in peace with all men" (Heb. 12:14) and to "love their enemies, do good to those who hate you" (Luke 6:27-28).

Days before the vote, there was a "Yes" Campaign concert to reach young voters and get publicity in Belfast's new pride and joy, The Waterfront Hall. Ash, a local rock music success story, was to play. On stage, the leaders of the two sides of the community—Trimble of the Protestant Unionist Party and Hume of the Catholic Nationalist Party—would appear together. What put the icing on the cake was U2 agreeing to make an appearance. U2 had offered its services to northern groups before but had always stipulated that it needed to be across the divide. At last, here was the country's greatest opportunity.

Many watched the events on television. After a version of the Beatles' "Don't Let Me Down," Bono told the crowd: "It's great to be in Belfast in a week where history is being made. I would like to introduce two men who are making history. Two men who have taken a leap of faith, out of the past and into the future." Hume and Trimble walked out, and Bono held both their hands up to a loudly affirming crowd. It was a moment that many watched in utter disbelief. It was a defining moment in history. It was a moment of grace. U2 had brought that "victory Jesus won" into a tangible reality. Seventy-one percent of the people in Northern Ireland took the leap of faith with Hume and Trimble. The future was filled with hope, and U2's role in this should not be underestimated. In her balanced and informative book *Northern Protestants: An Unsettled People*, Susan McKay describes the two men holding Bono's hands: "They looked awkward, but it was a winning gesture which had revived a floundering campaign."[2]

Hence Bono's consternation when he played the two poignant songs "North and South of the River" and "All I Want Is You" for a Remembrance Day special for the Omagh bombing victims on the Republic of Ireland's national television channel six months later. "North and South of the River," which could be seen as a grown-up "Sunday Bloody Sunday," has profound lyrics and was written with a legend in Ireland, folk singer Christy Moore. It first appeared on Moore's *Graffiti Tongue* album a year before U2's minimalist version became the B side of "Staring at the Sun."

The folk tradition where Moore has been a superstar for three decades has been known as a place of Republican propaganda. Moore himself supported the IRA's armed struggle for many years but turned his back on it around the time of the Enniskillen bomb. In this co-write with Bono and The Edge, there is an awareness that religion has led minds astray, and there is yearning for repentance, reconciliation, and mutual understanding without any need for surrender—a reference to the clarion call of Ulster Protestants: "No Surrender!" The lines that became most powerful and poignant as U2 performed the song for the TV special were those that suggested the loneliness of hurting your own. There are also fragments of hope in the midst of the evil that love is not lost and has its place in the future. "All I Want Is You" moved from a yearning for love in a romantic sense to a lament for those who lost loved ones in the bombing. Omagh was the only bombing in memory where everyone in Ireland felt they lost someone. Northern Ireland has a tiny population of 1.5 million people, and that afternoon everyone in the country feared they lost a friend. The entire population listened fearfully to news reports for names and wondered about friends who might have been in Omagh's town center that day. Bono sang for everyone, but especially the families of the murdered, about the desire for peace, the wisdom of hatred not having a place, and promises made. Those promises looked back to that Good Friday agreement, to that moment in the Waterfront Hall, and to that resulting referendum.

U2 believes that the Gospel of Jesus Christ has an agenda for peacemaking and justice and a kingdom coming. They also believe that kingdom could come now on this side of eternity. As Bono said in *Hot Press* at the end of 1988: "I don't expect this pie in the sky when you die stuff. My favorite line in the Lord's Prayer is, 'Thy Kingdom come, Thy will be done on earth as it is in heaven' (Matt. 6:10). I want it all, and I want it now. Heaven on earth—now—let's have a bit of that."[3]

As the band dusted "Sunday Bloody Sunday" off for the Elevation tour in 2001, the song had become a celebration of the positive, if cautious, steps Northern Ireland had taken toward a lasting peace. During the Pittsburgh, Pennsylvania, concert of the Elevation tour in 2001, Bono introduced the song by telling the crowd, "If you're Irish, you got something to sing about on this song." It is as if there has been a change from the shame of the Irish situation to almost a pride in what had been achieved. As someone passed him an Irish flag during the song, he acknowledged, "There was a time when you couldn't hold this flag so high." The peace process was again in jeopardy as U2 set out on the U.K. leg of the Elevation tour. Bono threw his encouragement to the politicians across the Irish sea when he told the crowd in Manchester, "Our prayer is that this week brave people make brave decisions, and this little island does not go back to war ... Compromise is not such a bad word after all." The chant at the end of "Sunday Bloody Sunday" had changed in the new hopeful, if fragile, climate. Instead of the screaming of "no more, no more" at the end of the song, Bono invited the crowd to "sing into the presence of love, sing into the presence of peace." There was a hope that these words would be sung for a long time.

chapter 05

LIVE AID

July 13, 1985, was an unforgettable day in U2's history. Still on the cusp of success, the band took the stage on Wembley's Live Aid bill at 5:20 in the afternoon. It was five hours before the event's finale, a signal of U2's still up-and-coming status at the time. Perhaps it was this day that launched the band into the next stratosphere of success. As Bono's natural charisma mingled with the emotion of the day to flood his body with big-stadium adrenalin, he decided to bridge the gap between the stars and the people. In one of the most memorable moments of the day, he pulled some girls out of the crowd and slow-danced with them before millions of viewers worldwide. Somehow, in one of the biggest and widest television audiences ever, he made the dance feel intimate. Fan and performer united in the day that rock music changed the world.

The spontaneity of the dance cost U2 a song that night. "Pride," which was to be the band's last song and was the crowd favorite at the time, had to be sacrificed. However, only playing two songs—"Bad" and "Sunday

Bloody Sunday"—didn't affect the band's sales, which tripled in the coming months. The band's live reputation was enhanced beyond measure, yet Bono left Wembley shattered by the experience. Perhaps the contradictions of the day were on the mind of this young, emotional, deep thinker. Was there not something incongruous about a great rock celebration aiding people who were starving to death? That might have been part of the cause of Bono's post-gig depression. But he also seems to have felt his dancing embarrassed the band. He actually took off by himself around Ireland to come to terms with it, maybe on a similar soul search as when the band had considered giving up around *October*. Somewhere in west Ireland, the story goes, Bono met a sculptor who was working on a piece called "The Leap," inspired by Bono's moment of letting go. It was quite a symbol on all kinds of levels for the band, the industry, and mankind. The leap at the crux of Bono's 2000 movie *Million Dollar Hotel* may have begun here.

"TO ME, FAITH IN JESUS CHRIST THAT IS NOT ALIGNED TO SOCIAL JUSTICE—THAT IS NOT ALIGNED WITH THE POOR—IT'S NOTHING." —BONO

Of course, Live Aid was not about Bono's personal journey, nor was it about selling more albums or enhancing the band's reputation. That may have been the view of the cynics. But if rock music ever laid its ego down for a day, this was it. For U2, Live Aid reinforced the band's belief that music could change the world. As a result of the Band Aid and Live Aid projects, Bono and his wife, Ali, went to Ethiopia in 1985. This event had a marked effect on both of their lives, as well as the band's music.

In some ways, it was at this point that U2 began to take over the mantle of the folk, pop, and rock protest movement that traces its roots back to Woody Guthrie, Bob Dylan, John Lennon, and even Boomtown Rats' Bob Geldof. Funny enough, in his band's first single Geldof sneered about not wanting charity but being all about "Lookin' After No. 1." It's ironic how the punk rocker from Dublin who sang about looking after number one selflessly fed the world, while those who say "love your neighbor as yourself" (Luke 10:25-37) only look after number one. Geldof himself would say that God looked down and saw he who was least likely and decided to use him. Maybe in that light, Band Aid was meant to embarrass the Church.

It is John Lennon who has been Bono's soul mate from beyond the grave. Lennon always has been a big influence on Bono's music and life. Bono once said of Lennon, "For somebody like myself, John Lennon really did kind of write the rule book ... As a tunesmith, as an irritant, as a willing taker of pratfalls."[1] That they hold a spiritual affinity even though Lennon never had much faith in God may seem a little unfitting, but true. U2's "God Part II" was, in some ways, meant to bring the atheist viewpoint together with the Christian believers.

Bono and Lennon's connection was more in their honesty and desire that the platform of music be used to change the world. More than using the injustices around them to stoke the fires of their songwriting, they wanted to get out there and bring on the revolution. Of course, Lennon was part of the great hippy idealism of the sixties, and there was a belief that flower power could instigate a new world. Sociologist and Christian writer Tony Campolo suggests in his book *Who Switched the Price Tags?* that the hippies of the late sixties had much in common with the kingdom of God. He writes:

> While they were arrogant and haughty, they did seem to have the right kind of dreams. As a matter of fact, in their idealism, I found values that I wished were more evident in the churches I attended and served. There was something noble about their visions of the future, and those of us committed to a radical theology of the Kingdom of God began to think that these young people were more Christian than those who filled the pews of churches ... Those long-haired males and braless females possessed a childlike

> innocence that made them seem exceedingly fit for the Kingdom of heaven.[2]

Lennon's much-publicized bed-in for peace spawned his song "Give Peace a Chance." A few years later, he released *Some Time in New York City*, a political manifesto that touched on feminism and support for the Black Panther movement and the Irish terror group, the IRA. It could be said that *War* was an early, naive, and youthful attempt by U2 to write and record a *Some Time in New York City*-type album. There was a look at global issues and, of course, "Sunday Bloody Sunday." Lennon's was a more vehement attack on the British soldiers and their policy in Northern Ireland—a less peaceful rage than U2's. For sure, Lennon was the artist who encouraged the young U2 to look out.

From *War* on, U2 began to become a politically active, cause-carrying, justice-driven band. In 1987, just after the release of *The Joshua Tree*, Niall Stokes commented on the changes in U2: "One thing is that Bono has become far more political. There was a time when a discussion of politics would have seemed irrelevant to him. He was more interested in spiritual issues. Now they have become more political, and the new album is an awareness of that."[3]

This new campaigning heart was in no way a change in perspective for the band. It was not that the members had left spiritual issues behind. They were not replacing one with another. Rather, they were opening up their spiritual quest to take in all that their faith was about. Bono said in 1988: "To me, faith in Jesus Christ that is not aligned to social justice—that is not aligned with the poor—it's nothing."[4]

Their faith went this direction for many reasons. Leaving the insular shelter of Dublin in the late seventies and stepping out onto the world stage was magnified by the band's being asked to take part in the Band Aid single in late 1984. Boomtown Rats' Bob Geldof, one of the few success stories to come out of Dublin before U2, had seen the horrific pictures of the famine in Ethiopia on the news in late 1984. He was so moved that he phoned his mate from Ultravox, Midge Ure, and the two wrote a song. They got several pop stars to sing a line in the song, and they made it into the top-selling single of all time in the UK. The proceeds from that song went to famine relief. Bono got the God line: "Well, tonight, thank God it's them instead of you."

It was around this time that U2 began to give their wholehearted support to Amnesty International. Bono campaigned for victims of injustice around the world. He later said one of the things he was most proud of in his career was highlighting the work of this charity in his music. U2 always would give space on its album sleeves to highlight a few cases and give details on how to join the organization. U2 was part of the Conspiracy of Hope tour in 1986, as was Sting, Peter Gabriel, Lou Reed, Bryan Adams, and others. The tour across America promoted the organization's mission.

For some reason, many Christians were suspicious of the band's political awareness. They feared it was another sign of moving away from the heart of the Gospel. Was U2 ashamed of the Gospel that it had proclaimed so vigorously on *October* to be going on and on now about social issues? Evangelical Christianity seems to have forgotten that Jesus asked His disciples to do just what U2 was doing. In one situation, Jesus told His followers that if they wanted to know who was going to heaven, they just had to look at who fed the poor and visited the sick or the prisoners. He said those people were doing those things unto Christ Himself, as He was manifested in "the least of these" (Matt. 25:31-46).

Many Christians find comfort on Sunday mornings in the Bible verse that says where two or three are gathered in Jesus' name, He is there with them (Matt. 18:20). For some reason, they prefer that verse over the one that says the prisoner and the tramp in the street is Jesus, too. When it comes to which place Jesus would prefer to be met, you have to wonder. Would He rather see His kingdom come by His followers praying for His kingdom to come, or by them putting their faith into action? Perhaps in working to bring social justice and compassion to the world, the members of U2 were more certain of their place in heaven than when they just talked about it.

Jesus wasn't the only one in the Bible who saw social justice as the vital manifestation of the life of faith. The prophets, particularly Amos, suggested that God was not interested in their song of worship or their holy days or their spiritual gatherings unless "they let justice roll down like waters and righteousness like an ever-flowing stream" (Amos 5:24, NASB). Far from being a move away from their faith, U2's political activism was in keeping with it. In those seeming throwaway lines from "Please" on *Pop*, Bono pleads, "Get up off your knees." He was asking the Church to get out of prayer meetings and into the everyday dirt and pain of bringing the kingdom. This band believed in a kingdom coming where all colors would bleed and blend into one, and they were going to run until they found what they were looking for: an earth as it is in heaven.

chapter 06

FOR THE REV. MARTIN LUTHER KING—SING!

When Bono joined Bob Dylan onstage at Slane Castle for a memorable performance on a sunny Sunday in July 1984, he did so as the underdog. U2 was at the top of its class, but the band had not yet graduated to the level of the great Dylan. As Bono bluffed his way through Dylan's "Leopard Skin Pillbox Hat" and improvised the words to "Blowing in the Wind," no one knew U2 was actually in the process of making the album that would propel their journey to greatness.

The band's most recent album at the time, *Under a Blood Red Sky*, released in late 1983. With its accompanying video, the band seemed to have mastered its show—The Edge's chunky, chiming guitar perfectly balancing Bono's prancing, posing, flag-waving, and high-powered emotion. This was a group that had become good at what it did. But at the same time, the band members realized that to get better, they would need to leave behind the security of repeating proven formulas.

1984's *The Unforgettable Fire* was U2's first reinvention. It was also the band's first album after they decided their faith could live alongside their art. If this album showed anything, it was that. The band realized that cliché-ridden Christian couplets were not necessary or helpful in sharing their faith. Being impressionistic would do. They were artists, not missionaries, in a proclamation sense.

Bill Graham put it well when he said, "Insofar as the album is Christian, the Holy Spirit is the presiding member of the trinity."[1] There is a spiritual feel to the piece. *The Unforgettable Fire* seems to describe the thin places where heaven and earth are so close that you can almost scratch some of the gold off the streets of glory. Graham also describes the album as "a travelogue of the soul."[2]

Given this, *The Unforgettable Fire* was a bold shift in direction—which would become a trait of the band. The guys of U2 made some brave decisions, throwing themselves into a deeper sea where the first question was always, "Can they avoid drowning?" Choosing Brian Eno as producer was radical. Eno had been a member of Roxy Music and producer for Talking Heads and David Bowie, but he had never so much as heard any of U2's material. Initially, Eno turned down the band's request. He finally agreed and brought to the equation Canadian Daniel Lanois. This set in place a team that would collaborate on some of the strongest music of the next fifteen years.

The Unforgettable Fire was a mysterious, meandering album. It was big, big music and had Lanois and Eno's imprints all over it. In a word, it was impressionistic. Though it still has The Edge's trademark guitar shuffling and scuttling along, it is a much more mature performance by the band. Bono's lyrics were just lines and poetic shades whose meaning rarely extended beyond each couplet. The themes of hope, home, belief, and giving away were all there, but there was little in the way of clear statements of faith, as on *October*, or of the world, as on *War*. Of course, there was "Pride (In the Name of Love)," which became U2's biggest hit to date and apart from "Bad" is the only song on the album that still rates in the U2 classic canon. It perhaps remains the band's trademark song, with the anthemic sound, spiritual core, and political edge. It also happens to be the only song on the album where the title is in the lyrics.

"Pride" and the album title *The Unforgettable Fire* were both inspired by a trip to Chicago's The Peace Museum. A series of paintings and drawings by survivors of the Hiroshima and Nagasaki holocaust at the end of World War II was on display, and the title of the exhibition immediately struck Bono as a good name for U2's next album.

While at the museum, the band saw another exhibit dedicated to the life and campaigning of Dr. Martin Luther King Jr. The guys immediately felt empathy for him. In their lives, as well as in "Sunday Bloody Sunday," they advocated pacifism. King's belief in nonviolence was something they would echo in all their political campaigning. They had expressed hope that a Martin Luther King Jr. would emerge in the Northern Ireland troubles.

King was an interesting hero of the band at this stage of their spiritual development. As the members of U2 had been exposed to more of the world and more of what masquerades as "Christian," there was much heart- and soul-searching. They were looking for new definitions of the faith they had taken hold of in their teens. There were new questions and realities, and they were deciding what to toss out from the baggage of their past Christian experience and what to hold onto. This was many believers' experience. After a time of dealing with the inner soul, being almost nurtured on milk as the apostle Paul puts it in one of his epistles, born again gives way to growing up again, and the world of the adult takes on very different issues than that of the infant.

As the band members were discarding some of their role models from Shalom and finding it hard to involve themselves with another local group of believers as such, a figure like King and his writings, thoughts, and behavior was just what the soul doctor prescribed. He was someone to look up to. He was someone to help them sort out their questions. He, in some ways, was a Christ figure who gave himself for the betterment of others. His politics and investigative spirituality, where he was not afraid to question the givens of the evangelical world in which he was brought up, were things to which the Christians in U2 could relate. His writings were far more inspirational than to just give them two great songs.

Yet two great songs they got. The song "MLK" took the same role on the album that "40" had on *War*—the haunting, moody finale. It was a song of deep sadness as it reflected on the tragedy of King's death. Almost the opposite of "MLK" was "Pride," which was all about celebration in spite of King's assassination, because his death was not the end of his life or his cause. His soul and his pride and his victory could not be taken away.

"I GO TO AMERICA AND I TURN ON MY TELEVISION SET, AND I START SWEATING PROFUSELY BECAUSE THOSE GUYS HAVE TURNED FAITH INTO AN INDUSTRY. IT'S APPALLING." —BONO

That Bono's words took a step back from the soapbox proclamation of his earlier work was due largely to the fact that the band had become suspicious of right-wing American evangelicalism. Bono would talk about this quite a lot in the years to come. He told Robert Hillman in 1987: "I go to America and I turn on my television set, and I start sweating profusely because those guys have turned faith into an industry. It's appalling. It's ugly—the guy's hand is virtually coming out of the television set."[3]

The Unforgettable Fire was the band's first post-Shalom fellowship release, and the guys would never have a very healthy relationship with the Church again. Of course, they have not exactly lived a life that is very conducive to church commitment. Around the time they left Shalom, they were becoming one of the world's busiest rock bands. Their schedule did not make it too easy for them to attend church regularly. And their fame made it hard for them to slip into the back pew unnoticed. Bono has said that even if he could and wanted to attend church on a regular basis, it would become the biggest church in Dublin—not because of anything God was doing but because of his being there.

A few years later in the song "Acrobat," on 1991's *Achtung Baby*, it seems Bono admitted to his loss of not having a place of regular liturgy, creed, and accountability. He sang of wanting to join a movement and receive bread and wine if there was somewhere he could believe in. He acknowledged the hypocrisy of how he looked like an acrobat talking one way and acting another. Bono, as he is never afraid to do, showed a vulnerable, honest side. He was almost embarrassed that his thought and art were so rooted in the Christian faith, yet his actions didn't live up to the belief.

Bono has returned to this idea again and again over the years. He has spoken of not being a great example of the Christian faith. He has made many references to having been drawn to peacemakers like Ghandi, King, and Christ—not because he has himself been by nature a pacifist, but because he has been the opposite. He told Liam Mackey in 1988: "The reason I'm attracted to the light of Scriptures is because there's another side of me that is dark. The reason I'm interested in men of peace is because I'm not like them and would like to be. I'm not someone in real life who turns the other cheek."[4]

Twelve years later, he took up the same thread in a *Q* magazine interview. In it, he said: "I get discouraged by my base emotions. I write songs about high ideals and aspirations, and I admire Martin Luther King and John Hume, peaceful people, but ... I'm capable of aggression of a really brutal kind. If that rears its head and I give in to it and thump somebody, then I feel really low."[5] He went on, "I wish I could live up to Christianity. It's like I'm a fan; I'm not actually in the band." This is the same Christian who told Joe Jackson while discussing Elvis' demise: "I think it was guilt that made

Elvis lose the will to live. Yet in the Scripture there is another line: 'There is, therefore no condemnation for those who are in God' (Rom. 8:1). There is no guilt. Guilt is not of God. It is false teaching."[6]

This seems to be a normal response to the contradictions that any believer experiences between the idealism of what can be achieved in the cross, the resurrection of Christ, and the outpouring of the Holy Spirit and the sometimes slow progress in attaining it. In Ireland there is a lot of talk about Catholic guilt, when someone who partakes in Mass on Sunday lives a life devoid of that spiritual belief the rest of the week. There is a similar Protestant guilt that lurks in the temples of those who claim to be free from having to earn their salvation by works. There are always expectations of behavioral codes and ecclesiastical dues that when not achieved or even sought leave us feeling that salvation is either lost or not as sure-footed as it was.

Evangelicals believe they are saved by grace through faith (Eph. 2:8-9), but then add a man-made waiver that you have to work as hard as you can to meet middle-class behavioral patterns to hang onto it. It seems to be contrary to the Gospel, where among the many teachings of Jesus regarding servanthood, the last become first. It is an upside-down kingdom contradicting what seems the natural order of the first being first and the best winning. The Church therefore should be radically opposed to such a success syndrome. It seems this affected Bono. Another strange quirk about the Church is it has specific qualities that indicate whether you are an "acrobat." Usually, they have to do with swearing, smoking, and drinking. For some reason, there are biblical teachings that do not—but perhaps should—hold so much importance. Among them: materialistic greed, bigoted prejudice, the oppression of women, or the neglect of social justice. Somehow you can ignore many of the rallying calls of Christ and the prophets, and because you are teetotal and less flowery with your language and attend church twice a week, you are declared spiritually strong.

Bono spoke of grace being the great attraction to Christianity. Then he said he'd like to be a Christian but could never shape up or that he was a bad example of Christianity. Either he was trying to deflect the press's ability to pigeonhole him, or he was duped about what a Christian is. Like his critics, he was blind to his own radical following of Jesus in his social justice commitments, such as giving an enormous amount of his time to Jubilee 2000. He pushed back his career and new album by more than a year to try to rid the Third World of crippling debts, keep the poor alive, and restore equality and justice to the world. And he said he was not a good example for Christ. Jesus told a parable about the kingdom of God where the sheep enter the kingdom, and the goats are left outside (Matt. 25:31-46). Jesus didn't say the goats smoked, drank, or swore too much. He said they didn't get involved in changing the circumstances of the marginalized by feeding them when they were hungry and visiting them in prison. These were the issues of His kingdom.

When it comes to the dilemma of the Catholic and Protestant guilt complexes, Bono is both and, at the same time, neither. He has consistently talked of how he despises religion but is a great believer in Christ. For Bono, The Edge, and Larry, the God that they met and have pilgrimaged with down the amazing road is a God who is bigger than Church or religious boundaries. They discovered Him outside of the straightjacket of traditional religion, and they have continued to see a God Who has gotten bigger and bigger in every way.

In 1990, at the Greenbelt Arts Festival in England, rock journalist, biographer, and poet Steve Turner did a seminar on how the Church was not good at being involved in conversations in the real world. He spoke of how many believers were not involved in the world at all and saw it as a bad place, not a place where Christians should be. Other believers were uninformed. They ran headlong into the world with clichéd religious slogans that made sense in church but were not understood outside it. These believers didn't relate in any ways that were understood or relevant. The third group consisted of believers who were unintegrated. They were involved in the culture but were so cut off from the Christian Church that they just blended in and thus made no impression.

Turner has used U2 as an example of a rock band that had been involved successfully in the conversation going on in the band's little corner of the vineyard. Turner co-wrote the official book for the movie *Rattle and Hum*[7] with Pete Williams and included a lengthy spiritual insight into the band in his book *Hungry for Heaven.*[8] There is little doubt that due to circumstances outside the band's control, U2 could have ended up among the unintegrated. Turner said not only did U2 get involved in that conversation at the cutting edge of the rock world, but the band even changed the language of the conversation. As one example, he asked if Simple Minds would have ever recorded a song like "Sanctify Yourself" before U2 got in among rock's movers and shakers and started using religious imagery.

"RELIGION HAS TORN THIS COUNTRY APART. I HAVE NO TIME FOR IT, AND I NEVER FELT A PART OF IT. I AM A CHRISTIAN, BUT AT TIMES I FEEL VERY REMOVED FROM CHRISTIANITY." —BONO

In Turner's analysis, where U2 would always be in danger would be in their integration. For Bono, Larry, and The Edge, their church has had to be the "coffee table fellowship," or dare I say "the barstool fellowship." They have kept their spiritual dialogue going through friends who share their faith, whether that might be old friends in Dublin, or fellow musicians such as T-Bone Burnett or Bruce Cockburn, or journalists and writers such as Turner. There have always been fellow believers involved within U2's inner circle professionally, artistically, and socially.

Probably most significantly, Bono has been able to sharpen his faith and continue to get inspired about his spiritual worldview by opening himself to "fellowship" with those who do not share his Christian viewpoint. He is always open to talk about the Christian faith with whoever will listen.

Though they have been known to attend churches locally or around the world on various occasions, they have been mainly limited to these informal means of spiritual nourishment and accountability.

U2's lack of integration with the Church is not entirely due to their fame and itinerant lifestyle, though. The band took a huge step back from Christian structures around the time of *War* and *The Unforgettable Fire.* Bono said at the time:

> Well, religion has torn this country apart. I have no time for it, and I never felt a part of it. I am a Christian, but at times I feel very removed from Christianity. The Jesus Christ I believe in was the man who turned over the tables in the temple and threw the moneychangers out—substitute TV evangelists if you like. There is a radical side to Christianity that I am attracted to. And I think without a commitment to social justice, it is empty ... When I see these racketeers, the snake-oil salesmen on these right-wing television stations, asking not for your $20 or your $50, but your $100 in the name of Jesus Christ, I just want to throw up.[9]

According to that statement, there is another reason for the band members' stepping back. After *October,* they openly quoted scripture and happily confessed their faith during several interviews. This was when they were most intensely involved with Shalom, and coming from their sheltered Christian base in Dublin, they were fairly unaware of what born-again Christianity meant throughout the rest of the world. They would soon find out. During a tour of the United States not long after the *October* publicity campaign, they came across a brand of evangelicalism that they simply could not understand or stomach. As Bono said, it made them want to throw up. They also began to realize that when they stated their Christian belief in the music press, people were equating what they were saying with right-wing, fundamentalist Christians in America. U2 was unhappy with such a comparison and stood back from it. This was why the guys quit being so open with the press about the definitions of their faith. It was not a silence imposed by Island Records for commercial reasons. It was the right-wing Church that was forcing them to shut up. But they never really did.

Not only did they stand back from such right-wing churches, they started to criticize them openly in interviews and from the stage. To some, this may have been seen as a betrayal of their previous spiritual allegiance. The band probably would have seen it as developing that allegiance. As they shone the light of their faith across the world to critique politics and make a stand for justice and change, they would shine that beam of truth across the Church, too, to illuminate the dross that has caused its decay.

This could be seen on the *Rattle and Hum* movie, when Bono, in one of his characteristic monologues, ends "Bullet the Blue Sky," which is about American foreign policy in Central America, with: "But I see no difference between the *CBS News* and *Hill Street Blues* and a preacher on *The Old Time Gospel Hour* stealing money from the sick and the old. Well, the God I believe in isn't short of cash, mister!" The link between televangelists, right-wing fundamentalism, and the bombing of innocent people in El Salvador was a potent cocktail of prophetic anger.

In 1994, The Edge said to John Waters, "We probably, at this point, have deeply disappointed a lot of Christians because what I perceive as freedom, they would perceive as complete decadence and self-indulgence."[10] This showed that U2 was aware of the wariness with which the Christian world looked upon the band, but the three Christians in the band lost no sleep over such opinions. There was a point in their career when they made a conscious decision to deflect any kind of allegiance to conservative evangelical Christianity and attempted to break that mass movement from giving any allegiance to them. There may be many reasons for this break, but it's important to remember that U2 has never denied its allegiance with Christ. That some have not been happy with the outworking of such a confession does not negate what the band members believe.

It might be that the members of U2 had to distance themselves from the

Church to be able to be faithful to their sense of vocation. There are hints here of the messianic secret of the Gospels. There are many recorded instances in the Gospel accounts of Jesus' life where He told His disciples and people He had healed not to tell people who He was (Luke 9:21). The reason was that if people knew, they would put the wrong expectations on Him and draw Him away from the heart of His vocation. U2's vocation was in no way messianic, but that evangelical Christians' expectations might distract the band from its vocation was a danger. Maybe what U2 has achieved for God has been as a result of not being tied to any particular denomination. So many of those who try to take Christ into the world, whether it be as missionaries or artists, are tied by those who look over their shoulders. There is a lot of peer pressure within churches or in Christian movements to dot all the i's and cross all the t's of a precise and perfect faith. The late Christian artist Rich Mullins had told audiences he once was not allowed to record a song because his record company felt it was not the sort of message the target audience would buy.

By being outside the pressures of Church expectations, U2 has been able to take risks and do its own thing. This is not an ideal scenario for any Christian, especially those facing the temptations and dilemmas of the rock world. But as a result of the uniqueness of the band's situation, it has been able to make a unique contribution to the culture without having to compromise it or water it down.

chapter 07

YOU KNOW I BELIEVE IT

The Joshua Tree was U2's finest moment. Until the album's release in 1987, the group had been all potential and promise. With *The Joshua Tree,* U2 achieved it. The album welcomed their status as rock legends. Yet as U2 sat at the top of the music charts around the world, the Christian community used the album's release as reason to write the band's spiritual obituary. One of the songs in particular sparked the backlash. It had the band's former Christian community in Dublin, as well as many believers around the world, mourning—and in some cases celebrating—the evidence that the band's days of being torchbearers of Christian truth were over. "I Still Haven't Found What I'm Looking For" was a pivotal song in the band's artistic intentions and spiritual development. The Soul Patrol and Theological Police were out in force, though, and they concluded their case that anyone who had not found what they were looking for could not have found Christ.

It was a remarkable response that not only highlighted a shoddy piece of listening to the song's lyrics, but also showed a great error in what was masquerading in some quarters as Christianity. There seems to be a belief that once someone makes the initial connection with Jesus Christ, he has arrived. Immediately, a watertight box of solutions is handed to him. No more questions need to be asked—Jesus is the answer! Everything is now explained; there is nothing left to search for. This view is built on a need for precision and perfection, which have always been enemies of art, which is all about coloring outside the lines. It is also an enemy of the reality that following Jesus is a journey, not an arrival.

"AT ONE TIME, I THOUGHT YOU HAD TO HAVE ALL THE ANSWERS IF YOU WERE GOING TO WRITE A SONG, SO IT WAS EMBARRASSING TO MAKE A RECORD THAT WAS FILLED WITH DOUBTS AND QUESTIONS." —BONO

The members of U2 knew what they were stirring up. By now, disillusioned with formal fellowships or churches of any kind and growing in their spiritual thinking, they were making a statement about a less dogmatic approach to their faith. Yet the dogma in the song is widespread. Even with the song's dichotomy, it could be regarded as their clearest confession of faith. Daniel Lanois spoke on *The Making of The Joshua Tree* video about having suggested that Bono write a gospel song. Up to that point, the band had been writing songs with Christian content. A gospel song was another category entirely, and Lanois seemed to have seen it as a natural place of inspiration for a band that was so wrapped up in all things Christian. Bono listened to his producer's advice and wrote "I Still Haven't Found What I'm Looking For," calling it "a gospel song for a restless spirit."

The Joshua Tree was the album on which Bono discovered the art of the song. Before this, there had been a lot of impressionistic improvisation. But somewhere between *The Unforgettable Fire* and *The Joshua Tree,*

Bono began to hone his craft. It could have been that sharing stages with the likes of Dylan, Baez, and Sting and hanging out with great writers had provoked Bono to try to imitate his peers. Perhaps it was a new sense of belief in what the band was becoming. Whatever it was, *The Joshua Tree* took the experimentation of Eno and Lanois' *The Unforgettable Fire,* melted it into the tighter sounds of Lillywhite's first three albums, and added more attention to lyrical detail. The result: "Our most literate record yet,"[1] according to Bono. His focus on the song made "I Still Haven't Found What I'm Looking For" a concise creed of redemption: Jesus breaks bonds, looses chains, carries the cross and all of our shame. After the confession there is the clear and confident assent of "I believe it."

Redemption, atonement, and the substitution death of Christ. There would be no more succinct a theology of the cross in all the songs that were coming from the Christian bands that U2's Christian critics would hold as models of sound theological content. The band, which many condemned for not proclaiming the Gospel and being ashamed of it, could not have spelled it out more clearly or poetically. Surely, this is what the Church needed. Christians in the real world being salt and light (Matt. 5:13, 16)—and in this case with a dirty great big fog horn, proclaiming the faith with the attention of the nation if not the greater part of the world. The song held the number one position on the singles charts for more than a month.

Instead of being a rejection of faith, "I Still Haven't Found What I'm Looking For" is an indication that U2 might have been closer to biblical truth than the narrow and precise Christians who pointed their fingers. In the book *The Post-Evangelical,* English vicar Dave Tomlinson states: "Evangelicalism is good at introducing people to faith in Christ, but unhelpful when it comes to the matter of progressing into a more grown-up experience of faith."[2] Tomlinson may generalize, but it is true that the evangelical wing of the Church spends a lot of energy on being "born again" but little time on "growing up" again. There is a failing to encourage newborn believers out of the maternity ward and into a big world where they will spend the rest of their spiritual lives trying to find what they are looking for.

The New Testament contains a letter from the apostle Paul to the church in Philippi. Paul makes his beliefs clear. He tells the Philippians he has given up striving to get to God by being a religious Pharisee and has put his belief in the "righteousness that comes from God and is by faith" (Phil. 3:9). After years of working on some kind of way to God by adhering to his Jewish rituals, rules, and regulations, he has set them aside and now believes in the Gospel that U2 so elegantly describes in its hit single. Paul could not find what he was looking for by being religious.

He says: "Not that I have already obtained all this, or have already been made perfect, but I press on to take hold of that for which Christ Jesus took hold of me ... Forgetting what is behind and straining toward what is ahead, I press on" (Phil. 4:12-14). Paul had to take the belief, then go where that belief would lead him. Proclaiming a new doctrinal statement did not bring with it an overnight holiness. He had to keep "pressing on to the higher calling of my Lord," as Bob Dylan had paraphrased on his song "Pressing On" from his *Saved* album in 1980.

If Christians look at the events of the past few years in Rwanda, Angola, Mozambique, Sarajevo, the Middle East, or Belfast City, they cannot say those tragedies are what they have been looking for. If they look at a Church filled with gossip, malicious lies in the name of truth, the bondage of legalism, or the bigoted hypocrites who sometimes hold power, they can't say this is what they are looking for. As they look into their own lives and see the egotistical, selfish, sinful spouse, parent, child, workmate, or friend, they can't say they have found what they are looking for. It is the realization that they haven't found what they are looking for that should draw them back to the only hope for being born again or growing up again: that someone broke bonds and chains and carried the cross in our place. It is only God's grace, through that work of redemption, that has brought them safe this far. And it is only His grace, through that work of redemption, that will lead them home. Until believers take that breath out of this world and into the hope-filled eternity of the next, they will be searching.

Bono's running and climbing and crawling toward that kingdom of oneness and realizing that as well as speaking in the tongues of angels, he sometimes holds the hands of the devil—this is perhaps a truer description of the pilgrimage of faith. Bono has been honest about his failings when it comes to his life and Christian journey. While the Church might ignore the darkness within and try to cover up its hang-ups with a shirt and tie, Bono has continually shown us himself, warts and all. That the Church has covered its eyes perhaps is a hint that it fears such honesty. In admitting to their doubts and weaknesses, the members of U2 got condemned from the very place where everyone should have raised their hands and said, "Hey, this is a perfect description of my yet imperfect faith. I believe all this, but, man, I need to keep running."

As well as another proclaiming of the band's beliefs, this was no doubt a loosening of the dogma and narrow lifestyle of U2's early spiritual days. They had left their Shalom bubble and headed out across the world. What they saw and the people they met had given them a whole new perspective. It not only gave them a more realistic picture of the walk of faith, it also gave them a lot more flexibility in what they could write about when they realized they didn't have to be so intense about perfection and precision. As Bono said around the time of *The Joshua Tree*'s release:

> I think there was a certain uptightness to the first three albums ... At one time, I thought you had to have all the answers if you were going to write a song, so it was embarrassing to make a record that was filled with doubts and questions. Then I began to see that many of the artists who inspired me—Bob Dylan, Patti Smith, Van Morrison, Al Green, Marvin Gaye—had similar feelings of awkwardness and spiritual confusion. I realize now it's OK to say you still haven't found what you're looking for.[3]

This became a theme for the U2 albums that followed. U2's songs became more and more honest about the struggles of personal faith, as well as the confusion that faith suffers from facing the world. In later songs, the theme would be raised in lines such as faith needing a doubt in "Hawkmoon 269," less knowing needs more believing in "Last Night on Earth" and knowing you need to believe whether you can explain it or not in "The Playboy Mansion." In these songs, Bono seems to be trying to give a few clues of what faith really is. It hangs around with doubt and lives far from the scientific certainties of the modern world. Maybe postmodernism was a better canvas to throw out the truth of God's interaction with man.

"I Still Haven't Found What I'm Looking For" had followed "With or Without You" to the top of the charts, the latter being voted *Rolling Stone*'s eighth-best single of all time. The previous decade—from Mount Temple to Live Aid and beyond—seems to have led U2 to this moment. The band members had taken the best aspects of their previous four studio albums and put them together, and all their hopes and dreams came true. *The Joshua Tree* varied in its textures from the almost orchestral build of "Where the Streets Have No Name" to the gospel classiness of "I Still Haven't Found What I'm Looking For" to the raging "Bullet the Blue Sky" to the minimalist "Exit." While *The Unforgettable Fire* painted almost so far outside the lines that lines could not be seen, *The Joshua Tree* drew up new lines that were not confining the band's creativity but mysteriously enhancing it. Consistent and articulate in words and instrumentation, the album was almost flawless.

The only boundary of the subject matter of *The Joshua Tree* was planet earth. But even then transcendent places beyond the space and time of earth are alluded to in "One Tree Hill," "I Still Haven't Found ... " and "Where the Streets Have No Name," which seems to be about some hopeful future place. Niall Stokes said, "He could be talking about heaven. Maybe even offering us a glimpse into some kind of private hell." Ethiopia has been cited as the place with no street names. What about Belfast as a geographical and political anchor? In a city where by your name, or the name of your school, or the name of your street, you can be defined into either sectarian camp within seconds and judged accordingly, it would be great to be in a place where the streets have no name and everyone is equal. Maybe the best thing about the song is that everyone can claim these streets as his own.

The Joshua Tree is global. North America is constantly under the bright light of interrogation in both "Bullet the Blue Sky" and "In God's Country." The character in "Exit" is an American living in a country where guns and fundamentalist religion are two preoccupations. "One Tree Hill" was written in New Zealand and has its reference to Maori religious ritual. "Mothers of the Disappeared" touches on injustices in Argentina. "Bullet the Blue Sky" was Bono and The Edge's response to American foreign policy in El Salvador. The miner's strike in England is the focus of "Red Hill Mining Town." And Bono found himself around the corner from his childhood home as he dealt with the drug problems of Dublin's Ballymun in "Running to Stand Still." The members of U2 were like documentary journalists investigating the world that their faith had been caressing and colliding with as they crossed the globe frequently in their touring and extracurricular activities. Without doubt, this is a look at the dark from the place of light, the band allowing their faith to shine around their world and draw questions and conclusions.

IN THEIR FIRST DECADE, BONO ONLY SCRATCHED THE SURFACE OF THE HEART IN HIS OBSESSION WITH THE SOUL, AND HE PURPOSELY SHIFTED DIRECTION WITH THIS ALBUM.

"Exit" was as interesting in the spiritual direction of U2's work as "I Still Haven't Found ... " This was a band that had been giving alternatives to the sex, drugs, and rock 'n' roll rebellion. This was a band that was singing the most uplifting and positive of songs—made even more inspirational by The Edge's trademark guitar. On "Exit," Bono, for the first but certainly not last time, eyeballed the love and goodness of the Christian faith with the demonic, darker side. This was U2's darkest song to date, as Bono disappeared down inside the mind of a psychotic killer who shared Bono's belief in "the hands of love." Now here was a contradiction, one without neat and tidy conclusions. Bill Graham suggested that "only a committed believer could have gotten inside the skull of the protagonist of 'Exit.'"[4] The song communicated the truth about a disturbing reality. There must be questions asked about any Christian worldview that would rather sweep that beneath a theological carpet than wrestle with it. U2 would wrestle with it for years to come.

The Joshua Tree sessions were a productive time for U2, and the B sides on the album's singles could have been an album all by themselves. "Spanish Eyes" became a concert favorite, and "Sweetest Thing" became a number one single in the U.K. eleven years later when it was remixed for *The Best of 1980-1990* compilation. Another brooding piano piece that is closely related to "With or Without You" but wasn't finished in time for the album was "Luminous Times (Hold on to Love)."

"Luminous Times" has a few crucial lines in otherwise interesting but improvised *The Unforgettable Fire*-style lyrics. The love Bono has comes from God, and though God holds him in His fist, he still needs the lover's kiss. He has one eye in the heavens and the other firmly on earth. Bono always did say that the guys of U2 had their heads in heaven but their feet in the mud. Bono is held in the security of God's love, but still he finds his insecurities throwing him onto the dependence on his wife Ali's kiss.

Bono's relationship with Ali has been an absolute rock in his journey, both personally and artistically. Alison Stewart was a schoolgirl sweetheart whom Bono has been with since he was sixteen and married to since he was twenty-two. In the world of pop music, their relationship is an exceptional success. Bono is the first to acknowledge this is due to Ali's strength of character and spiritual steadiness. She has never been satisfied being the wife of a rock star, nor has she been uncomfortable with that. She has studied for a master's degree. She has founded a charity that helps the children of Chernobyl. She is known as a human being of some renown in her own right in Ireland, and she has brought up the couple's four children.

When it came to love songs, U2 was a slow starter. It wasn't until the band's third album that its first clearly defined love songs appeared. Bono had written "Two Hearts Beat as One" in August 1982 about his marriage. *The Unforgettable Fire* touched on their love and domesticity in "Promenade." But *The Joshua Tree* is where U2 really began to look into the romantic heart with the song "With or Without You." Adam told *Rolling Stone*: "The thing is to challenge the radio. To get 'With or Without You' on the radio is pretty good. You don't expect to hear it there. Maybe in church."[5]

Even "With or Without You" is not a plain-sailing love song. There are moments when it appears that it is focusing on the old cliché, "Women—you can't live with them; you can't live without them." But then the lyrics twist and turn and deal with a whole lot more than a relationship between men and women. Weaving two or three themes into one song has been another trait of U2's lyric-writing. Niall Stokes, in his song-by-song account of the band's entire catalog, is accurate when he sees erotic love and agape love mixing around here, and also another great U2 theme of surrendering the ego in the lyrics "give yourself away" (Luke 9:24). Of course, a person does give himself away in love and marriage, but this kind of surrender could be spiritual or even in opening up to hundreds of thousands of fans every night.

This new discovery of the love song developed even more in *Achtung Baby*, the group's first album of the nineties. In their first decade, Bono only scratched the surface of the heart in his obsession with the soul, and he purposely shifted direction with this album. Bono has commented often that U2 did everything the wrong way around. Other bands started singing about girls and then found the issues of the cosmos and started singing about God; U2 started out singing about God and eventually ended up doing a love album. It wasn't until after twelve years and six albums that Bono stepped up to a mic and used words such as "baby" and "sugar."

Bono has always held his women, at least his mother and wife, on a pedestal. He told Niall Stokes, "I do tend to idealize women."[6] This is a result, no doubt, of having lost his mother at fourteen years old. This leaves her, whose face he says he cannot remember, as a bit of a legend. It was a turning point in his life that certainly sent him off seeking God for some solace and direction. "I Will Follow" on the first album is another mingling and interweaving of his fascination with the loss of his mother and his discovery of God. Later on *Pop*, "Mofo" would weave the two again. Not long after his mother passed away and around the same time he ran into God, Bono fell in love with Ali. The fact that Ali is who she is would leave anyone seeing the wonder in womankind. In "Ultra Violet (Light My Way)," Bono sings again about his need for Ali and how when he feels like trash, she makes him clean. He asks her to light his way. There is good reason to read this song as being about God as much as his wife, but he is asking that Ali would be a path for his feet. In many ways, Ali has always been just that.

Bob Dylan's *Blood on the Tracks* is the quintessential heartbreak album. He wrote it coming out of a time of separation from his wife, Sara, and it was the delicate chiseling of beauty out of pain. *Achtung Baby* is U2's version of the same kind of album, less delicate maybe but just as painful and poignant. Heartache is the overriding theme. The songs seem to have their origin in two sources: First, the love that Bono and Ali have and that Bono cherishes. He is aware of her as a spiritual guru filling the gap left by no church connection and being a sense of reality in a rock world where it is easy to lose all perspective on who you are and what life is all about. The other case study is the sadder one. The Edge had married Aislinn O'Sullivan about the same time Bono and Ali wed. The Edge and his wife, too, had a young family but went through a separation that ended in divorce. This is one of the few hiccups in the scandal-free lives of U2's members. Even then, the quiet way the divorce was dealt with is a radical alternative to the tabloid soap operas of most celebrities' love lives.

Bono believes in the miracle of love and has never seemed to doubt that the God dimension is vital to keeping it together. He dealt with this sticking together on *Pop*'s "Do You Feel Loved." On "Staring at the Sun," he seems pretty sure of where the miracle of the sticking together comes from, suggesting that he and Ali are stuck together with God's glue. He suggests, too, that the glue gets stickier as it goes, the secret of their longevity.

chapter 08

HEARTLAND

U2 has always had a good relationship with America. The band's first gig on the soil of the Promised Land was at New York City's The Ritz in December 1980. Unlike so many bands before them, U2 didn't wait until they broke through in Britain before cracking the United States. America has loved U2 since the beginning, and the band has been wrapped up in the country even more. When Anthony DeCurtis came to review *Rattle and Hum* at the end of 1988, he confirmed this: "Recorded almost entirely in the United States, the album also carries forward U2's near obsession with the brave new world of America."[1]

Often, Irish kids look to America rather than Britain for their inspiration. Dublin in 1977 had a very different culture than American cities, but the city was exposed to heavy doses of America daily on its televisions. If you are into music, then you are constantly gazing across the Atlantic Ocean to the place your influence comes from. It becomes a mythological land and always leaves you wondering. Sun and big skies and deserts and skyscrapers and those big, big cars. It may be that unless you get in a car on a California highway with the top down and the radio turned up, you will never fully understand rock 'n' roll.

Then there is the other side of the connection. There are more Irish people living in America than in Ireland. As the result of the mass exodus from Ireland to America at the time of the famine and ever since, there are millions upon millions of Americans who claim Irish ancestry. Saint Patrick's Day parades are taken more seriously in New York than in Ireland. There is a strong affinity between the two nations. As Bono would say in the song "New York," the Irish have been coming to New York for years and think that they own it. Maybe it was that Irish-American thing in the back of Bono's mind, but America always had a magnetism for U2.

As the members of U2 set out on tour after Live Aid in support of *The Unforgettable Fire*, they were getting more and more drawn into the American dream and its landscape and nightmare. They were starting to read lots of American writers. Ginsberg, Burroughs, Kerouac, and the beat poets must have been intriguing for a band that was on the road so much. Bono said, "Allen sort of turned us onto the road, and he broke me into America."[2] He also credited Ginsberg with getting him into the poetry of the Bible: "Howl was the one that turned me on because of its biblical roots and discovering how, in the Psalms, ideas rhyme rather than words. The Bible became poetic to me again after reading Ginsberg." Flannery O'Connor also must be seen as one of the influences on a song like "Exit," with its twist and tragic end to religious experience and deepest darkness related to light.

As with "Exit," there was a lot of America on *The Joshua Tree*, including "God's Country" with its crooked crosses and Statue of Liberty coming to rescue the immigrant. It was a big, mysterious, barren American desert on the album's cover. Twelve years later, the band would throw out a phrase that would echo back to the image when in "Mofo" on *Pop* they would be "looking in the places where no flowers grow" to find something to save their souls. They were seeking meaning and hope in the desert-scapes.

But if the members of U2 have a lot of questions about the American dream, and even more angry opinions about her foreign policy as in "Bullet the Blue Sky" and "Mothers of the Disappeared," there was still enough fascination and love to go in search of their rock 'n' roll roots. *Rattle and Hum* was a study, a thesis almost, of all the influences of rock 'n' roll. In 1983, the band released its first live album, and it seems Paul McGuinness probably thought it would be a good consolidation idea to do another live album and video. Live albums have been the object of more and more suspicion in recent years, but in the seventies and eighties, they were a way to gain a little time for the band between albums and make a cheap buck from an album that is inexpensive to record. Of course, U2 was not so keen to do something as mercenary or artistically freewheeling as that. On *Rattle and Hum* the band members stretched themselves again. They not only wrote and recorded new songs, but they made a movie that followed a journey through America on tour as well as in a historical search for their influences. Interestingly, when they looked deep into their influences, it was not traveling down the west coast of Ireland to find fiddlers and pipers and the seannos (unaccompanied Gaelic Irish singers). It was in America.

"DREAM UP THE KIND OF WORLD YOU WANT TO LIVE IN. DREAM OUT LOUD AT HIGH VOLUME. THAT'S WHAT WE DO FOR A LIVING." —BONO

Though the Beatles' influence on the band gets recognized in the raucous version of "Helter Skelter," even the reason for its inclusion on *Rattle and Hum* had origins in the United States. The reason was to steal the song back from the notorious American murderer Charles Manson, who had used a lot of the lyrics off the Beatles' *White Album,* including lyrics from "Helter Skelter," as prophecy from God that he should indulge in wanton killings. When U2 trawled through its musical heritage, there was Billie Holliday, that "Angel of Harlem" whose jazzy gospel soul singing lit up the forties, and B.B. King, whose blues had stretched out more than half the century. Then there were Dylan and Jimi Hendrix in abundance—Hendrix's version of "The Star-Spangled Banner" and the Dylan song that Hendrix made famous, "All Along the Watchtower." His Bobness himself appeared as a co-writer for "Love Rescue Me." There were also name checks to Miles Davis and John Coltrane. There were delta suns, deserts, and ghost ranch hills. There was a "preacher in a traveling show," a spiritual entrepreneur, the likes of whom is rarely found in the Republic of Ireland. There were death rows, skid rows, and gangs. In the movie, there were journeys to Sun Studios and Graceland, and it is a wonder that "Can't Help Falling in Love" came along some years later and not somewhere on the four sides of the vinyl version of *Rattle and Hum*.

"ALL I HAVE IS A RED GUITAR, THREE CHORDS, AND THE TRUTH." — BONO

The movie and the album have never been seen as a highlight in U2's career. Written off as self-indulgence, they no doubt suffer from being sandwiched between two classics, *The Joshua Tree* and *Achtung Baby*. They were not without merits, however, and the movie had people standing on their seats applauding back home in Dublin as though they had been to a concert. The album did more than simply regurgitate U2 live favorites, though. Similar to what Neil Young had done on *Time Fades Away* in 1973 and Jackson Browne had done on *Running on Empty* in 1977, the stage and places along the road were used as the setting to release new material. The live stuff is emotionally powerful, especially on "Sunday Bloody Sunday," captured on the day of the Enniskillen bombing, and "Bullet the Blue Sky." "Silver and Gold" from the *Sun City: Artists United Against Apartheid* album recorded with Little Steven gets a rockier outing with Bono ordering The Edge to play the blues, which he does in a way that makes it the song's definitive version. The album has at least nine new songs that, maybe apart from "Van Diemen's Land," all stand unembarrassed in the U2 song lists. U2 continued to feature "Love

Comes to Town," "Angel of Harlem," "All I Want Is You" and "Desire," the band's first U.K. number one song, in its live set right up to Popmart, and "Hawkmoon 269" has been described as one of U2's finest moments.

In a quick panorama across the spiritual landscape of *Rattle and Hum*, there is much to cause the listener to stop and ponder. Jesus is called upon for some relief in "Silver and Gold." Again, the cohabitation of good and evil in the same home is disturbingly pointed out in the line "praying hands hold me down"—an indictment on the use of the Christian faith to excuse the atrocities against the black majority in South Africa and many other places across the world.

The first rays of lamenting Psalms dawn on *Rattle and Hum*, too. Bono's line that salvation is in the blues in "Angel of Harlem" is a reference to what Bono would come back to again and again: that the Psalms were the blues. Then, of course, there is "Love Rescue Me," where he and Bob Dylan revisit Psalm 23 in the lamenting way that U2 would return to throughout the nineties. In some ways, it's a follow-up song to one of Dylan's greatest moments: "Every Grain of Sand," a wonderfully tender and vulnerable testimony of spiritual frailty. "Love Rescue Me" is about a similar spiritual struggler who sees dark shades and reflections and is losing his ability to believe that there is any comfort in King David's rod and staff (Ps. 23:4). But there is still a dim, flickering belief that love will come to bring salvation in the end.

The love that Bono and Dylan are crying out to rescue them is defined in the blues song on the album that delivers that salvation. The love in "Love Comes to Town," written for the great bluesman B.B. King, is clearly the cross of Jesus. "Love Comes to Town" evokes the old gospel hymn "Were You There When They Crucified My Lord" when it declares that he was indeed there and helped the soldier with his sword and threw dice for Jesus' clothes as well as realizing in conclusion that this was the place where love conquered "the great divide." Again, it is a spelled-out proclamation, this time Bono seeing himself as having put his Lord on the cross like the centurion who stood guard at Christ's crucifixion and suddenly realized He was the Son of God. Here, as in "I Still Haven't Found What I'm Looking For," which was given a black gospel remake in the *Rattle and Hum* movie, there is a pointing toward the atonement—"I saw love conquer the great divide."

Love here obviously is made flesh in Jesus, and it is that love that the band claims to believe in on "God Part 2." On this track, the band takes up a dialogue of sorts with their hero, John Lennon, and are happy to stand up for their faith by disagreeing with his 1970 conclusions of who God was or was not. Lennon's song "God" appeared on his *Plastic Ono Band* album, where he railed off a long list of things that he no longer believed in, including the Beatles, Elvis, and Jesus. "God," he exorcised, was merely a concept to measure pain—pain being his obsession at the time, having just gone through Primal Scream therapy. "The dream is over," he depressingly announced, and all he now believed in was himself and Yoko. U2's "God," labeled "Part 2," took a more positive angle on belief. Though it also listed what not to believe in, it was much more constructive in its negatives. The list included Uzis, excess, riches, drugs and sexual abuse. The ultimate item, though, was in the opening line that they didn't believe in the devil or his lies.

It is a behavioral manifesto. This is a clear code of biblical living. It is close to being a sermon against the world's vices that the kingdom of God opposes. In the end, there is more fighting talk against the devil and his rule across the world: the darkness needs a darn good kicking til it bleeds some light. What a wonderful motto for the kingdom builder. The lines come from a song by Canadian singer Bruce Cockburn called "Lovers in a Dangerous Time" from his album *Stealing Fire*.

It is hardly likely that the band heard it on the radio. For thirty years, Cockburn has been releasing exquisite albums and never received the recognition he is due. He does have a rabid little following, though, as a result of his virtuoso guitar playing and the poeticism of his lyrics, which, like U2, have dealt mainly with spirituality, politics, and justice. He has a Christian faith and, again like U2, avoided the ghettos. It is hard to imagine that U2 came across him any other way than because he was a fellow pilgrim. Bono's friend T-Bone Burnett, who later produced some of Cockburn's albums, would no doubt have moved in his circle, and he probably is the link. They also visited South America with the same Christian-based relief agency, though not at the same time, and wrote similarly angry songs about the experience. U2 has even gone on record as saying the band recorded Cockburn's "If I Had a Rocket Launcher," but as U2 couldn't beat his version, it remained unreleased. They did meet in August 1987 when Bono went to the Greenbelt Arts Festival in England just to see Cockburn perform. They spent that night in a hotel room with two of the festival's seminar speakers, John Smith and Gustavo Paragon. Such moments have been U2's church for some years. Interactions with stimulating Christian leaders worldwide in more informal settings have kept U2 members sharp in their Christian worldview.

Maybe the most memorable line on *Rattle and Hum* is not sung but shouted by Bono in the middle of the band's impromptu version of Dylan's "All Along the Watchtower," which they cobbled together, seeking anyone in their road crew who knew the words to enlighten them as they sang in the downtown business district of San Francisco. Bono cries, "All I have is a red guitar, three chords, and the truth." Again misconstrued as an egotistical rant, it was another humble cry that these guys had little to offer even musically, but they were trying to make something of their privileged position by being honest and seeking some truth in a world full of fraud and anything goes.

The Love Comes to Town tour that followed *Rattle and Hum*'s release took U2 to the end of what was in many ways its decade. It culminated where it all began, in Dublin, Ireland, with four sell-out nights at the Point Theatre. The New Year's Eve gig was relayed live on radio across Europe. Listeners were encouraged to tape it, and several magazines, including *Hot Press* and *Q*, printed a cut-out cover to put inside cassette boxes. The end of the decade live on the radio was too good an opportunity for Bono to miss. So as midnight approached and a few bars of "Auld Lang Syne" were played, he made the speech that not only raised the emotions of the moment but put a stop to another phase of the band, opening up a door to the nineties. Bono said: "Here she comes: the future. Forget about the past. We're gonna celebrate the future ... Seeing as it's New Year's Day, you probably expect me to get all sentimental, yeah? Well, you're exactly right. Here's to the future! The only limitations are the limits of our imagination. Dream up the kind of world you want to live in. Dream out loud at high volume. That's what we do for a living."

This was a wonderful comment on what was a fulcrum moment in U2's history, a throwaway line in the heat of a heightened adrenalin buzz that could be a thread between the serious political stances of the eighties and what was about to be dreamed up in the nineties. But that wasn't all. This speech was full of a preacher's prophetic intent. If anything was to come of any of U2's passionate concerns in the eighties, their audience and those to whom they campaigned would need wild imagination to dream up the kind of world that U2 had come to visualize from their kingdom-of-God perspective.

Imagine a world where the blacks in South Africa could learn to forgive and live alongside their white oppressors. Imagine a white government in Pretoria that could see a new South Africa with, by some kind of miracle, Nelson Mandela as president. Imagine that there could be a ceasefire in Northern Ireland where the paramilitaries would lay down their weapons and sit together in a new Northern Ireland government. Imagine if enemies could be loved (Luke 6:27). Imagine if the hungry could be fed (Luke 6:21). Imagine if the meek could inherit the earth (Matt. 5:5). Imagine a world where the first would be last and the last would be first (Luke 13:30). Imagine. Without the turbocharged engine of imagination, nothing can change in our world. God told His people that they would dream dreams and see visions (Joel 2:28). Imagining another world and how it could be and how it could work and where to begin to put it together is where the kingdom begins.

At the end of the eighties, Bono and U2 beseeched their faithful audience to imbibe their passions and dreams and to dream out loud. They would repeat that phrase again as they do their artistic dreaming and imagining in a whole new concept of U2 that will soon be born.

chapter 09

REINVENTION

The video footage conjures up an Eastern European mood in the drabbest, grayest, and most ominous way. Every shot is close up. Bono is in shiny black leather. There's an onslaught of sound. The Edge's guitar sputters and stutters and shudders onto a different avenue of his trademark minimalism. It's a new, strange incarnation of the familiar. It's almost like he turned down the brightness of the echo effects unit and threw shades of darkness across the U2 horizon. Then there's Bono, his distorted voice heavy, breathing, mumbling out confusion and doubt. Stars are falling, and there are liars and thieves and all sorts of characters struggling to survive in a world as harsh as the new industrial sound.

"The Fly," U2's first single of the nineties, made some of the band's fans shudder. U2 singles have never been predictable. Starting with "Desire" and through the video singles "Numb," "Discotheque," and "Beautiful Day," U2 tends to make its first single from a new album a wake-up call to the radio-listening and video-watching public. "The Fly" was the statement that an album with "Achtung" in its title should make. This band takes great pleasure in pushing its audience to the boundary with the first single. Then, after weeks of uncertainty and doubt, the fans are reacclimated.

A few weeks later, when *Achtung Baby* was released, what the fans would hear on the next track would continue the discomfort. "Zoo Station" came over all industrial, with The Edge giving this funky "grinding of the girders" riff, Bono singing distortedly, and the whole thing seeming to be out of sorts, disturbed, turbulent, and disconcerting. Bono was ready for the laughing gas and what was coming next. The one certainty was that what's next was going to be very different from what had been. When Bono told the Point Theatre audience two years earlier that the band was going away for a while to dream it all up again, no one could have expected this. Not even U2.

"THERE ARE A LOT OF PEOPLE A BIT PUZZLED, TO BE HONEST, ABOUT WHAT WE ARE UP TO AND WHAT WE ARE TRYING TO DO." —THE EDGE

It was a remarkable reinvention. As *Rattle and Hum* looked back to the past in an attempt to discover the roots of what U2 had become, *Achtung Baby* sent the band hurtling into the future. U2 hit the road of the nineties heading even faster than the historical changes in Eastern Europe. It may be the band's best work, eclipsing even *The Joshua Tree* in songwriting, performance, and vocals. The photographs and videos revealed Bono behind shades and dressed in hedonistic shiny leather. There were belly dancers and cross-dressing and television screens with weird and wonderful slogans. There was even a naked picture of Adam on the cover. There are more songs about love on *Achtung Baby* than the band had ever written before.

Why? What had happened? Had the U2 camp finally broken its ties with Christianity and headed out into the modern world? Here is an album of songs full of irony and lust and betrayal and almost sleaze that seemed to indicate a band that had strayed to the edge of lewd sexuality, just leering over the precipice into a hedonistic abyss. Surely there could be no explanation to this one. The video released a year later has a lot of historical footage and snippets of band interviews. On it, The Edge said, "There are a lot of people a bit puzzled, to be honest, about what we are up to and what we are trying to do."

Certainly, this is true of those within the Church. U2 has suffered at the hands of the great Christian art theft. The band has been misunderstood and maligned and judged for what it does, in many cases because the Church has little desire or ability to understand the arts and is rarely given help from within to look critically at the arts. The robbery has meant that for the vast part of four hundred years, Christians have not thought artistically and have not encouraged the creative among them to develop their gifts. As U2 moved from being a polemic chanting band to an impressionistic and later a persona-wearing, ironic cultural prophet, it largely fell on the deaf ears of the robbed.

North Belfast is a place of division and community tension. There exists the most concentrated microcosm of what has become known as the Northern Ireland troubles. There is a "peace wall," which is actually quite the opposite, that divides the Roman Catholic nationalists from their Protestant loyalist neighbors, literally a stone's throw away. In such an environment, many of the area's youth workers are involved in reconciliation programs, creating safe ways for the youth of both communities to interact, listen, learn, and hopefully come to understand one another's religion, political conditioning, and culture. In one such program, a youth worker was showing a group of Roman Catholic youth around a Protestant church. As the group came through the building and into the main sanctuary, a startled Roman Catholic boy shouted, "You've been robbed!" Compared to a Catholic chapel, with its statues and icons and multiplicity of artistic representations, the basic, empty, dull, drab Presbyterian building was quite a culture shock.

On the other side of the cosmos, on the other side of time, God moved across the chaos and began to imagine. Colors—blue and green and red and yellow. All the colors somehow mixed together. What would green look like alongside blue, with a little thin band of gold to join the two? Mountains. Oceans. Beaches. Rivers. Trees. Canyons. Valleys. Shapes and textures and smells and taste. All these things existed in God's imagination, even before He decided to make them into a reality and create His artistic masterpiece—the world. God was a Creator (Gen. 1:1). The first thing we learn about Him in the Scriptures is that He was an artist. When we read that man was created in God's image, the only thing we know about God is that He was an artist (Gen. 1:26).

That should have a deep impact on how those who claim to believe and worship and follow His ways work out their salvation and bring in His kingdom in these dawning moments of the twenty-first century. Yet that young man in north Belfast may have uttered more than a humorous squeal of naive surprise. Maybe he was speaking in prophetic terms. The Church has been robbed. Robbed of art. Robbed of the creative image of God. Who has robbed the Church? How did it happen? The Church has robbed itself, and many well-meaning worldviews and ideologies down through the centuries have been the tools that were used.

The Reformation robbed us of art. When Martin Luther discovered that he could be justified before a holy God by God's grace and the work of Christ (Rom. 3:21-26), it was a crucial moment in Church history. In the ensuing division within Roman Catholicism, many decisions were made in the early days of Protestantism that were taken as being in reaction to withdrawal from Catholicism. With many good reasons at the time, the Reformers reacted to the statues of saints that sometimes replaced God as the focus of people's prayers. To rid churches of any art seems to have been a rather imbalanced response. The Reformers were quick to quote the second of the Ten Commandments, in which God tells His people, "You shall not make for yourself an idol in the form of anything in heaven or on the earth beneath or in the waters below. You shall not bow down to them or worship them" (Exod. 20:4-5). The commandment, though, does not forbid art in church. Eleven chapters after the commandments, we find that the first person in the Bible to be described as being filled with the Spirit of God is Bezalel, whom God has given "skill, ability and knowledge in all kinds of crafts" (Exod. 31:1-11). And he is to use these divinely given gifts to decorate the Holy Place of worship. Today most meeting places for worship do not evoke in people the creative heart of God. People are more likely to think churches have been robbed. The arts are peripheral.

Modernity also has taken its toll on all things artistic. In the past ten years, there has been an amazing amount said about postmodernity, and there have been evangelicals warning against it as a dangerous new worldview. Any of the lenses by which the world is assessed have to be critically studied, their weaknesses pointed out. For Christians, all worldviews taint definitions of belief and need to be stringently critiqued. Holding postmodernity up to the light of modernity as its winnowing sieve is giving an authority to modernity that is dangerous, but seemingly natural within the evangelical world. Modernity itself is a faulty worldview. It is the failure of modernity in fulfilling its great promises of a better world that has led to its demise.

Under the influence of modernity, the Church became obsessed by definitions and seamless doctrine. Modernity was based on a scientific and rational reasoning that everything could be proven by human experimentation and that this exploration of the scientific field could come up with a superior world and a greatly improved human being. In many ways, this worldview was seen as a huge threat to the mystery of faith. Modernism was driving out the mysteries and belief in a supernatural unseen world, one that was being replaced by a world that could be explained in clear scientific terms. That Christianity should be taken captive by such a system of thought seems a little incongruous, but it led to a couple of centuries of clear systematic theology, apologetics, and an overemphasis on the word spoken and written in the communication of Christian truth. Most of these things in themselves are great aids to

Christianity's case in the world, but the loss of mystery, experience and any artistic representation of the Gospel was detrimental.

The Bible uses a wide array of creative ways to communicate truth: law, history, poems, songs, literature, lament, prophesy, proverbs, dreams, angels, miracles, parables, preaching, epistles, and visions. When the evangelicals of the world decided that the Word preached was God's most efficient way of communicating, they overlooked the fact that when Jesus was born, God was saying, among other things, that those ways were not sufficient and that the Word had to become flesh (John 1:1, 14). God's Word is much more than words. Modernity coerced Christianity into taking the flesh and making it into words again. Art suffered. It was not a clearly defined and conclusive kind of rationalism. It left feelings hanging. Stories or songs might stress some points of theological truth and fail to cover other aspects of the Gospel. They missed the fact that Jesus left the crucial doctrine of atonement out of the parable of the prodigal son (Luke 15:11-32). Jesus, in fact, was much more an artist than a preacher, preferring stories to open the truth and in sometimes oblique ways promising the disciples that those with ears to hear would hear. It could be said that the only writer in the Bible with any interest in theological definition is the apostle Paul, and though we thank God for him and the theological explanation of his letters, we must never lose the balance between this and art.

The Puritans also left a negative legacy on art. Though they were sincere in their attempts to lead their followers into good biblical behavioral patterns, there were side effects. There was a tendency to set up boundaries to help progress toward holiness, but that quickly slipped into a judgmental legalism. The general premise to stay safe from any dangers of "the world" led them into an almost dualist approach to the "spiritual" and the "worldly." Art had a tendency to fall into the worldly camp. The Protestant work ethic, which also seems to have its roots in the Puritan legacy, pushed the arts to the fringes. H.R. Rookmaker, in his influential book *Modern Art and the Death of a Culture*, wrote, "We can only conclude that the Calvinistic and

Puritan movement (at least from the seventeenth century on) had virtually no appreciation for the fine arts, due to a mystic influence that held that the arts were in themselves worldly, unholy and that a Christian should not participate in them."[1]

So what had caused the shift within the U2 camp to this new image on *Achtung Baby*? For some time, the members of U2 had been a little uncomfortable with touring. It had become a job. They had been on the treadmill of the circus that followed the release and phenomenal success of *The Joshua Tree*. There was a feeling in the ranks that they could not go on like this. There was little evidence of this in their high-spirited live performances throughout those three years, but it had taken its toll. They needed to change something.

"I DON'T HAVE AN IRONIC PERSONNA LIKE DAVID BYRNE OR DAVID BOWIE TO STAND BEHIND. IT'S ME UP THERE ON THE SCREEN, AND IT MAKES ME CRINGE." —BONO

Then there was fame. The dreams of fame and the hard work that gets people there never really prepared them for it. Since the beginning, Bono and Adam had believed with little doubt that the spark of U2 was destined to take them to the top. Now that they were at the pinnacle of their field, they discovered the dilemmas and struggles of being the biggest act in rock. Bono was feeling that he was losing who he was in the madness of being a rock star. Lines around his sense of identity were blurring. Being the spokesman for a generation and being constantly out there exposing his beliefs and causes and fighting for this and that had taken its toll. The press had begun to see him as much too serious, and, after a decade, the press was beginning to turn. He felt he needed to step back. How could that be done? How about putting on a pair of shades and stepping into a character like the Fly? Personas and play acting would bring with it some protection.

Critically, *Rattle and Hum* had been seen as a bit of a pretentious overindulgence. Critics felt that the band members had gotten a little carried away and were not just tapping into their roots in singing Dylan and Beatles songs and bringing B.B. King on stage and singing about Billie Holliday but were setting themselves up as their equals. That the band constantly admitted to its failings, on and off vinyl, seems to have been missed. There is no doubt, though, that these guys felt they were becoming caricatures and needed to change the whole darn thing. To go from the critics' caricatures to their own, imagined cartoon personas was the new strategy.

Then there was the challenge. U2 had been assured of its place in the high echelons of rock, but the band members had never made that their goal. That was something that came with their art. Nor was money the most important issue. While most bands set out to get famous, get laid, and get rich, these were not the goals of the Christian-hearted U2. The band members were obsessed about something different: Their art. Being good at what they did. Becoming better at what they did. Stretching their abilities as far as possible. By the end of the Rattle and Hum tour, they were ready to see where they could take it. They needed to spark their imaginations all over again.

How could they do it? Where would they go in their imagination to come up with a reinvention? There had been clues for some time. These clues were hard to see in foresight, maybe even by the band members themselves. But looking back, "Desire" seemed to be a major transitional song. It was heading toward the sexual language of *Achtung Baby*, and the preacher who went around stealing hearts would be a character that the band would spend some time irrigating and bringing to fruition. "God Part 2" was almost a confession of the weaknesses of *Rattle and Hum*, giving up belief in the sixties and suggesting you only elevate the past when the future is lacking in inspiration and innovation. It was a huge hint that U2 needed a new source of inspiration. There was also a lack of belief that rock music could change the world, which was another window into an album that left those high ideals and issue-based songs behind.

It also was becoming obvious in interviews that the boys were at the end of one rich vein. The seam was becoming used up, and a new mine needed to be dug. Bono openly discussed his frustration with being himself when he said: "I don't have an ironic persona like David Byrne or David Bowie to stand behind. It's me up there on the screen, and it makes me cringe."[2]

The scary truth is that when the band members got together in Berlin to crack the top of the new mine and see if the seam was as rich as before, they had little idea what was there. It seems that excavation was a rather difficult job, and it took some time to strike anything at all. At times, they even wondered if the game was over. There had been rumors after the Point Theatre gigs when Bono said it was the end of the road for U2 that maybe he meant it. In the Hansa studios, people wondered if he had been prophetic. That U2 persevered and came out with something as essential as *Achtung Baby* must have at least fulfilled the band's artistic needs.

A year off before the *Achtung* sessions started gave the band time to read and think and be influenced by conversations in the vacuum of commercial or work pressures. The band always has had an artistic, loyal, and long-standing inner circle, and in those down times, the members' hanging out and dialoguing and debating constantly threw out ideas. When the guys were wrestling with the need to divide their public and private lives and also to dream it up all over again, their old friend Gavin Friday was in on the conversation. Both Bill Flanagan[3] and B.P. Fallon[4], whose books on the band describe this phase wonderfully, suggest that Friday is in on all the band's social and artistic dealings. As late as *Pop*, he is credited on the album cover as a consultant poptician, and Bono recognized him and Guggi in interviews post *All That You Can't Leave Behind* as the "no" men in the camp. They are who the U2 guys call when they fear they have lost the plot.

Gavin Friday grew up on the same north Dublin street as Bono. The two have been friends for more than thirty years. Friday has been a huge influence on the U2 singer. The former Virgin Prune may have even inspired the entire persona-toting U2. Friday's Prunes were a performance art band that Bono said was twenty years ahead of its time. Why these two guys didn't form a band together way back when is a mystery, apart from the fact, of course, that Bono answered Larry's ad on the school notice board and hooked up first with the band that would change the world. Friday started the Prunes, a Lypton Village gaggle, with Guggi, another lifelong friend of Bono's.

The Prunes were wild onstage and off, and it would seem that Gavin was first to leave the Shalom community. Just as he had been another voice back in the days of the dilemma with rock and faith, so he continues to be a man of constant friendly and healthy friction, always throwing another slant. His natural penchant for throwing other slants headed U2 down the persona road. Friday, having long been the thespian rock star, obviously had been living out of characters for some time. When Bono looked to find some new angles, of course he might look to a close friend whose work he greatly admired. Friday was a huge Oscar Wilde fan. He even wrote a song around Wilde's words. It's the title track on his 1989 album *Each Man Kills the Thing He Loves*. The song titles and lyrics on that album contain words such as "Tell Tale Hart," "Another Blow on the Bruise" and "Dazzle and Delight." You can sense what U2 might have been listening to before heading off to Berlin.

Bono's friendship with T-Bone Burnett was another constant at the time. Burnett is the tall, lanky American guitarist on Bob Dylan's Rolling Thunder Review tour who had formed the Alpha Band with the other two coverts of that tour, Steven Soles and David Mansfield, before making a highly acclaimed solo EP, *Trap Door*, in 1982. Bono would co-write "Having a Wonderful Time Wish You Were Her" with T-Bone Burnett for that album's follow-up, *Behind the Trap Door*, and "Purple Heart" for *The Talking Animals*. Burnett had a habit—particularly on his *Proof Through the Night* album—of writing songs that could be seen as being written to a woman or to America. Similarly, Flanagan has said that *Achtung Baby* is a suite of songs that could be interpreted as referring to women or God.

Certainly that could be said of "Until the End of the World." Some have seen it as another song of betrayal, and that may be the only way to fit it into the rest of the album's songs of sexual politics. But it can only be about one thing: the betrayal of Christ (John 18:2-6). Judas is not someone to whom Christians have given a lot of time. He was Satan incarnate and sold his soul for thirty pieces of silver. If only Judas' story was that simple. Judas and his story were so complex that Bob Dylan had wondered if Judas Iscariot had God on his side?[5] It's a mighty question that like so many other things we want to ignore. As always, Bono faced it head on. For him, it seems to have been one of those rich seams he had been trying to tap.

Bono got inside the story. The closeness of the bride and groom was a wonderful image of the return of Christ at the end of the world, and missing too much, if you stop to think, seems to have been a shot across the bows of postmodern culture that U2 would take on. It could also be an ironic dig at those who would get nothing from this album because they wouldn't stop to think. Kissing Jesus and breaking His heart was a bringing to life of the passion story that seems to have lost its flesh and blood and feelings and pain. Judas' emotions after the act was done are a musical moment of genius. No sermon or Easter reflection could quite conjure such a roller coaster of insight into this vital event to the redemption of the world. In the end, we are left to wonder. When Judas reaches for the One he tried to destroy, Bono uses the words of the song title—"Until the End of the World"—which intriguingly in the Gospel are said to the disciples as they head out to convert the world (Matt. 28:20). The promise that He had given to His friends of His eternal loyalty is spoken here to Judas. Does the song conclude with his salvation or damnation?

Without doubt, the spark that lit Bono's Gethsemane flame was a book of poems by Irish poet Brendan Kennelly called *The Book of Judas*.[6] When the book and albums appeared around the same time, both men reviewed each other's work. Kennelly's work is quite a tome, eight years of poems, where profanity sits alongside Christ as he looks at the Judas of Gethsemane, the Judas in our culture, and the Judas in us all. In his preface, he questions:

> Was Judas the fall guy in some sublime design he didn't even begin to understand? What was he trying to prove? Was he a not-so-bright or too-bright politician? A man whose vision of things was being throttled by another, more popular vision? A spirit not confined to the man who bore the name Judas but one more alive and consequential now at the famined, bloated, trivialized, analytical, bomb-menaced, progressive, money-mad, reasonable end of the twentieth century than ever before?

It's obvious how such questions, and the poems that explored them, would have caught Bono's eye. It's biblical. It's contemporary. It's different from what U2 had been doing. It's not something else, though; it's the same thing from a different angle.

Is that not what poets and songwriters should be doing? Let the systematic theologians spell it out. Let the artists throw out thoughts and slants, maybe even slants no one else has thought of. They should give another view of something familiar to help us learn more about it. They should deal with love, life, good, evil, God, the world, and faith. Many of the biblical writers were poets more than they were theologians. Poets and prophets ranted and raved, and storytellers wrote great yarns that all had different slants on God and life and faith. Perhaps the poet's absence from the Church for many centuries has left it deprived of much insight.

One of the most telling aspects of *Achtung Baby* may be how it reveals the artistic heart of U2. Whereas many bands are interested primarily in filling their bank accounts and are not too fussed about saying anything in their music, the members of U2 are artists who need something to say. As they set out in the reinvention of 1991, they were probably trying to make a shallow, not serious U2-type work. They probably were thinking, *Let's just rock.* As the recording process gathered momentum, however, what became obvious was that these guys could not be frivolous. Since they were teenagers and found faith in Christ, they had been asking cosmic questions. It was not going to be possible to back out now.

In some ways, the cover and title were the only funny things about the album. It seems Joe O'Herlihy used the phrase "Achtung Baby" endlessly during the Hansa sessions in Berlin, having picked it up off the Mel Brooks film *The Producers*. It's a title that has been highly criticized as foolish, and Bono felt the press would have been even harder on the band had it not been frivolous in the packaging. He said at the time: "It's a con, in a way. We call it *Achtung Baby*, grinning up our sleeves in the photography. But it's probably the heaviest record we've ever made."[7]

The Edge's divorce was part of the reason for the "blood and guts" on the album. Bono would say, though, that The Edge's struggles at the time were far from the only influence. The songs were about what many of his friends were struggling with at the time. The whole miracle of two people finding love and then the hard work of maintaining it was a universal theme. That the band was recording the album at the end of communism in East Germany and that the guys were watching the Persian Gulf War between sessions had to have an effect, even though there is little point of reference to all that in the lyrics, apart from "Zoo Station." This song was the gateway to the East or West, depending on which way a person was heading, and that crossroads image was a perfect lead track for a band heading toward its own kind of freedom.

The opening lyrics to "Zoo Station" about being ready for what is next were clearly a sign that this song was simply about the band and the reinvention. What was happening in the band would be tangled up or woven into what was going on in the relationships around Bono, as well as what was going on in his own head, heart, and soul. "One," which is the torch song of the album, seems to have evolved around Eno finding two melodies that the band decided to play over each other with Bono ad-libbing as he played them. Hence, we can be one but not the same. It then becomes more, but it's a tapestry of Bono's thoughts.

It is inevitable that another intricate part of the tapestry would be his faith. As they couldn't be frivolous if they tried, they couldn't leave God out if they tried, either. As well as in "Until the End of the World," which was written for the Wim Wenders movie of that name, Jesus appears in "One" and in the song of Bono's spiritual hypocrisy, "Acrobat." Following Flanagan's suggestion to hear all U2 love songs as songs to God and see how they change becomes as interesting as ever on *Achtung Baby*.[8] There are those who would see "she moves in mysterious ways" as a clear nod at that phrase's original usage for God. In 1993, there would be more echoes of such a thought on Bono and Gavin Friday's title song for the movie *In the Name of the Father*, where the lyrics say it was about a father and his wife, the spirit. God as a woman is something that would raise many Christian heckles, but U2 was not the first to use the feminine for God. Jesus used it in the parable of the widow's mite (Luke 15:8-10) or to describe God as a hen looking after her chicks (Matt. 23:37), and Isaiah used "mother" as a way to describe how God comforts His people (Isa. 66:13). To limit God to the male gender would be to make Him something less than God and mean that women are not made in His image.

"Mysterious Ways" ends with the female fusing into the Spirit moving in mysterious ways lighting up days and nights. The song shows that God is there in the midst of all the struggles, that He sees the man inside the immature behavior of the child, and that if you're going to reach for anything in this life, you've got to get on your knees.

chapter 10

EVERYTHING YOU KNOW IS WRONG

As the lights went down, there was a bugle call. The thirty-six televisions that were scattered across the stage were fuzzy and flickering, seeking to catch some kind of signal. Suddenly, slogans spilled across the screens in split-second, fit-inducing flashes. TV pictures of sports and politics and science and fashion mingled in a good, bad, and ugly of what was postmodern entertainment. The frivolous sat alongside the serious so they blended into one another. There was a flickaholic in the room, as there now is in every living room across the world, changing channels at a speed that allows no one to get bored, but lets no one get a handle on what's happening. Television screens arrayed the entire stage, and a video wall was drowning out the band. Welcome to Zoo TV.

Dreaming it up all over again had never sounded or looked so true. There had been feverish anticipation as U2 took the stage in Lakeland, Florida, for what would be the first U2 gig in America in almost five years. Those who came looking for news were not disappointed. It is hard years later to remember the impact these first Zoo TV shows had. Here were four former bohemian young men who, in the guise and tradition of the hippy years, had shouted out their causes and slogans in rock 'n' roll music, all glitzed up like a glam rock band or back to the new romantics they had helped rid the world of. It was as if they had left their crusty trailer park and relocated on Wall Street or in Hollywood. There were even hints of Vegas Elvis. It was some transformation. Up until this point, backdrops were about as exciting as U2 stage shows got, maybe with Bono taking hold of a big spotlight and shining it on a feverish Edge guitar solo. That night the band was almost a backdrop or soundtrack to a stage show like never before. It was hard to imagine, but imagination was exactly where it was all born. Bono said at the time, "We've got all this technology available, and it's our duty to abuse it."[1]

Dwarfed by the images flashed in glitzy, fast-moving colors and a noise that could be described as "dreaming out loud" was Bono, in shiny leather and throwing shapes. Acting. Fooling. Mocking. The images continued to flash around him.

EVERYTHING YOU KNOW IS WRONG
ENJOY THE SURFACE
AMBITION BITES THE NAIL OF SUCCESS
BELIEVE EVERYTHING
TASTE IS THE ENEMY OF ART
BELIEVE
WATCH MORE TV
CELEBRITY IS JOY
MOCK THE DEVIL
GUILT IS NOT OF GOD
EVOLUTION IS OVER
ROCK 'N' ROLL IS ENTERTAINMENT
SERVICE IS NOT INCLUDED
IT'S YOUR WORLD & YOU CAN CHANGE IT

Words to confuse and words to depress. Words of truth and words to inspire. Words to slit your wrists to. Words to worship to. Where do you look? What do you believe? The audience's senses were bombarded with stimuli and assaulted by the truth and lies of the word-bites that pummeled them. It was manic and thrilling. It was gripping and overwhelming. For the first few songs of the set, it was hard to focus on any particular thing. Whereas Bono's charisma had been central to U2 gigs for some fourteen years, suddenly he had to compete with the flashing words and brightly colored images. But that was the point. This was a spectacle, not Bono. U2 was in hiding, behind its art form, its technology, its music, and the modern world.

It was a postmodern overload of subliminal messages that contradicted one another and left the audience screen-shocked and confused. At the same time, it almost celebrated and denigrated the postmodern world. That, in itself, is what postmodernism is all about. And in some ways, that might be its strength. Evangelical Christianity has been scathing of the onset of postmodernism. It has been seen to be the purveyor of relativism. Zoo TV was not about the answers of truth as much as it was about asking questions about what truth is and using those questions to question what the human race in the Western world is all about at the end of the second millennium. Maybe God was not so much answering prayer as He was asking questions that He's already given us all the resources to answer. The members of U2 always have been able to live with the questions of faith and have said they were just asking a different set of questions. They have been able to live with contradictions, too. They have been able to live in the heart of the contradictions to give life to their art and journeys.

Flanagan saw the start of Zoo TV as during the recording of *Achtung Baby* when Bono and The Edge watched the Gulf War live on television. This was the first time you could watch cruise missiles heading down the streets of Baghdad. It was fascinating, gripping, and frightening. Entertainment and real-life war were blurring where "fact is fiction and TV reality." Flanagan said, "When U2 tours behind this album, they have to figure out a way to represent this new reality."[2] In the midst of the Zoo TV spectacle, there was a lot more happening than just humor and irony and a rock 'n' roll extravaganza to beat all rock 'n' roll extravaganzas. This was as carefully put together as a play on Broadway or in London's West End. Bono's words and postures were scripted, and his personas were to hide behind. But the disguise would allow him to reveal so much more.

When the final outworking of those thoughts while watching the Gulf War became Zoo TV, one has to wonder if Bono in the meantime had been reading Neil Postman's book *Amusing Ourselves to Death*.[3] The premise of this influential 1985 book was: "All public discourse increasingly takes the form of entertainment. Our politics, religion, news, athletics, education and commerce have been transformed into congenial adjuncts of show business largely without protest or even popular notice. The result is that we are a people on the verge of amusing ourselves to death." In his foreword, he looks at the prophecies of George Orwell and Aldous Huxley. Postman said he thinks Huxley got it right when he feared that we would not have truth concealed as Orwell thought, but that truth would become irrelevant in thoughtless, trivial culture.

"Amusing Ourselves to Death" would have been a wonderful strap line for Zoo TV. If Postman had used the very technology he feared to communicate his point, then he would have come up with Zoo TV. What U2 conveyed so powerfully on stage in the early nineties was that we were trivializing life. We were making the absurd normal. Canadian novelist Douglas Coupland, most famous for his books *Life After God* and *Generation X*, has taken on a similar theme in his book *Polaroids from the Dead*. He points out that "soon the planet will be entirely populated by people who have only known a world with TVs and computers." He then asks, "When this point arrives, will we continue with pre-TV notions of identity?"[4] The reality of the unreality of this TV-shaped world was portrayed on Zoo TV.

As part of this play to expose the absurd, Bono took on two personas.

The Fly, with his shiny leather suit and shade glasses, is an over-the-top hedonistic rock star. Bono played this character onstage and off. Frivolous, rude, and foul-mouthed, he would avoid the serious issues of life, contrary to the serious young Bono Vox from U2. He even removed his clothes during an interview with U.K. magazine *The Face*. The Fly himself had another persona in the Mirrorball Man. Coming out for the encore to sing "Desire," Bono—dressed in his gold-lamé suit—brought a mirror so he could pose in front of it. In a bizarre twist of fate, or thoughtless critique, this led to Bono being labeled as an egocentric poser. Yet there is nothing so humble as to make fun of yourself and of the position people think makes you important. To stand up and expose the seeming nonsense of it all seems far from egotistical. But many had lost the real Bono beneath the personas. In some ways, that had been the whole point. It was all about ego and raunchy postmodern Elvis sexiness. For many, it was what they had always believed: Bono was full of himself, and they were seeing the real him at last.

"IT WAS ABOUT WORLD-WEARINESS ... WHICH—IN A SENSE—IS WHAT U2 IS GOING THROUGH." —BONO

In reality, it was one of the absurdities to be exposed. He said at the time that rock music was absurd—"four jerks in a limousine" was his phrase.[5] The band was keen to show the lunacy of what it had been made into. Why should four guys who played guitars and drums and sang a few songs be taken so seriously and put into such positions of power and money and sexual idolatry? That was, pretty much, the theme of the whole shebang—to expose modern culture and let people see the shallow nonsense that it was.

The idea of mocking the world was closely linked with the third persona in Bono's new repertoire. This character threw Christendom even more. McPhisto was a horn-wearing devil, and Bono played the part so well that many within the Church thought he had sold his soul to the opposition.

Bono told Joe Jackson a story of how he had encountered a concerned Christian girl who did not understand:

> One night I was doing my Elvis-devil dance on stage with a young girl in Wales, and she said, "Are you still a believer? If so, what are you doing dressed up as the devil?" I said, "Have you read *The Screwtape Letters*, a book by C.S. Lewis that a lot of intense Christians are plugged into? They are letters from the devil. That's where I got the whole philosophy of mock-the-devil-and-he-will-flee-from-you." She said, "Yes," and I said, "So you know what I am doing." Then she relaxed and said, "I want to bless you."[6]

In *The Screwtape Letters*, Lewis sought to expose the cunning plans of the devil so people would be shocked into realizing where they were being duped and lied to and deceived. U2 took on this strategy, too. On the American leg of the Zoo TV tour, Mirrorball Man appeared as something of a shady rock star who could have been a cross between Jerry Lee Lewis and his cousin, Jimmy Swaggert. Mirrorball Man wore a cowboy hat and threw away dollars like confetti. When the tour came to Europe, Bono felt the televangelist would need a new slant for a different context. Somewhere along the way, Mirrorball Man metamorphosed into McPhisto, the place where Satan meets insincere rock star ego. It is all the worst of what Elvis could have become.

C.S. Lewis' influence on Bono's life and work should be no surprise. Bono has always had a bit of a soft spot for Christian writers. Way back in time, the band mentioned Christian writer Francis Schaeffer in interviews as being a significant influence on them. In addition, in 1998, Bono chose Eugene Peterson's poetic paraphrase of the New Testament, The Message, as one of his books of the year. Lewis was born in 1898 in Belfast. He spent most of his life in Oxford as a lecturer and writer. In literary terms, he is best known for his wonderful allegorical children's books *The Chronicles of Narnia*, which took Christian thoughts and made them into books that sent children's imaginations racing long before the birth of Harry Potter. Though

Lewis was selling books of apologetics within the Church, he had a strong desire and sense of vocation to bring the truth he believed into a wider market through his fiction. Here, he had a lot in common with U2.

In an essay called "Sometimes Fairy Stories Say Best What's to Be Said," Lewis wrote, "I thought I saw how stories of this kind could steal past a certain inhibition which had paralyzed much of my own religion in childhood. Why did one find it so hard to feel as one was told one ought to feel about God or about the sufferings of Christ? I thought the chief reason was that one was told one ought to. An obligation to feel can freeze feelings. And reverence itself did harm. The whole subject was associated with lowered voices, almost as if it were something medical. But supposing that by casting all these things into an imaginary world, stripping them of their stained-glass and Sunday school associations, one could make them for the first time appear in their real potency? Could one not thus steal past those watchful dragons? I thought one could."[7] That is a succinct appraisal of what U2 was trying to do in Zoo TV.

A few years after the birth of McPhisto, Bono said a character in *The Black Rider*, Tom Waits' 1993 theatrical collaboration with William Burroughs and Robert Wilson, inspired McPhisto. The Edge said, "Bono and I saw that show in Hamburg, and I thought there was a certain license in that figure that would be interesting for Bono. It wasn't just Bono. It wasn't the other three members of the band going, 'Oh my God, he's wearing devil's horns! How embarrassing!' We were into it."[8] As the character was in the thought-stream, Bono's best buddy, Gavin Friday, suggested the horns. Whether it was at or before that moment, or later in McPhisto's incarnation, somewhere along the line he became a Screwtape.

Around the same time, Joe Jackson interviewed Bono for a book he was writing, tentatively called *In Search of Elvis*. Jackson had been aware of the Elvisness of much of Zoo TV, especially the ending where Elvis and McPhisto kind of duet. Bono said:

The whole encore section is kitsch, it's Elvis/second-hand car salesman/the devil, before I got into McPhisto. That's what I saw him as: an Elvis-devil. It was about world-weariness, about being in a jaded, fat Elvis period, which—in a sense—is what U2 is going through. But part of it all was "stardom" and the decadence implicit in that supposed lifestyle. So we began with "Money, Money, Money," then "Desire," and ringing up the president, whatever. It's the derangement of stardom. And we paint that kind of portrait until finally we come through to the soul of that with "With or Without You" and "Love Is Blindness"—the repentance.[9]

To U2 and most thoughtful artists, the problem with Christians is the Church has for many years taught people what to think and not how to think. Everything has to be explained in such linear terms. Whether it was that night in Wales, or whatever it was, Bono seems to have thought it important to throw out clues to the rest of the Christians who were not getting it. In the video cartoon for "Hold Me Thrill Me Kiss Me," McPhisto is knocked to the ground by a car, and a book flies out of his hand. The camera follows the book, which hits the ground, and the front of the book says, "THE SCREWTAPE LETTERS—C.S. LEWIS."

THAT WAS THE THEME OF THE WHOLE SHEBANG—TO EXPOSE MODERN CULTURE AND LET PEOPLE SEE THE SHALLOW NONSENSE THAT IT WAS.

The Screwtape Letters begins with two quotes, from Thomas More and Martin Luther. Luther said, "The best way to drive out the devil, if he will not yield to the texts of Scripture, is to jeer and flout him, for he cannot bear scorn."[10] More said: "The devil ... the proud spirit ... cannot endure to be mocked." So the devil hams it up and tells the audience that he is in control of the world, from politicians to religious leaders, and thanks the audience for making him who he is.

If we just take the Dublin monologue as an example, Bono ended a stage of the Zoo TV tour with this message from McPhisto:

> You know who I am. Oh I know who you are. I know you probably even better than you yourself. What a night. What a show. *Zooropa*. It's all over. So many have turned out to see us, I don't know what to say. Thank you, thank you, thank you ... But you know there is someone who used to come and see us all the time and who hasn't been around for a while. We used to be so close. People think I have forgotten about him, but I haven't. I used to find him so inspiring back then. He invented me. I was his most magnificent creation. The brightest star in his sky. Now look at me. A tired old pop star in platform shoes. I try to speak to him all the time, but he won't take my calls. And I get blamed for everything. All the wars, all the famine, all the trouble in the world. I get blamed for it. Even the *Evening Herald* slags me off. Who can I get to make me make peace with him? Who will mediate for me? Shall I call the United Nations? Maybe they could help me. Off with the horns, on with the show ...

It's a marvelous monologue. Bruce Springsteen, of course, was the inventor of the long story in the middle of songs, but here is one man out on a stage in front of thirty-thousand people holding them in the palm of his hand without a band suggesting that they would rock back into some hit song at any time. This is a fantastic piece of showmanship, with all kinds of nuances as Bono slips into his character as the devil and then pop star. From a biblical sketch of who the devil is, he turns into himself being ripped apart by the Dublin press, then almost spelling out what the Christian fraternity thinks, that he has left God behind somewhere, then bringing it all to a fervent preacher's final questions: Who will bring us peace with God? Who will mediate for us? That he then brings in his other nightly prop of technology and phones, the United Nations could be seen as a frivolous ending or the most poignant of all endings. Who does mankind trust? C.S. Lewis would have been proud.

chapter 11

MIDNIGHT IS WHERE THE DAY BEGINS

The very sound of the title track of *Zooropa* conjures up images of a futuristic European city, at a time just after midnight. *Zooropa* is about what lies beneath the neon lights, the promises of fame and fortune, and the pleasures of the modern world. It's the place where the day begins at midnight ("Lemon"), where it is cold but bright ("Zooropa"), where man builds banks and cathedrals ("Lemon"), where the streets are paved with gold ("The Wanderer"), where we are still looking at the world through television and cinema screens ("Babyface," "Lemon," "Zooropa"). In some ways, Bono again is giving a bit of a commentary on what U2 is doing. This is so in "Stay (Faraway So Close)," as the band describes Zoo TV as bringing the far away up close with static, radio, and satellite television.

In this collection of songs, we are also given a look beneath the surface of this night time, fun time cityscape—and the heart of it all is found wanting. Underneath the streets, paved with gold, the stones are lifted to reveal the outside of a city that has no soul underneath ("The Wanderer"). The things that are being held onto so tightly are already lost. The victim of this darkness, as described in "Stay," has her wheels spinning, but as she is upside down, she is going nowhere. "Numb" is maybe the conclusion of the soulless city. The technology, the promises of the advertising, the bright lights, and the good looks of the surface of things have you realizing that everything is numb, and no matter how much, it is never enough.

Achtung Baby and Zoo TV had revived U2's desire to make music. With all the paraphernalia that the Zoo TV world tour brought with it, the band just wanted to make new music. Feeling music-weary after *Rattle and Hum*, the band members' passion was back. The reinvention had reignited the old fires. The new angles that they had given themselves were giving their imagination the head of steam needed to keep the U2 journey hurtling on. In 1993, U2 was a band picking up a fresh impetus, having run on momentum alone for far too long.

Literally recorded between the U.S. and European legs of the band's Zoo TV outside broadcast tour, *Zooropa* was originally planned as an EP to keep the inspiration fuse lit, but it turned into an extra album. Bands of U2's stature were not in the habit of releasing two albums in such a short time. Being recorded so quickly during a tour perhaps has caused *Zooropa* to be taken less seriously in the U2 canon. It may not have been seen as a follow-up to *Achtung Baby* as much as a stopgap release. It also lost out in that since it was recorded so quickly, there was little room left for maneuver between its completion and the first gig of the tour's next leg. That meant it didn't get the live exposure new albums need to register in the minds of fans. The band just didn't have time to rehearse it. Bono would explain on stage, "Well, it was a fine thing writing some songs and putting out a record while you are still on tour, but it's another thing trying to play the ------ things." As a result, only "Stay," "Lemon," and a version of "Numb," where at times The Edge read the lyrics off a music stand, made it into the set list.

In musical terms as well as in concept, lyric, persona, and creative storytelling, *Zooropa* deserves serious consideration. The band members had broken free of their old selves, all the expectations of their eighties caricatures. They had found irony and humor. They had hidden beneath image and new personas. They had paddled in the shallows of investigating and then exposing the postmodern and technological age. Then they had been dragged into the deep whirlpool of it all, where the culture they feared was drowning. As they exposed it to others, more and more they were uncovering the darkness beneath its shiny surface. So when it came to the downtime between tours, there was so much to say and too little time in which to say it.

AT THIS STAGE OF U2'S MUSICAL JOURNEY, THE BAND HAD HIDDEN BEHIND CHARACTERS. BONO WAS NARRATING SOMEONE ELSE'S STORY.

Zooropa is full of complex characters looking at life from a plethora of angles and from a darker perspective than the band was used to. There are those very different, bizarre, almost perverted views on life—and especially faith. The cold and almost wicked way Bono sings "Daddy's Gonna Pay for Your Crashed Car" could almost be a snide attack on the wealthy father who throws money foolishly at his spoiled children. It could be about the devil being someone's sugar daddy. *If you sell me your soul, I'll bail you out.* Then again, it could be a reworking of the story of the prodigal son.

When Jesus told the story of the prodigal son (Luke 15:11-32), it was a scandalous yarn. This boy was a rogue who had lived the wildest end of hedonism and, in the process, blew his dad's hard-earned inheritance. He partied and whored it away. He was irresponsible and lived the model sinner's life. As he was heading back home, the crowd, the Pharisees in particular, were getting ready for the most justified and harshest of judgment. When Jesus stung the tail of the tale with a merciful tenderness, kindness, and warm-hearted love, the sense of heckles that must have gone up in the hearts of the Pharisees could almost be felt and heard. That Jesus then went on to expose their response in the good son's lack of grace to his brother and abhorrence at his father's grace made it even more outrageous. "Daddy's Gonna Pay for Your Crashed Car" could be Bono trying to invoke a similar disbelief and outrage. Could grace really be this ridiculous? Could it really be such nonsense that God would let you drive the most reckless of lives, then when you crash, offer another chance? It is scandalous, irrational, and revolutionary.

"The First Time" is one song that has topped the conversations of the most discerning of believers. What on earth? Throwing away the keys of the kingdom and leaving by the back door? Again, many from within the Christian fold saw this as another renouncement of the band's faith—signed, sealed, and delivered. One of the misconceptions with any artist is that everything they sing, write, or create is subjective and always in the character of the singer, author, or artist. At this stage of U2's musical journey, the band had hidden behind characters like the one in "The First Time." Bono was narrating someone else's story.

Niall Stokes' book shows how Bono was playing around with the angles of the camera on the biblical stories. It seems "The First Time" had been written for Al Green in the same way that "Daddy's Gonna Pay for Your Crashed Car" apparently was written with John Lee Hooker in mind, and "Mystery Girl" had been given to Roy Orbison. There was also "Slow Dancing," with Willie Nelson in mind, and "Two Shots of Happy, One Shot of Sad," with Frank Sinatra in mind. Bono said about the Green song: "We decided to keep it for ourselves. Brian really loved it. But instead of doing an 'up' version, we just emptied it out, deconstructed the song and ended on this line about throwing away the key, and the prodigal doesn't go back. He sees all this stuff there for him and he doesn't want it and he goes off again. That's a really interesting take on the story."[1] It sure is. Isn't that what art is all about? Let the theologians fight over how it is. The artists are there to get around the corners of the story, to ask how it might have looked from here or over there, to ask what might have happened if this had happened instead, and what light that might shed on the whole deal.

"The Wanderer" is another almost blasphemous yarn to the puritanical listener. Apparently, Bono had Ecclesiastes in mind for this conclusion to his own little thesis on the futility of a life without God. In some ways, *Zooropa* might be U2's version of what Douglas Coupland was talking about in his book *Life After God*.[2] The working title to this final track was "The Preacher." (The writer of Ecclesiastes in the King James Version of the Bible is called "The Preacher" in the first chapter, first verse.) The Edge was the one who suggested "wanderer" as an alternative, but a preacher still he is, and in some ways, he might be the inspiration for the Robert Duval movie *The Apostle*. As in the Old Testament book of Ecclesiastes, which sits snugly alongside the work of nineties U2, there is someone searching for where he might find meaning, exploring the breadth and depth and height of every human experience before he repents. As an album, *Zooropa* is a wander through modern culture, and that is where the whole thing concludes.

Bill Flanagan, in his book *U2 at the End of the World*, said there was debate as to whether Bono should replace Cash as vocalist: "I think that the real reason Bono does not want to sing 'The Wanderer' is because when Bono sings the song, it comes off as a mea culpa for all the glitz and surface that U2 has spent the last two years creating. When Bono sings 'The Wanderer,' it seems like a public confession that beneath the fly shades, he is hoping to find God by searching through the glitter and trash."[3] Finding the divine in the trash is paraphrased in "Mofo" from *Pop*.

Flanagan's book also speaks of debate between him and the band about antinomianism.[4] This is a heresy that has the sinner almost creating and performing as much sin as possible so grace can abound as much as possible. Around the time *Zooropa* was being recorded, Maria McKee, a friend of U2's, was releasing an album called *You Gotta Sin to Get Saved*. McKee was a Christian who had jumped headlong into the world of rock music with her band, Lone Justice. In her late teens, she wooed the rock world with her voice, good looks, and Bono-type charismatic stage performance. She also had talked openly about her Christian faith. One of her most successful singles was "I Found Love," where she testified about finding a wishful vision and an idea of a glorious kind which she has no choice but to surrender to. Her musical life could have been weaned on a strict diet of *October* and *War*. Live, she went into a celebratory rant in the middle of "I Found Love" that had her giving an American preacher's ecstatic exclamations of redemption and salvation.

McKee had moved to Dublin at the end of the eighties, drawn by the creative rock music vibe of the city, the tax breaks for artists, and her friendship with U2, which had its origins in their shared faith. Maybe Flanagan was onto something when he brought up antinomianism with the band. Maybe it was as much a pastoral discussion as it was a journalistic investigation. Maybe the band members were living too close to the experimental end of their art. Maybe after their sheltered late teens and early twenties, the temptations of the world were beginning to entice them. Maybe as they looked at the dark and the light, the dark was becoming too appealing.

Even if this were true, this band probably had the fewest tabloid gossip-column appearances in the history of rock music. Adam, who lived the most hedonistic life of the four, never taking hold of the whole Christian ethos, was the target of a drug bust in Dublin and missed a concert in Australia as a result of alcohol abuse. He later came clean. That is the sum total of scandal in this band in an industry where the public could be mistaken for thinking sensational headlines were part of the job description. For a Christian to get a little fond of Jack Daniels and openly confess to be enjoying the party life may be some great evangelical scandal, but in the world this band moved in, it was tame, almost boringly good behavior.

chapter 12

. . . UNDER THE TRASH

It was a brief second in the Popmart set. It was a tiny moment with enormous meaning. It was a throwaway gesture in which the whole Popmart thesis is understood. Perhaps it was even the whole point of the U2 dissertation of the nineties. The band was cranking up the volume in "Mofo" when Bono came to the line "Looking for the baby Jesus under the trash." As he sang those words, he gestured his arm to the biggest TV screen in the world, that huge golden arch and that mighty lemon. It was almost just a shrug, but the illumination it threw out was as bright as every spotlight, special effect, or image Willie Williams was flashing up from the light desk. All of this paraphernalia the band had around it night after night for most of the nineties was trash. What was more important was underneath it all. The use of Baby Jesus could mean the genesis of this thought is in the commercialization of Christmas, when Jesus, the real meaning behind the season, is lost beneath wrapping paper, tinsel, stuffing, and Santa Claus. But it is a picture of a general loss of meaning or hope or truth. As we glance across the horizon of the loudest and brightest culture in the history of humankind, is there any chance we might find in the midst of all the shallowness something deeper, something more precious, something more lasting? Is Jesus lost? Or can He be retrieved from the garbage?

Pop and Popmart, the next U2 live extravaganza, had much more kitsch, glitz, and, well, pop than the Zoo TV and *Zooropa* period. *Pop* was the third album in the trilogy of technology, loops, irony, humor, and persona. It did move away from the European underground city sounds of both *Achtung Baby* and *Zooropa*. Musically, there was a nod in the direction of dance music. Scottish hip-hop expert Howie B came on board to keep the band sounding youthful and still involved in the musical technological conversations of the nineties, when bands such as the Chemical Brothers, Massive Attack and Prodigy were becoming major players.

U2 took some time off after *Zooropa*. It was the band's first lengthy break in nearly twenty years. When the members reconvened to look at what they might do next, a lot of fresh ideas were buzzing around. Adam told Robert Hilburn of the *Los Angeles Times*: "I think we needed that break to get away from each other for a while and explore music without worrying about what U2 should be doing ... At the end of that period, we started to realize that we were actually all listening to the same music. I was listening to bands called Leftfield, Massive Attack and Underworld. Bono and The Edge were listening to Prodigy and the Chemical Brothers, as well as Oasis and some others."[1]

Bono had seen two distinct directions going on around the band members and was interested in what they would add to U2. Bono said, "We liked the tendency in England toward pop songwriting in the (traditional) way of Lennon-McCartney and Lou Reed—something that Noel Gallagher and Oasis are doing. But we also liked the energy and adventurousness of the techno, hip-hop world. So we decided to explore bringing these two disciplines together. That's what this record is about."[2] It would be wrong to simply pigeonhole *Pop* as U2's modern dance record. It was experimental, and it was a band competing with its peers, but at no stage did it degenerate into any kind of gimmick to be trendy. The album was still U2. No matter how the band members decided to re-dream it, it always sounded like U2.

When U2 went on tour for *Pop*, there was a visual shift of stagescape, too. From a television studio, U2 took its inquisitive investigations to the other great altar of the late twentieth century. It was as if the band had built a stage slap-bang in the middle of a shopping mall. In fact, the U2 guys launched the tour at a Kmart. It was back to America, the world's Capitol Hill of capitalism. This time, it was out of the desert and into the malls of the city. Here they were again, setting up their spot to give another exposé of the modern ills. While *Zooropa* looked at fame and power, *Pop* looked at the consumerist dream of progress with its empty philosophy of "I buy tacky products, therefore I am."

Again, it was that searching for Jesus under the trash. "Mofo," which kicked off the shows, begins with that statement of intending to look for something to save his soul and fill the God-shaped hole. The seeking will be done in a barren desert place. Bono is peering out from behind those shades again, and "Mofo," with its nod in the direction of John Lennon's song "Mother," is again Bono in intimately subjective muse as he tries to deal with the death of his mother and how that loss has shaped him through the years. It finds him looking very personally at his own life. He's a singer wanting to make music that will take on the world. He's wanting to find a better father of his daughters. He's going further inside and beyond the material things to seek out who he was intended to be before the world was made. There is something of the pop star, the family man, and the spiritual pilgrim. It's as if Bono is crying out to God that in finding those three in balance, he will find that something he needs to fill the God-shaped hole. There are still no comfortable refuges in the life of this Dublin boy, but the search continues. The compass points have not changed even though he may be in the wilderness in some kind of Old Testament wandering. It is still that God-shaped hole that captures the thinking of his heart, soul, and mind.

Further into the Popmart concerts, Bono shouted, "I went looking for spirit and found alcohol; I went looking for soul, and I bought some style; I wanted to meet God, but they sold me religion." U2's latest mission in dadaism was to erect the cathedrals of today's religion, expose its emptiness, and then try to dig deep down somewhere for Jesus in the midst of it all. He isn't even as easily found in the places you might expect to find Him. As the song "If God Will Send His Angels" says, they have brought Jesus into show business, and it's hard to get in the door to meet Him as a result. It seems that rather than digging for Jesus beneath the trash, the Church has unforgivably allowed the trash to come inside and water down whatever there was left of God. Christianity had become commercialized on many levels, and Bono may have been turning over the tables of various modern Christian temple courts, but the most obvious victims of his wrath would be his age-old friends, the televangelists.

Whether listening to the *Pop* album, enjoying the Popmart experience, or just watching the *Popmart* video filmed in Mexico City, there is an overwhelming feeling that the book of Ecclesiastes is being made into song to live among us. Irish journalist Stuart Baillie evoked that in his review of the album when he described it as "watching the world dancing and shagging and shopping and suggesting that it is ultimately joyless."[3]

The book of Ecclesiastes implies that there is nothing to live for under the sun unless you get some kind of connection to what is above the sun. The writer says everything goes around and around forever on the same old circle. It's almost like it was written in Ireland. The rain falls into streams and flows into rivers and into the sea and then rises as clouds and blows across the mountains where it falls into streams and then into rivers and into the sea where it rises into clouds and blows across the mountains where it falls ... Life can be very much like that. Every day can be the same old drudgery.

The wisdom of the teacher, as the writer of Ecclesiastes described, deals with fame as well (Eccles. 1:11). The first chapter also suggests that no one is remembered. It is all vanity. It's pointless even to try to make an impression. And so the teacher wanders around the houses of wealth and pleasure and even philanthropy, but ends up concluding that's all meaningless—unless there is a God. A vertical connection with the divine changes everything about how we relate to the horizontal.

"I WENT LOOKING FOR SPIRIT AND FOUND ALCOHOL; I WENT LOOKING FOR SOUL, AND I BOUGHT SOME STYLE; I WANTED TO MEET GOD, BUT THEY SOLD ME RELIGION." —BONO

Pop and Popmart were like the dramatic soundtrack of that teacher's wanderings. The Old Testament philosopher would have no idea how decadent and ridiculous the trash would have gotten 2,500 years later, but he could have related well to U2's interaction with it. He could have found only empathy with the band's interrogation of the meaninglessness of the horizontal and its constant probing for something else—the search for hope that might be found above the sun to make sense of all the nonsense below it. As U2 went for a ride along the surface of things, Bono confessed that his heart was where it has always been, but his head was caught in between. Finally, walking and staggering down the ramps center stage, Bono reached to the heavens, screaming desperately, "Don't walk away!" The teacher could have emerged authentically with this modern-day pilgrim and realized the enormous difficulties he had in his longing to get beyond that trash.

Pop could find a home, too, in the New Testament. It could be a huge theatrical performance of Paul's mission in Athens (Acts 17:16-34). In the early days of the Christian Church, Paul was the great missionary to the Gentiles. In Acts, a historical book written by Luke, the same doctor who wrote a Gospel, we read about the spread of the Christian faith throughout the world of that day. In chapter 19, Paul arrives in Athens and is trying to communicate the Gospel into a Greek culture. Before that, he had been preaching in the Jewish synagogues. In Jewish situations, he had been expounding Old Testament theologies like atonement, blood, lambs, and sacrifice. When he arrives in Rome, he seems to be giving it much of the same until he realizes it is culturally ineffective. The listeners had no comprehension of the concepts Paul was using as his hooks.

Paul's response was as wise as a serpent. Jesus told His disciples to be wise as serpents and gentle as doves (Matt. 10:16). Sometimes the Church can be accused of getting these traits reversed. Not Paul. He readjusted his thinking and rewrote the script to make the truth relevant in another culture. The Church has been slow to do the same. There is an attitude birthed in the Enlightenment that says truth is a form of words in a particular order, and there is no wisdom or creativity to poetically take the same truth and describe it in ways more digestible to the world outside Church gates. Paul took his time and walked around the city, imbibing its art and listening to its philosophers and poets. When he gave his sermon to the Athenians, it was on the cutting edge of where that culture was, stating as his points of references all he had seen and heard and read. The truth didn't change; it was just clothed in more relevant outfits.

In some ways, this was U2's reasoning throughout the nineties. In his February 2001 *Hot Press* interview, Bono said: "At the start of the nineties, we realized that to touch and reach people during a new decade, we had to come in a different guise. So we did."[4] Touching and reaching people is so crucial to all that U2 is about. It's not just tickling their ears with pleasant pop songs, but wanting to touch them deep down in their souls in the midst of whatever is going on in their world. It's to assess that world, point out a few of its dilemmas and dangers, and prod its edifice with a stick to see if there are possible lessons or alternatives. As Bono strode across the Popmart stage, he was not trying in any way to be an evangelical preacher that seeks converts, but he was trying to dialogue with his audience about what a soul might look like and how that soul might be nourished or starved in the contemporary landscape of the world's gods and philosophers and poets.

A trawl through the treasure trove of lyrics on the album would give good evidence to the Athenian nature of the piece. Love was a recurring theme throughout *Pop*, but not in any throwaway, silly love song-type vein. As on "Please," there is another conclusion that love is talked about and defined in all kinds of ways, but in the end that kind of love is not what is being thought of or lived out. Love needs to be reassessed in light of the definitions thrown out daily in our condensed packets of thirty-minute soap operas. "Do You Feel Loved" asks how it is being defined. Reviewers and interviewers have been writing a lot about Bono's healthy fourteen-year-old marriage, and perhaps the "stuck together with God's glue" line in "Staring at the Sun" hints at some of love's solutions.

The album also deals with eternal issues in songs like "Wake Up Dead Man" and "The Playboy Mansion." The latter is clearly walking around the world's ideas of heaven and showing them up as both transitory and out of reach. It's about people waiting in the hope of moments of luck to take them out of where they are to where they hope they will find salvation. The song is a weary and desperate acknowledgement that if we are depending on fashion, celebrity, commerce, and luck, then we are doomed. Then there is a turn and a twist toward Christian belief and the words of John on Patmos, as written in the New Testament book of Revelation: "There will be no more death or mourning or crying or pain" (Rev. 21:4). The alternative to the gods and hopes of the heaven in this age is another kind of mansion altogether.

"Please," with its references to Northern Ireland, seems to be a call for belief to be about more than words and religious practices and the cry for authenticity in the following of Jesus. "Get up off your knees now please" seems to be the cry of one who longs for the ideas and clichés of faith to become a living reality. In Northern Ireland, as in many parts of Bible-belt America, people have heard the truth of the Gospel until they can almost recite it back to the street preachers. They have heard it. But have they seen it? Get out of your self-indulgent prayer meetings and start to be available to God to answer those prayers.

Elsewhere there are name checks to Michael Jackson, Big Macs, the lottery, and even flute bands. As Bono said to Jon Pereles of *The New York Times*, "Musicians, painters, whatever, they have no choice but to describe where they live."[5] So it is all described, reflected on, and questioned, and the conclusions are matched up against the alternative kingdom values spoken of by Jesus. He was suggesting not to store up treasure on earth where it will not last, but to invest in heaven where the contradiction of saving your soul is that you've got to give it away. Thus, when Bono imagines a girl faced with the reality of living her "Last Night on Earth," as one song is titled, she concludes, "Give it away."

When the reviews for *Pop* appeared, there was a preoccupation with all things Christian. In *The Boston Globe*, Jim Sullivan said, "U2 remains identifiable as U2, and this work might also be titled 'Conversations with God'!"[6] He continued, "On *Pop*, U2 finds itself asking us to look for meaning, be it love or faith, amid the chaos and media onslaught of the modern age. 'Last Night on Earth,' with its urgent 'You got to give it away' refrain, is about living each day as if it might be your last." Mark Brown of *The Orange County (California) Register* finds similar themes: "Not as complex as *Achtung Baby* or *Zooropa*, and more accessible than either of those discs, *Pop* completes a trilogy of searching, questioning works where Bono looks for meaning in a modern world by alternately embracing and disdaining its trappings."[7]

chapter 13

WAKE UP DEAD MAN

"But you see, David was the first blues singer. As well as praising, he was there shouting at God—you know: 'Where are you when we need you?' ... 'We're surrounded.' ... 'Your people are starving.' ... 'Are you deaf?' That type of thing. He'd be wailing, this militant mind, this poet musician with enough faith to believe he had a deal with God ... believed it enough to get angry when it looked like He wasn't coming through."[1]

If ever Bono described himself, it is in those lines from his foreword to John Waters' deep book *Race of Angels,* about U2 and its Irishness. Bono's belief is one that reflects his personality. He's a big character. He is passionate about the things that matter to him, which seem to be his music, his family, his friends, and his faith. He is a volatile ball of energy. He is a creative whirlwind of an imagination. He is a dreamer in the apostolic succession of John Lennon, whose honesty he also embraces. But unlike Lennon, he has even more belief in his dreams coming true because he has all his wishes tied up in a dialogue with a transcendent God. So when it all seems to be a nightmare instead of a dream, he is not the kind of man to hide that. He just tells his world and his God what he thinks.

Bono has said that he had been into the Psalms since he was twelve years old. When many children were being turned off from Church, he seemed to be able to find interest amid what was becoming increasingly archaic and irrelevant, seeing cinema in the stained glass and heroes in Old Testament stories. King David seems to have been the hero who caught his imagination most. David was one of Israel's most successful kings, a man of deep-seated godliness on a throne that most of the time compromised both religiously and politically. He was also credited with being the writer of a great number of the psalms. David had a major failure in his life (2 Sam. 11:1-17): He committed adultery with a woman named Bathsheba and then orchestrated her husband's death in battle. His repentance and reconciliation with God turned out to be another honorable part of David's story. It earthed his holy image. It inspired many psalms of honesty and humility (Ps. 51).

BONO TAKES IT ALL ON. HE LONGS FOR HEAVEN ON EARTH AND TELLS HIS GOD HE IS TIRED OF WAITING.

Bono would call David "a star, the Elvis of the Bible."[2] Bono called himself a fan and could sense empathy between the Israelite's big life and his own rock star absurdities. He also could sense what made the difference in David's successes and failures. He said, "And unusually for such a 'rock star,' with his lust for power, lust for women, lust for life, he had the humility of one who knew his gift worked harder than he ever would."[3] In the end, across 2,500 years of history, the two got to write a song together. When another track was needed for *War*, and the band was looking for something more spiritual to complement the political nature of the rest of the album, something that would be a bridge between the album and its predecessor *October*. They found a psalm and gave it their own musical treatment. "40" was from the psalm of that number, adding a line from Psalm 5. It became the closing anthem for U2 concerts throughout the eighties, with thousands of people leaving stadiums across the world singing an old scriptural hymn.

His public interest in the Psalms, which again was made evident in his references to David as "the first blues singer," made Bono an obvious choice for the publishing house Canongate to introduce the book of Psalms in an intriguing series of books called the Pocket Canons. The idea for publishing the books of the Bible individually came when someone went looking for the Song of Songs for his wife's birthday gift and was told that it was only possible to buy all sixty-six books of the Bible. Then to add another dimension to the ancient literature, modern writers, poets, novelists, and songwriters were asked to write their thoughts, almost like little reviews, as introductions to the books. Writers such as Faye Weldon, Blake Morrison, Peter Ackroyd, Ruth Rendell, and P.D. James, as well as the likes of singers Nick Cave and Bono, got to dialogue at some level with Saint Mark, Saint John, Saint Paul, Isaiah, and, of course, King David.

The publicity for the project was enormous. The Bible was on display all around bookstores. Most of the broadsheet newspapers did reviews and articles. Evangelical Christians had been campaigning for years in a wide array of projects to get the Bible back into people's hands. The Bible was back in the news and in conversation. Prayers had been answered. Then, in a twist, the company that produced the books was not hailed as an answer to prayer but was taken to court for blasphemy. The fundamentalist end of the Church was unhappy that the introductions were not always glowing in their support of scripture. Some writers would question the literal belief in certain events and would not claim to have had any Christian conversion from reading their designated book. Some admitted to reading it for the first time. Yet most of the writers were enthusiastic, not only about the books as literature but as good, life-changing advice.

What the opposition to the Pocket Canons exposed was a lack of faith among those who claimed faith. If, as many of these fundamentalists believed, God's Word was unique and special, holding with it some kind of authority beyond any other literary work, then there seems to have been nothing to fear in having it thrown into discussion, discourse, and even disagreement. It is a surprising outworking of a belief in an all-powerful God to be so defensive and protective of Him and His Word.

Bono's contribution appeared in the second batch of books released. It was his introduction that drew the most publicity. The U.K.'s *Sunday Express* printed the whole introduction. Again, Bono was seeing much of himself and his belief and his art in David. He also wrote about the psalms that he has a particular empathy with: "Abandonment, displacement is the stuff of my favorite Psalms. The Psalter may be a font of gospel music, but for me, it's in his despair that the Psalmist really reveals the nature of his special relationship with God. Honesty, even to the point of anger. 'How long, Lord? Wilt thou hide thyself forever?' (Ps. 89) or 'Answer me when I call' (Ps. 5)."[4] Bono likened the psalmist to bluesman Robert Johnston and said the book of Psalms prepared him for the honesty he later discovered in Leonard Cohen and John Lennon. The blues, and indeed full-frontal naked honesty, had not been predominant in the worship of the modern evangelical Church. Where the Church has been growing in the Western world, it has been nurtured by the sensational. At the same time that U2 was exposing the absurdity of fame and the deception that big is always better, many churches were being sucked into its absurdity and were seduced by the success of numbers and the spectacular event. Healing extravaganzas and sell-out worship concerts where the worship leader became a new kind of pop star was the modern-day order. Triumphant victory was the best sales pitch, and the songs of the faithful became obsessed with God, high and lifted up, conquering all and dealing with every ailment physical, emotional, and spiritual at the touch of a hand.

U2 was like an antidote to that reality. The band members looked the dark side of life right in the eye. They never felt a need for glib solutions or shortcuts to what the kingdom was taking time to bring. Believers in the Christian faith, who, as a result, are deeply engaged in the writings of the

Old and New Testament, are caught in the horns of dilemma many times. Believing these ancient manuscripts of scripture to be the inspired Word of God (2 Tim. 3:16-17), they often are thrown by the reality of the news on television clashing with divine revelation. An example is every Christmas, when those angels glide above the astonished shepherds and tell them, "Glory to God in the highest, and on earth peace to men on whom his favor rests" (Luke 2:14). This peace on earth usually clashes, literally, violently with the year-end reviews of twelve months of tragedy, disaster, violent crime, terrorist atrocities, and war. Where is the peace? What were those angels talking about?

How do you answer such questions and not play gymnastics with scripture or ignore the reality of the news? It's a hard position for a Christian whose worldview has been dictated by the seamlessness of modernity. U2's postmodern worldview, though no better or worse than modernity, allows mystery and confusion to sit alongside faith. As Bono put it to Neil McCormick: "Belief and confusion are not mutually exclusive; I believe that belief gives you a direction in the confusion. But you don't see the full picture. That's the point. That's what faith is. You can't see it. It comes back to instinct. Faith is just up the street. Faith and instinct, you can't just rely on them. You have to beat them up. You have to pummel them to make sure they can withstand it, to make sure they can be trusted."[5]

Instead of separating the tussle of his faith and the confusion, Bono is always able to bring the two eyeball to eyeball. That's what happens in "Wake Up Dead Man" and "Peace on Earth." If you are watching the 1998 year in review, in the midst of your children's nativity plays, how do you reconcile the twenty-seven lives so violently and needlessly ended by a bomb on a Saturday afternoon in a market town with the song of the angels? Honesty, vulnerability, and a good amount of courageous faith allow you to cry out in your bewilderment and not lose your belief in the process. These things allow you to wrestle with your faith rather than lose it. They allow you to cry out for Jesus to throw you a lifeline. Bono takes it all on. He longs for heaven on earth and tells his God he is tired of waiting. He asks his God to answer the cries of those who have lost their children. He concludes by telling Jesus that the words of that Christmas nativity stick in his throat, and he asks Him what it is worth—"this peace on earth."

This is why the Church needs Bono. This is why everybody needs Bono. He is willing to take what he believes and the world around him, and wrestle with them and not let them go. "Peace on Earth" is upfront and without apologies. It's a rant at God. It sits precariously close to slushy and sentimental when he names some of the victims of the Omagh bombing and links them with Christmas peace words. It works because the sentimentality is given the roughest of edges by the confrontation with God. It is by no means a new theme on a U2 record. It could be seen as a direct follow-up to the last track on *Pop*, "Wake Up Dead Man," when Jesus again is asked to help him because he feels alone in a "f---ed up" world.

U2'S POSTMODERN WORLDVIEW ALLOWS MYSTERY AND CONFUSION TO SIT ALONGSIDE FAITH.

For most Christians, the use of the F-word would not help the medicine go down. Initially, the song seems to portray Jesus as dead and impotent with His hands tied behind His back, unable to bring any help to a troubled world. Closer inspection sheds a little more light. Struggling with why things are as they are and why God does nothing about it is common to everyone at one time or another. "Wake Up Dead Man" is trying to make sense, without actually making any, of the problems of pain and suffering under the eye of a loving God. It is the prayerful seeking of help and wanting a reminder of how things will be in eternity. It confesses belief in God as Creator—"He made the world in seven"—and in Jesus as the "Boss." It's a ranting plea to intervene and bring a solution to humanity's conundrum of evil: "Are you working on something new?"

Bono said of the song: "It's the end of the century, and it's a century where

God is supposed to be dead. Seeing the world in two dimensions doesn't have the appeal that it had for a lot of people. People want to believe, but they're angry, and I picked up on that anger. If God is not dead, there are some questions we want to ask Him. I'm a believer, but that doesn't mean I don't get angry about these things."

This dynamic of dilemma has been at work in U2's songwriting for many years. *Boy* was an honest struggle with adolescence, and even the charismatic enthusiasm of *October* had its admission of failure. "Sunday Bloody Sunday" took the voice of the psalmist in the despairing cry, "How long must we sing this song?" "I Still Haven't Found What I'm Looking For" would become quintessentially U2's soul-view. Another song from *The Joshua Tree*, "Bullet the Blue Sky," would be cut from an Old Testament lamenting rock. After a trip to Central America, where he witnessed the horrific things the country was doing to the native population, Bono returned to Dublin and asked The Edge to do his best to put the rage of El Salvador through his amplifiers. There perhaps has never been a more turbulent and warlike rock track in the history of music. In the midst of Bono's lyrics, there is an almost throwaway line that might just be the crucial clue to "Wake Up Dead Man," "Peace on Earth," and so much more. Bono sings about Jacob wrestling with an angel and the angel being overcome.

In another Old Testament story, Jacob was a scoundrel, a man who deceived everyone he came in contact with, from his father to his brother to his father-in-law. Somehow the grace of God "sees beauty in ugly things" and "sees goodness in everything." We are told that Jacob and a man tumbled and wrestled one entire night. In the dawn, Jacob realized something supernatural was happening and would not let his assailant go until he blessed him. The mysterious aggressor eventually was understood to be God, and Jacob got a new name, Israel, which means "wrestled with God." A nation was born (Gen. 32:22-32).

It is that same wrestling that Bono has been doing in his art. He has never let go. Since the early days in the fervent and zealous and a lot more naive Christian fellowship in Dublin, Bono has tried to make sense of his unflinching faith in God and Christian redemption and hope. He never hid it from the difficult issues that faith has to wrestle with in the unbelievable world he has seen as a rock star, humanitarian, and courter of popes and presidents and prime ministers.

chapter 14

LEAP OF FAITH

In 1988, as U2 promoted *The Joshua Tree* and was building up the idea of embarking on its study of America's heartland, the band members found themselves on the roof of a Los Angeles hotel for a photo shoot with Anton Corbjin. It was a place that dropped a seed into the fertile imagination of Bono, a seed that would take some twelve years to be harvested. At one end of the roof, there was another building just a few meters away. It seemed so close that apparently The Edge told Bono he could reach it. "If you have the faith and really believe you can do it, then you'll make it," he said.[1] Thirteen years later, Bono took journalist Sean O'Hagan to the edge of that same roof and echoed The Edge's thought: "It would take a good run up."[2] The building on which they stood was the Million Dollar Hotel.

The hotel fascinated Bono. More than just the roof, it was the clientele that hung around the lobby and lived in the hotel that captured Bono's attention the most. Built long ago as the biggest and best hotel in America and given its title to attract rich travelers, the Million Dollar Hotel had become the hangout of the underbelly of L.A. life. Those on welfare and Social Security would congregate there, and Bono's mind raced about those people, their stories, their lives. This was a movie.

For twelve years following that initial seed, Bono developed the story. He brought on board Nicholas Klein, who would eventually write the script, and Wim Wenders, who would be the director and producer. Wenders is most famous for his movie *Wings of Desire*, and his movies *Until the End of the World* and *Faraway, So Close!* have obvious links with U2 as they share song titles. The band also contributed a duet with Sinead O'Connor, "I Am Not Your Baby," to yet another Wenders movie, *The End of Violence*. It was this movie that Klein probably was best known for writing, and the three came together to work on and improve Bono's original idea for the film *Million Dollar Hotel*.

Million Dollar Hotel was a slow burn. Mel Gibson, its star, could not find himself anywhere further from *Braveheart, The Patriot* or *Lethal Weapon*. The film is about freaky characters with darkness and a lot of soul. Bono does with his storyline what he so often does with his lyrics. Like a magpie, he goes about knitting together scraps of ideas into one whole piece. In *Million Dollar Hotel*, there are a few Bono obsessions. Hotel culture is the most obvious. Bono pointed out repeatedly during interviews how he knew hotels rather well from all the band's world tours and how he'd even bought one, The Clarence, in Dublin.

His fascination with John Lennon is exposed in the brilliant performance of Peter Stormare as Dixie. The character basically lives out Bono's John Lennon fantasy, believing to have written the Beatles songs and at one point declaring that it was the first time he'd left the hotel since December 1980. Television is also a recurring theme in throwaway scenarios, where it seems to be omnipresent—in the way the TV media descend on the hotel to deal with the art scam and in the confession of the killer, which appears not in a police report but in an interview replayed on prime-time news.

The trumpet player on the film's soundtrack, Jon Hassell, described the film as being a "screwball tragedy,"[3] but there are moments of real beauty, oft tenderness and glimpses of fulfilment and how life could be if love had its way. Here is another one of Bono's constant themes, maybe one that is appearing more and more as the years go by—unconditional love. He himself said: "It was initially going to be a play about a leap of faith, but then it mutated into something bigger and darker. I'd call it a dark fable on the redemptive power of love."[4]

"IT WAS INITIALLY GOING TO BE A PLAY ABOUT A LEAP OF FAITH, BUT THEN IT MUTATED INTO SOMETHING BIGGER AND DARKER. I'D CALL IT A DARK FABLE ON THE REDEMPTIVE POWER OF LOVE." —BONO

This is where the light shines in *Million Dollar Hotel*. Tom Tom, the narrator, is the most lovable and innocent angel-like idiot and falls in love with the vulnerable and beautiful prostitute Eloise. Played stunningly by Jeremy Davies and Milla Jovovich, it is in the interaction of these two characters that the film finds its soul. In each other, they find a love that neither of them has ever known. Tom Tom is so innocent he really is not even sure what sex is and is certainly not pursuing Eloise for any momentary wantonness. Eloise has never known anyone who just wants her for herself. They both find the redemption that Bono speaks of in one another. Bono is speaking about how earthly love—which he often has referred to as a miracle in itself—can make broken people whole. But there is the transcendent idea of divine love shadowing the whole escapade.

Bono's storytelling always repels any hints of a happy ending. The movie begins with its most successful cinematic scene, where the camera pans across downtown L.A. and fixes upon the twenty-foot letters that spell the movie's title. As this happens, U2's "The First Time," originally on *Zooropa*, sets the storyline and mood. The use of songs is another one of the movie's most successful tools. In "The First Time," the prodigal gets the keys to the kingdom, and just as Bono said he could not sing such a happy ending but wanted to look at the other angle, so it is in the movie. Tom Tom, with his salvation assured in the arms of Eloise, runs across that roof with the most peaceful and joyous smile as he waves to Eloise—who is at the roof door trying to save him. He takes the leap, a leap out of this world, or a leap into the next world. As he falls, he says, "Wow, after I jumped, it occurred to me: Life is perfect. Life is the best. Full of magic and beauty, opportunity, and television and surprises, lots of surprises, yeah. And then there's the best stuff, of course better than anyone ever made up because it's real."

Million Dollar Hotel is yet another study in the tangled web of darkness and light that life is all about. It is a web that shimmers and shines much more in the mind of a Christian who has to deal with all the contradictions of the juxtaposition of those shadows and shades. There are similarities to a much more successful Hollywood flick of the time, *Magnolia*, which looks at the darker shades of the underside and then breaks through with the brightest moments of illumination. The need for salvation and redemption is deeply embedded in both movies.

Art is everything that the members of U2 have been about, exploring the world and faith and love in whatever creative ways stimulate them and leaving the door ajar for whatever insight they stumble upon. Bono's idea of a film script was a natural outworking of that. It was no surprise that the final product was independent, mysterious, poetic, divine, provocative, and lingering. If the film did anything, it left deep-seated emotions and a haunting sense of love for the characters for weeks after it left the cinema. It was the speed of the chase that foxed the audience, especially those who had been attracted by Mel Gibson's FBI role.

The soundtrack to *Million Dollar Hotel* was released before the movie. The soundtrack gained credibility even before it was fully understood by its use in the film. While only three of the songs got a U2 credit, three others include Bono with either The Million Dollar Hotel Band or Daniel Lanois as on "Falling at Your Feet." This song is strong and insightful in the vein of Bob Dylan's "Gonna Serve Somebody." Bono layers image upon image of people "falling at your feet." The lyrics include some of Bono's most clever one-liners about faces being spoiled by beauty and adults being dulled by their sense of duty. Whose feet they are falling at and why comes through in the song's conclusion when he asks that he might learn to surrender and quotes Christ's prayer of commitment on the night of His betrayal in Gethsemane: "Not my will, Thy will" (Matt. 26:39).

It is a wonderful piece of Christian hymnody. Bono, as he had done before, seems to be delving into Paul's letter to the church in Philippi. If "I Still Haven't Found ..." could be linked with Philippians 3, then "Falling at Your Feet" is very much rooted in Philippians 2:9-11. In this passage, Paul is encouraging those at the church at Philippi to humble themselves as servants as Christ did. It is about Christ's surrendering to the will of God, and having done so, Paul concludes that "God exalted him to the highest place and gave him the name that is above every name, that at the name of Jesus every knee should bow, in heaven and on earth and under the earth, and every tongue confess that Jesus is Lord, to the glory of God the Father."

This song, in its gentle, understated way, takes us to the grand culmination of history. Here, falling at the feet of God, is every lonely, broken, confused, tragic loser or seeming winner who doesn't even realize it. In such a moment, the conclusion comes, "How can we stand? Whom shall we trust?" The solution is in surrender: "Not my will, Thy will." The movie does not use much of the song or its conclusion. It is in this song, and not in the final cut of Bono's storyline, where that "leap of faith" is found. It is a song about surrender. It's a song about letting go to transcendence and finding some grace. From the pop star to the prisoner, everything one day will fall at the feet of God. Ultimately how do you find salvation? Surrender.

Like so much of U2's work, this theme can be traced back through the band's entire catalog. Surrender has been a constant theme in songs such as "I Will Follow" and "Out of Control" on *Boy*, "Surrender" on *War* and "The Last Night on Earth" on *Pop*. Ever-present in U2 members' lives and songs has been this secret of spiritual living, bowing down to a higher power and the losing of self to gain eternity. In a *Rolling Stone* interview, Bono said: "Christ says, 'If you love your life too much, you've already lost it' (Luke 9:24). Which is an interesting one. As a younger man, I remember I didn't understand what that meant because I loved life. You're holding on so tight to it you're incapable of doing anything with it. It's about fear."[5] There are signs here of Bono's maturing as a human being as well as his ongoing meditation on scripture.

Whatever we make of the more-than-reasonable soundtrack or the intrigue of the characters and jazzy storyline, Bono's first foray into movies did not see as much commercial success as his band had. *Million Dollar Hotel* was released in Europe in 2000. By the time it reached the United States in the first months of 2001, the reviews had been written, the critics had dismissed it with all other rock star attempts at Hollywood, and even the star of the show, Mel Gibson, was denouncing it as boring. It only hit a few big screens in the United States. Apart from its Silver Bear Award at the Berlin Film Festival, it's safe to say that it is Bono's biggest failure since *Rattle and Hum*, that other movie. Like with *Rattle and Hum*, though, there is no reason to dismiss *Million Dollar Hotel*, especially if you are a U2 fan. The movie is a slow-paced mixture of love story, art scam, and whodunit all wrapped up in more than its fair share of the bizarre and offbeat. But there are characters, beauty, sadness, and an ecstatic sense of salvation that linger with the harder-working viewer for a long time after the credits have rolled.

chapter 15

GRACE

When U2 released its first album of the new millennium, *All That You Can't Leave Behind,* it was almost as big a culture shock for the U2 traveler as *Achtung Baby* had been a decade earlier. Somewhere between the last concert of the Popmart tour in March 1998 in Johannesburg and the middle of 2000, the technology took leave, and U2 stood, once more, as naked as the proverbial jaybird—bass, drums, three chords, and the truth. In the *Achtung Baby* video, Bono mischievously looked at the camera and said, "I learned how to lie." Here the members of U2 were learning how to tell the truth again, revealing themselves again, dreaming it up all over again—again! They were going back to find the future. *All That You Can't Leave Behind* was no repeat of past glories; it was a rediscovery of U2 in the primary colors of their sound and their spirit of honesty and vulnerability.

After an album called *Pop,* they finally had found pop. Now all the harshness of the preceding trilogy was gone, and what remained was the purity of the song without clutter—just the most gorgeous melodies, dashes of great playing, and Bono's voice giving its best performance ever. Every track was a potential hit single, fully exposed in all its beauty. Beauty was one adjective rarely used in a U2 review in the nineties. But beautiful this was. One review even described Larry's drumming as "gorgeous." Along with the technology, the shades and horns had also been thrown out with the trash. Writer David Dark has said that on the first listen to U2 albums, people are always concerned that they have lost their faith, and then as they listen and allow the songs to play around in their minds and hearts and souls, they wish they were as Christian as U2. *All That You Can't Leave Behind* did not need any time to resonate with the soul. This was as upfront about faith as the band had been in twenty years.

It was quite a reinvention. What were the reasons? There may have been many. The cynic may have touched on something if he said one of them was commercial. Though *Pop* and Popmart probably would have been hailed as a success had they happened to any other band, U2 experienced a disappointment commercially at the end of the nineties. The band may have had a need to regain the bigger audience. The guys of U2 would never settle for being the Rolling Stones, touring greatest hits packages long after their artistic zenith. It was important that they remained relevant, accepted for their new work and not just past accomplishments. A more immediate sound may have been an important consideration as a new album project got under way. The marketing of the album and the Elevation tour that would follow were strategically different. A few smaller gigs, supposedly for the fans to see them in an intimate setting, had a publicity strategy and helped the band rekindle the fires of starting again. The return to an arena tour in the United States as opposed to playing in stadiums as in recent years was to guarantee a big demand for tickets, a demand that would grow, not diminish. The album and tour showed a band spilling over the brim with the inspiration, fresh enthusiasm, and best songs and performances of a band that was hailed as the best on the planet more than twenty years after it began.

There is a story, truth or myth, that during the Popmart tour, U2 found a dingy little room in which to rehearse, and without much gear available, the band members made do with what amps they had and practiced the best they could. In the middle of this makeshift rehearsal, their cool, cutting-edge, dance groove sampler Howie B happened in upon them. After listening for a few moments, he asked them, in not too Presbyterian language, what on earth was that amazing noise they were creating. The techno boy had been blown away by the stark naked drums, bass, and guitar of a rock 'n' roll band. Apparently, from that gig on, during the tour Howie B drew back the number of technological loops and sounds he was adding to the brew. Perhaps this was a turning point.

Author Salman Rushdie recalls a lunch at Bono's home in Killiney, south Dublin, when Wim Wenders "announced that artists must no longer use irony. Plain speaking, he argued, was necessary now. Communication should be direct, and anything that might create confusion should be eschewed."[1] U2 responded by taking the irony even further on *Pop*, but then they realized Wenders had a point and they followed their cinematic friend's advice into the next phase.

Though not recording, this was a seriously busy "downtime" for U2. As well as the soundtrack and movie *Million Dollar Hotel*, they took part in The Belfast Agreement Campaign, helped launch an Amnesty International petition in support of the Universal Declaration on Human Rights, inducted Bruce Springsteen into the Rock 'n' Roll Hall of Fame, had three babies, and released *The Best of 1980-1990* compilation, whose "Sweetest Thing" single was a huge hit. Bono sang on Kirk Franklin's "Lean on Me" and Wyclef Jean's "New Day," which benefited NetAid charity. Bono also had a dinner in his home for Northern Irish politician John Hume in commemoration of the Nobel Peace Prize he and David Trimble won, met former President Bill Clinton when he came to Dublin, and had an audience with the pope where he traded his glasses for a set of rosary beads.

The meeting with the pope was part of the Jubilee 2000 campaign that delayed U2's next album. The spirit of Jubilee 2000 could have contributed to the depth and openness of the soul in the band's next recordings and performances. Even as the members masqueraded in their hedonistic persona of the nineties, they continued to publicize Amnesty and support many other causes such as War Child, which had the focus of its attention on Sarajevo. That war-torn city's name was the title of arguably the best song on the *Passengers* album, in which all four band members were involved, along with their producer, Brian Eno, as a more involved collaborator. They even played a gig there in 1997. Even though Bono's voice was in tatters, the gig was broadcast on BBC Radio One.

As the end of the millennium neared, many organizations were exploiting the landmark event and possibility of the biggest party in history. From champagne companies to local government, money was being spent or earned in all kinds of reckless ways. That justice organizations would attempt to use the date to achieve worthwhile results would help redeem a New Year's Eve that would end up as singer/songwriter Aimee Mann once described the Fourth of July: "a waste of gunpowder and sky."[2] Bono wanted to exploit the calendar for the good of humanity, not just the pleasure drives of a hedonistic West. The guys of U2 are rock stars and live in a rock star stratosphere. They enjoy that world. Perhaps they even indulge in that world in a way that might be judged as a little excessive. Yet they never lose sight of what's important. They never strive for it or put it in the wrong end of the ladder of their priorities. Sure, on millennium night, these four Dublin guys partied with the best of them, but their individual enjoyment was never more important than the world issues that have been so much a part of their legend.

Jubilee 2000 was an interfaith effort that began in the offices of Christian Aid and soon became an all-encompassing campaign. At last, a Christian organization pioneered the cause and, as happens too rarely, showed that if something is essentially Christian, even those who might not hold to a Christian worldview or belief can benefit from the teachings of Jesus, which should be for the betterment of everyone. The idea of Jubilee is found in Leviticus 25, in the Old Testament, where God commands that every fifty years there should be a special year for liberty and restoration. People who had slid down the economic scales for whatever reason got a fresh start, a theme that is central to the whole message of the Bible—grace. Bono later said that you can't write lyrics about debt relief, but then pointed to the song "Grace," which closes *All That You Can't Leave Behind*: "It's about the right to begin again, the right to be free of your past. That's grace. So, yes, you can write lyrics about debt relief." In this phrase, Bono overlayed the crux of Christ's Gospel to the soul, which is souls being saved by the grace of God alone and having an opportunity for a new birth. The crux of Christ's Gospel to the body is bringing about heaven on earth.

FOR A LONG TIME, BONO AND THE REST OF THE U2 GUYS WERE AMUSED BY THE ABSURDITY AND OBSCENITY OF HOW IMPORTANT ROCK STARDOM HAD BECOME.

Leviticus 25:35-37 says: "If one of your countrymen becomes poor and is unable to support himself among you, help him as you would an alien or a temporary resident, so that he can continue to live among you. Do not take interest of any kind from him, but fear God, so that your countrymen may continue to live among you. You must not lend him money at interest or sell him food at a profit." You will not find these verses in the *Hit Parade* of sermon texts being preached in evangelical churches on a Sunday morning. But with the modern global village, the Jubilee 2000 campaign took this neglected principle and applied it to countries trapped in a never-ending cycle of debt repayments. The money given to Third World charities every year falls way short of the interest repayments those countries send back to the West.

Bono was drawn in by his interest in scripture and his applying scripture to justice and peace. The links that must have convinced him to participate in Jubilee 2000 were his involvement in Band Aid and Live Aid, and the month he and Ali spent in Ethiopia working in a relief camp. They had given him a heart and a rage for the cause. The fact that the $200 million raised by 1985's greatest show on earth was about the same amount African nations owed in debt repayments every five days must have brought back some of the rage and shown an older and wiser Bono that more than a bandage was needed. The cause of the gash needed healing. Providing relief was a good thing, but dealing with the very structures of poverty was a much greater cause.

It had been ten years since Bono had put himself on the front line of the abuse and suspicion rock stars receive when they put their names to causes. Sting got negative publicity for his involvement in the Amazon Rain Forest cause and, of course, the members of U2 stepped back from being protest rock singers at the end of the eighties because of the disparaging reaction their sincerity had caused. Ten years later, Bono seemed to be less concerned with the snide press he might receive than he was with the potential result he might be able to achieve.

For a long time, Bono and the rest of the U2 guys were amused by the absurdity and obscenity of how important rock stardom had become. He had laughed about this and at himself before the public on the Zoo TV tour. Now he was seeing how foolish it seemed that this Dublin singer should have the clout to affect world powers. When Jubilee 2000 earned him an audience with the pope, he said: "U2's music has taken me on some odd diversions, but this has got to be the maddest and most absurd experience of my life."[3] Laughable it might be, but Bono was cunning enough to exploit the seemingly foolish position his music had given him. Jamie Drummond of Christian Aid, who recruited Bono for the "foot in the door" job, seems to have been strategic in his planning. Drummond and Jubilee 2000 recognized that in the era of celebrity, they needed someone to catch the imagination of the media. He said: "Bono got meetings with people that we couldn't meet with. If you're looking for the X factor, it is that we managed to win over the attention of the media, which usually ignore a cause like this. And that was through Bono."[4]

This is the kind of potent contribution that Bono, as a Christian, could make to the world through being a rock star with belief and convictions. Had U2 given up at the command of its well-intentioned spiritual gurus in the early eighties, who would Jamie Drummond have been able to turn to? It was Bono's Christian faith that was the bridge to Christian Aid. It was his radical political and justice beliefs rooted in the following of Christ via the likes of Martin Luther King Jr. that caused him to be up for it. He is a classic example of a Christian living his life in the real world and having a natural influence in that world. Bono hadn't done Gospel altar calls during "40" at the encore of concerts, but he had been out there in the flowing tide of the real world, sometimes bouncing about in its stormier seas. In the end, he got the opportunity to be the spokesman of a campaign that would affect a significant portion of God's planet, finding some justice and hope and literally saving people's lives. Many would accuse Bono of doing nothing for Christ and being ashamed of the Gospel. In Jubilee 2000, Bono lived it out in the heat of the world's spotlight.

It was that very flowing tide where Jesus had commanded His disciples to live. Out there where the city gambles. Where no one believes. Out there among the thieves. In the face of abuse and mockery. Where love violently dies. Out there at their daily Calvary, to take up their crosses and follow. Not to holler but to follow. If only Jesus had said to Peter, "Pray this prayer and withdraw from the world and make sure you preach in every song." He didn't. He said, "Follow me into a daily dynamic of dilemma where they will misunderstand you and castigate you and call you all kinds of things. It'll be messy, and every decision will not always be on the white or black side of gray, but follow me. Get involved. Where I walked."

Bono's place in the world gave him a big foot in some important doors. The organizers of Jubilee 2000 were stunned at his commitment. Bono was not going to do a rock star conscience saver and do a concert, raise a lot of money, and give a week's news profile. Maybe he saw he could be Martin Luther King for a while. He wanted the bigger job. Drummond said: "We expected that [Bono's involvement] might be concerts and records, but it turned out Bono's a very brilliant political lobbyist."[5] He was going to get his hands dirty, at least as dirty as presidents, popes, and prime ministers get. It was expensive, white-collar dirty, but it was the equivalent of the blood, sweat, and tears of the corridors of political power. Bono walked through the doors of the houses of political might and took on the world's finest economists and bank managers. Holly Peterson put it well in the January 2000 *Newsweek*, which featured Bono on its cover. She explained that she called financier David Rockefeller and U.N. Ambassador Richard Holbrooke. She said: "I said I had a kooky proposal. 'I'm going to bring a rock star into your office in weird sunglasses to talk about Third World debt.' They were sceptical. But within five minutes, they were floored by his breadth of knowledge."[6]

Christians have been bringing about social change and campaigning for justice for centuries. Martin Luther King Jr., of course, is one great example. In the U.K., William Wilberforce campaigned for the abolition of slavery for twenty years before he achieved success. In the first half of the nineteenth century, Lord Shaftesbury entered politics not long after his conversion to Christianity, and he spent most of his political career dealing with humanitarian issues, especially working conditions. He got a ten-hour work limitation for children, got a ban on woman and children having to work underground, and improved many other employment conditions.

As the millennium ended, Jubilee 2000, with significant help from Bono, had encouraged the seven richest nations to promise the cancellation of $110 billion in debt that possibly would benefit some forty-one countries. There were still many conditions that would allow the rich nations to stall on implementing this, and it was still considered to be an opportunity missed to deal with the horrific effects of such crippling debts. U2 continued to use the concerts in the Elevation tour, which began in March 2001 in Florida, to encourage fans to mail or email President George W. Bush and other decision makers, asking them to take more action on the debt that would cause the deaths of 1 million children during U2's three-month tour. They were also campaigning for action against the HIV/AIDS crisis in Africa.

15 GRACE

Bono often has said it is his Catholic guilt that drives him. Just as this is another veil to protect him from being labeled in any particular camp—he asked if the pope was aware he wasn't a Catholic before he met him—there is truth in the statement. It is Bono's spiritual provocation that will not allow him to lie back and enjoy his own luxury. His obsession with Jesus Christ prods him to keep stirring up anything he can to improve the world. As he told Olaf Tyaransen in a *Hot Press* interview: "I can't live with acquiescence. I can't make peace with myself or the world. I just can't. To me, it's like rolling over. So in doing things like Jubilee 2000, I do feel better for actually feeling that I'm getting my hands around the throat of something I care about."[7]

The idea of grace that Bono mentioned as a theology for Jubilee 2000 has been a constant phrase on his lips in more recent years. Bono even sent a copy of Philip Yancey's book *What's So Amazing About Grace* to Oasis' Noel Gallagher after the two had an in-depth conversation about faith in 2001. In a *Q* article just before the release of *All That You Can't Leave Behind*, Bono said he was always more into grace than karma.[8] If karma was what it was all about, he was coming back as a frog! Sean O'Hagan, in his detailed article on the events of the Belfast Agreement Yes concert, said Bono was chatting with Unionist politician David Trimble about the merits of the hymn "Amazing Grace." Even before that, when asked by British broadcaster and television celebrity Chris Evans what song he would sing if the world was about to end, Bono immediately responded "Amazing Grace," and continued, "how sweet the sound." Then there was the final song on *All That You Can't Leave Behind*, "Grace," which in addition to being a girl's name is a thought that can change the world. In concert from here on, Bono would name check "Amazing Grace" neatly into the lyrics of "I Will Follow." That makes an interesting dovetailing of the U2 career, as "I Will Follow" was the first track on the band's first album, and "Grace" was the final track on U2's most recent album at that point.

The spirit of this grace came through in an interview Bono did with Irish journalist Joe Jackson about a Samuel Beckett Film Festival at the beginning of 2001 in Dublin. Jackson touched on the underlying sense of attitude within the U2 camp, as its decade hidden behind the shades of irony faded and gave birth to yet another reinvention.[9] Throughout the interview, Jackson constantly tried to caress and collide Beckett and Bono with each other. Under the surmise that these two Irish writers were very strange bedfellows, he probed Bono to conclude that they had nothing in common. As with the vast majority of interviews with Bono, the God question was raised, and Jackson pointed out that it's a godless universe that Beckett depicts and this must leave Bono cold. "No, it doesn't because a lot of my friends are atheists," he responded. "It's lukewarm believers that drive me out of the Church. It's the big questions, isn't it? If there's a God, it's serious; if there's not a God, it's even more serious. And Beckett did at least approach the question."[10] Bono's respect for the atheist is refreshing. Many believers distance themselves from those with differing views on God, sometimes even within different churches. Bono makes them his friends and then makes himself accountable to them. He has fellowship and sharpens his faith against those with whom he doesn't agree because they are discussing the same issues.

"IT'S LUKEWARM BELIEVERS THAT DRIVE ME OUT OF THE CHURCH." —BONO

Jackson quoted Beckett as having believed that "to be an artist is to fail as no other dare fail. Failure is his world."[11] Bono immediately responded: "I really identify with that because what I think Beckett is getting at is that you must get the fear of failure out of the way. Once you become a better failure, you can really go places. For example, I have discussed this in the past. The constrictions of being cool. It's useless. And Lou Reed said that to me. He grew up in the fifties with the fifties idea of what it means to be cool. It's a stranglehold." Jackson then asked if U2 had burst beyond that stranglehold. "We played it cool for ten years." Had the band members finally freed themselves to be hot and bothered? "Yeah, we are! But at the start of the nineties, we realized that to touch and reach people during a new decade, we had to come in a different guise. So we did. Now the real challenge is to turn up without a mask. And I must tell you, it's not as easy to take the shades off as I thought it would be."

Here is the secret to the reinvention. The U2 members had lost the need to succeed and had come to terms with being relaxed in failure if failure should come. Isn't this what *cool* really is? Not minding if the world thinks you are cool. Just being faithful to you, no matter what the consequences. Not that failure was about to descend upon U2. "Beautiful Day" hit number one on the U.K. charts. The forty-year-olds reigned supreme.

"Beautiful Day" was an interesting opening track for *All That You Can't Leave Behind*. The last track on U2's nineties catalog, as the entire world seemed caught up in a frenzy of apocalyptic doom and gloom, fearful about the ending of a millennium, was "Wake Up Dead Man." It was as though Jesus was in the tomb after His crucifixion, lifeless, with the disciples letting go of all hope. John Lennon's words "the dream is over" come to mind. "Beautiful Day" is like an ecstatic proclamation that Peter and James might have sung just after Mary came back to the disciples' hiding place with resurrection news. The biblical image used may be the dove going out from the ark to bring back the leaf that informed Noah that the old world had ended and a new one could begin. But even that depicts the whole celebratory mood of the dead man waking up and a whole new kingdom being birthed. The album and the Elevation tour would see a new resurrection shuffle of a mood in the U2 camp.

As well as the biblical reference in "Beautiful Day" and the band's theological take on "Grace," the whole album is drenched in an upfront spirituality. The cover even has a clue as to the state of U2's spiritual temperature as it features a cryptic Bible verse from Jeremiah 33:3. The band had gotten Steve Averill to doctor the cover shot of the band members taken at Charles De Gaulle Airport and change the gate number behind them to read J33-3. Bono called the verse God's telephone number, as it reads, "Call to me and I will answer you and tell you great and unsearchable things you do not know."

That cover shot of the band members in a place of departure with their baggage beside them and Bono checking his passport depicts traveling. Symbolically, the music was leaving in other directions, and the technology was staying behind. There has to be more, though, and "Walk On" gives an obvious clue with a clever twist and a familiar phrase, "You're packing a suitcase for a place none of us has been/A place that has to be believed to be seen." The song, dedicated to Burmese human rights campaigner Aung San Suu Kyi, seems to live in two dimensions. Bono is always running and climbing and crawling toward what he is looking for here on earth. A world of freedom and justice has to be first believed before it can be achieved.

It is another song about these guys hanging on to the fraying thread of faith in spite of what is going on around them. It is a song about groping in the darkness with little immediate hope of light. It is about suffering a broken heart and falling back but trying to stay strong in the midst. Bono's perseverance that he yearns to transmit to Suu Kyi may have its basis in his love of scripture. When the apostle Paul says nothing on this earth can separate us from the love of God (Rom. 8:38-39), it is a promise they could see through the many dark nights of the soul.

But the cover and title have yet another spiritual and heavenly dimension. When U2 sang "Walk On" at the telethon for the heroes of the tragic events in New York, Washington, D.C., and Pennsylvania on September 11, 2001, Bono spoke over the newly included "hallelujahs" on the emotionally charged climax, "I'll see you when I get home"—an obvious reference to eternal hope even in the midst of mourning. The evangelical Christian roots from which Bono, Larry, and The Edge came have a core belief that heaven is only achievable by belief. A new millennium, Jubilee 2000, and the loss of INXS singer Michael Hutchence may have brought a few spiritual issues to the forefront of the band's thinking. It was time to take stock and ask some serious questions. What goes in the suitcase, and what has to be left behind? What are the important things in life? What are the transitory things? What can last the journey? What is of the moment? These spiritual questions are an ongoing theme of the Bible.

Ecclesiastes has a basic thesis of "everything is meaningless" (Eccles. 1:2). Only a connection with God brings any sense to the meanderings of humankind. Jesus encouraged His followers to forget about the treasures of earth because they get stolen or rust or moths eat them up. Treasures in heaven are lasting. The apostle Paul told the early believers to put their trust not in things that cannot be seen because they are temporary, but to trust in things that cannot be seen because they are eternal.

At the end of the song, Bono lists the things that can be left behind: what you fashion, what you make, what you break, what you steal. It all can and must be left behind. They are man-made things, but he adds to the list all the wrong things or mistakes that the Gospel deals with. Jesus came and died and was raised to life to offer a new start, leaving the regretful things and guilt behind and heading on afresh. The song and the Gospel have the same conclusion that love is the only thing that you need and that can be in your suitcase. Jesus, when asked what the most important commandment was, told the inquirer, "'Love the Lord your God with all your heart and with all your soul and with all your mind.' And the second is like it: 'Love your neighbor as yourself'" (Matt. 22:36-39). Whether you're heading for justice on earth or a fuller realization of the kingdom of God in the next life, everything else can be left behind.

The soulful, Motown-sounding "Stuck in a Moment," which may become a U2 classic, was written about the suicide of Michael Hutchence, an event that hit Bono hard. He claimed that the song is an angry conversation between him and his dead friend."[12] Yet the title itself is another moment when the transcendent belief at the core of U2, and indeed this album, suggests that there is more to this whole charade than the material world or the clock that seems to hem us in like walls to our left and right. It is so easy to get stuck in the moment of our troubled and hassled and painful and angry lives. But there is the hope of escape. If we could lift ourselves out of the moment and see all our moments from a panorama above us, then this moment in which we are trapped would hold new perspective. Ecclesiastes deals with this concept as well. There is nothing new under the sun, and if there is nothing above the sun, then this is all "meaningless, utterly meaningless" (Eccles. 1:2, 9). But if there is something above the sun, then a different perspective comes to bear. That faith perspective, a belief in an eternal God, gives hope and strength in the moment to keep on keeping on, and the conclusion of the song almost becomes a brother of "I Still Haven't Found What I'm Looking For": if all goes wrong and you falter in your steps, the moment will pass.

"Elevation," which follows "Stuck in a Moment," is the song that would have sat most comfortably alongside the *Pop* material. From being stuck in that moment, it prays for elevation that would give a higher perspective. Becoming the title of the tour to follow, "Elevation," like many songs on the tour, would take on a spiritual Gospel feel. The "you" clearly becomes God. Elevation is about revelation and, in the power of the live show, touches close to transfiguration, a mystical experience that Jesus shared with a few of His disciples on a mountainside.

"Kite" seems to be Bono, the magpie, at work again, picking up scraps of thoughts and ideas and weaving them into another song of a hundred angles. From flying kites on Killiney Hill with his daughters, Eve and Jordan, to thinking about all that this world might throw at you like an unseen wind, this is a meditation on dying and pondering whether we live life to its fullest. During a gig in Manchester, England, in August 2001, Bono dedicated the song to his father, who was dying of cancer and had just a few days to live. "I wrote this for my kids, but now I feel like he wrote it for me."

There is an overriding thought from John 3:8, where Jesus tells Nicodemus that the wind blows wherever it pleases; no one sees where it comes from or where it is going. Jesus was referring to the believer in that conversation, but that's the root of Bono's idea. Like a kite blowing about in the Spirit unseen. This might be a moment when he is meditating on who his children will become in this unpredictable world and asking himself what they think of their father, up until recently dressing up in makeup and horns in front of thousands of people every night.

"In a Little While" is about journeying home, and in this home, the singer will no longer be "blown by every breeze." There is autobiographical information in it. Bono seems to look back at his love with Ali, and this line harks back to the early days of U2 when it lived this tension between Lypton Village, the world of rock music, and the Shalom fellowship: "Friday night running to Sunday on my knees." On the Elevation tour, after the death of punk rocker Joey Ramone, the song took a new turn. Apparently, Ramone was listening to this song at the end of his battle with cancer. Bono prefaced the song by telling the crowd: "He turned this song about a hangover into a Gospel song. That's how cool Joey Ramone is."

"When I Look at the World" is one man's desire to have a mind like Jesus. It is full of U2 honesty in that it speaks with Jesus about the difficulties of acting like Him in every situation. The song starts out as an affirmation of how Jesus changes the singer's life, then it addresses the struggle that no matter how hard he tries, he cannot see it through God's perspective. It is about trying—and struggling—to see the events of "Peace on Earth" from the other side of his dialogue with God.

"Grace" is an epic end to *All That You Can't Leave Behind*. It is an atmospheric ballad in the tradition of "One" or "With or Without You," but it is more like "40" or "MLK." The ethereal mood is topped with the most beautiful poetry that evokes the grace of that word's other definition: strong, not decadent but a pearl in perfect condition.

In a world where the Eastern religions get a great deal more acceptance on the scale of cool than Christianity usually receives, Bono pulled a subtle little punch for the Christian belief in salvation by singing about how grace exists outside of karma. There is something about grace that makes even those who believe in it find it hard to believe in. You can hear the words and take hold of the understanding that here is an upside-down world order where the first are last and the last are first and where acceptance is unmerited. In a world where the first are first and the only way to be affirmed is to be the most intelligent or best-looking or most successful, it is hard to get reconditioned to the conditioning of grace. A flower doesn't bloom in one hour of sunlight, and a believer's soul needs constant exposure to the rays of grace day after day, year after year, before it moves from an intellectual assent to a truth that our lives bask in and live by.

The fact that the members of U2 were all about to hit forty in the year of their ninth album's release must also have led to some soul-searching. You can drift through your thirties without noticing that middle age is a whole lot closer than youth. That you are being adored by fifty thousand young rock fans every night, dressed up in all the latest fashions, and rocking and rolling can hold back such an awareness. But the band members' seeing themselves twenty years older than those at the top of the charts must have had its impact on where they should go next. Could they compete? Grace may have become a friend worth getting to know at this stage.

As they took to the stages of the world on the Elevation tour to promote *All That You Can't Leave Behind*, U2 was experiencing the unmerited favor of God. The band had not shown such a spiritual openness or intensity for many years. As they ended the show with "Walk On," Bono shouted, "Unto the Almighty, thank you! Unto the Almighty, we thank you!" before leading the crowd in choruses of "hallelujah!" When *Rolling Stone* caught up with Bono in Atlanta, Georgia, he was open about what he thought was going on: "God is in the room, more than Elvis. It feels like there's a blessing on the band right now. People are saying they are feeling shivers—well, the band is as well. And I don't know what it is, but it feels like God walking through the room, and it feels like a blessing, and in the end, music is a kind of sacrament; it's not just about airplay or chart positions."[13]

chapter 16

THE GOAL IS SOUL

U2 had once described *Achtung Baby* as chopping down *The Joshua Tree*. Similarly, the Elevation tour chopped down the Popmart stage. The golden arch that hung over Popmart, a symbol of the neon glitz and kitsch of the god of commerce, was felled and in Elevation lay in front of the stage in the shape of a heart. The heart became the insignia of the entire tour. It also served as the ramp that would take Bono into the heart of the U2 audience. In the Popmart set, U2 astonished their fans by outdoing *Zooropa*. Elevation was U2 finally drawing back, but by no means did it have any less intensity. This band's calling card has been the minutiae of detail in their plot and play, and the removal of clutter allowed them to add more in the subtlest of ways.

When the band finally hit the stage on March 24, 2001, at the National Car Rental Center in Sunrise, Florida, the most startling effect was that the lights were still on. When Bono, in a gesture, threw his wraparound shades into the audience, the message was loud and clear. The personas were off;

the lights were up; and there was no hiding. Stripped back to the basics like the musical construction of *All That You Can't Leave Behind*, this tour was going to be a ride into the heart of the real U2. On Popmart the band had inhabited a land-of-the-giants type set where they appeared as miniatures in the midst of the vastness of the screen, the arch, and the spaceship-like lemon that they descended the steps of. Not on Elevation. On Elevation the band was what mattered. This tour, and the fortune that went with such a venture, was going to be won or lost on the songs, the players, and the performance.

The opening songs revealed the other intention of the tour: Soul. At the feverish height of fans' anticipation just before the band's entrance, the PA pumped out a snippet from "Elevation." The only words were a sample on a loop of "elevate my soul ..." Then the band kicked in, and the song went live. At the end of the next song, "Beautiful Day," which in the course of just six months had already become a U2 classic, Bono reached out from the heart and shouted at the audience: "The goal is soul." A more understated declaration decorated his boots as he raised them to the crowd in the heart's interior; the word SOUL was spelled out on the soles. It was more than a contrived wordplay or pun.

While Bono searched for soul and God and love and spirit across the Popmart stage and found fashion and alcohol and style instead, here nothing blocked his way. It was as if to paraphrase his "Helter Skelter" comments on *Rattle and Hum* that television (as exposed on Zooropa) and commercialism (as unmasked on Popmart) had stolen the soul from the world, and here was U2 on a worldwide crusade to steal it back to its premier place in life's priorities.

Bono, The Edge, and Larry have long spoken about being influenced by the writings of Chinese mystic and Christian Watchman Nee, and Nee has an interesting slant on the soul. In his book *The Breaking of the Outer Man and the Release of the Spirit*, he wrote, "God not only wants to break the outer man, but also to separate it from the inner man. He wants to dismantle our outer man so that our outer man does not become an encumbrance to the inner man. He wants our spirit and our soul, that is, our inner man and outer man to be separated from each other."[1] The use of the word *dismantle* is an interesting one and makes a later appearance in the U2 story.

Orthodox evangelical Christianity could show some concern at the seeming dualism of Nee's theology where the body is in direct opposition to the spiritual soul. The song "Yahweh" on U2's next album speaks about a soul that is stranded in skin and bone, which is again very Nee. This idea can turn into an unhealthy attitude toward the body and the material world, ironically art. Even more ironically, this kind of dubious distinction led members of Shalom, who were very influenced by Nee, to suggest that U2 give up the music. At the same time, Bono seemed to use this imbalance to balance his own life of excess and spirituality. A spiritual traveler picking up different strains of Christianity in a variety of places and experiences, Bono tempers the fanatical division of Nee's thinking and makes it healthy.

Oftentimes, theologians are very semantic, and a phrase like "the goal is soul" is taken absolutely literally and not in the spirit of the poetry. Bono's declaration of purpose is to seek spiritual priorities and to live in a way that dismantles all the hurdles that the modern world erects to block our God connection and take captive our spiritual core to trivial and momentary pursuits. The soul and its connection to the body are ultimately a mystery in evangelical Christianity, but no one can argue that the stains and shame from the outer bodies' interactions with the world contaminate the soul. The song "Grace," often played over the PA as audiences left the venues of Elevation, is about God dealing with those stains, a cleansing of the soul, grace's goal.

Bono's opening pronouncement about this goal of everything that follows being soul was the key to unlocking the entire production of Elevation. These songs in this context, with all that was added on to the songs and what filled the gaps between them, had the intention of finding the soul, excavating the soul, guiding the soul, freeing the soul, healing the soul, redeeming the soul, elevating the soul. There was always the menace of temptation, sickness, evil, pain, and death, but on the journey we took in this tour, we found the courage, the wisdom, the belief, and the hope that these irritants could be overcome and that we could walk on into another world having left a better world behind for our children.

BONO'S DECLARATION OF PURPOSE IS TO SEEK SPIRITUAL PRIORITIES AND TO LIVE IN A WAY THAT DISMANTLES ALL THE HURDLES THAT THE MODERN WORLD ERECTS TO BLOCK OUR GOD CONNECTION.

As the tour rolled on, there was an overwhelming sense of something transcendent that was happening. Fans and band alike were speaking of something going down that Bono best described as "God is in the house." This was spiritually intoxicating stuff.

The goal of soul music has always been about liberation, and the spirit of that old, black gospel, soul music shaped this song cycle. If Elevation was about the soul, it was also about the soul's journey. Where were we going to take soul? There was a place featured from beginning to end in these concerts—eternity. Whether remembering Michael Hutchence or Joey Ramone as they did early on in the tour or whether it's much closer to home with the passing of Bono's dad later in the tour, death and what comes after and songs to those on the other side were rife the whole way through. They were the thread that wove the entire set list together, night after night.

All That You Can't Leave Behind was built around that theme, and those were the songs that U2 went on tour to promote, so their influence weighed heavily. Yet there were other songs that added to that theme in the set list coming from every U2 album apart from *October*. "New Year's Day" has always hinted at another world in white that has imminent arrival. A new stripped-back, almost completely naked "Wake Up Dead Man," as beautifully sad a lament as U2 has ever performed, asks Jesus to tell the story of eternity where everything will end up right. During the climactic jam in "I Will Follow," Bono asked the crowd to lift him onto their shoulders and take him to a place where they'd never grow old—Club Paradise. "Where the Streets Have No Name" is a pilgrimage, running and crawling and climbing and reaching for another land. Heaven is in the ether. Indeed from their debut album's "I Will Follow" to the up-to-date "Walk On," there is a continuing journey of a bunch of guys heading toward the distant shore.

And on that journey with soul as the goal and eternity the destination, Christian imagery and posturing are rampant. Bono had the odd moment of prayerful genuflecting and endlessly looking skyward, raising his hands like a Christian worshipping at a church service. Laced sparingly but startlingly in songs throughout the concert were additional lyrics and angles. No surprise there, but considering they were prayers lifted straight from The Message, a paraphrase of the Bible by scholar Eugene Peterson, something was new. Through the entire tour, Bono read Psalm 116 at the beginning of "Where the Streets Have No Name":

> What can I give back to God
> For the blessings he's poured out on me?
> I'll lift high the cup of salvation—
> A toast to God!
> I'll pray in the name of God;
> I'll complete what I promised God I'd do,
> And I'll do it together with his people. (MSG)

It was quite a public declaration of allegiance. It was an offering up of not only a life, but a band and a concert tour.

Praise was just as much in evidence. On the song "Elevation," Bono ended with a tirade of "jubilations," another word for praising and rejoicing. It was a nod back to the use of "rejoice" on *October*. In "Beautiful Day" there was a subtle but strongly intentional addition to the lyrics when Bono would shout, "Lord, teach me."

When the Elevation tour set out in Miami, Florida, Bono improvised the ending with, "How long to sing this song ..." from "40," the psalm they used to finish their concerts in the eighties. He reprised the lament of yearning for what is to come once we've left it all behind. Not long into the tour, everything changed in the conclusion. "Hallelujahs" and "thanks to the Almighty" turned the song into a closing hymn. The "how long" had been answered, and the audience left the gig not yearning for, but welcomed to, the other side. The "hallelujahs" would become so inscribed in the song that when Nigel Godrich, most famous for his work with Radiohead, did a remix of the song, they were included.

The name of God was called on in "Mysterious Ways," too. Often, Bono uttered, "The Spirit is in the house," during his, "The spirit moves in mysterious ways." He also used *Jehovah* and *Jah*, two names for God, and names for God became a theme on the next album. This was an interesting song to spiritualize. The result was a belly dancer and the Holy Spirit dancing to Marvin Gaye's "Sexual Healing." American Christian writer Frederick Buechner defined sex as follows:

> Contrary to Mrs. Grundy, sex is not a sin. Contrary to Hugh Hefner, it's not salvation either. Like nitroglycerine it can be used either to blow up bridges or heal hearts. At its root the hunger for food is the hunger for survival. At its root the hunger to know a person sexually is the hunger to know and be known by the person humanly. Food without nourishment doesn't fill the bill for long, and neither does sex without humanness.[2]

It was the healing that drew it into "Mysterious Ways," a song from *Achtung Baby*, where U2 mixed the sensual and the spiritual and even more so in this revivalist Church version.

After the worship and prayers, what about the sermon? Nearing the end of the liturgy, U2 broke into the sphere of the prophetic with very strong pontifications against guns and poverty. "Bullet the Blue Sky" took a new slant as American arms turned on themselves. Instead of the poor Central American nations running into the arms of America, it was the American people themselves. Gun legislation had been a controversial debate in the States for some time, and George W. Bush becoming president gave the pro-gun argument papal power. This was the most theatrical moment in the set and also the most cinematic.

Introduced with a snippet of a gospel song that kept us in church and reminded us that soul was the goal, actor Charlton Heston appeared on the screens. Heston was the president of America's National Rifle Association and gave his credo on guns: "There are no good guns. There are no bad guns. A gun in the hands of a bad man is a bad thing. Any gun in the hands of a good person is no threat to anybody, except bad people." Suddenly a small child appeared on the screen, walking to a paper bag and lifting out a revolver. This chilling image led into a bombardment of clips that overloaded the screens with photographs of gun-related incidents. Bono walked around in front of these with his arm over his eyes. It could have been that he could not look on the carnage, or it could have been a comment on those who blindly ignore the facts. Bono said 676,000 is the number that will "go down on the streets of America with a bullet." A bullet drum clap ended the song.

U2 Go Home: Live from Slane Castle, Ireland is the visual recording of a unique moment that can never, for many reasons, be repeated in the history of U2 and the lives of the four individuals in the band. The passionate performance that resulted made it an indispensable document. U2 built, as always, an emotional powerhouse from what was going on around them. The newspaper headlines, their lives, their faith, and their country all blended into a Molotov cocktail that exploded into a great rock 'n' roll spectacle. Maybe never have there been so many such things to blend as in the two gigs that ended the European leg of the Elevation tour. Two days at Ireland's most famous open-air venue saw 160,000 tickets selling like hot cakes in a population of 3.5 million. This was as major a homecoming as U2 had had in a long time. National pride was evident everywhere and was coincidently added to on the September 1 concert when the national soccer team qualified for the World Cup Finals with a 1-0 victory over one of the world's most powerful soccer nations, Holland. The match and Jason McAteer's goal were shown on the big screen before the gig. Bono even joked in the link between "Elevation" and "Beautiful Day" that, "It's now two nil," and later that he was Jason McAteer.

The venue also had obvious historical significance to U2, who played at Slane Castle as support for Thin Lizzy exactly two decades before. Bono introduced one of their first songs, "Out of Control," as if it were indeed that day: "We'd like to thank Philip Lynott for letting us open the show. We are a band from the north side of Dublin. We are called U2, and this is our first single. We hope you like it." Ireland's premier rock writer Stuart Bailie remarked in his brilliant DVD booklet notes about how many vintage U2 T-shirts there were in the crowd. Yes, many would be seeing the band for the first time, getting hooked on the *All That You Can't Leave Behind* mania, but some were at Slane in '81 and even before that!

Bono reflected on that day and the dream of becoming the biggest band in the world. He spoke of how they promised that they would not only make it, but that they would not relocate to do it. They were going to remain in Dublin. This was their tribe! The roar that greeted such strong nationalism was not the usual going-through-the-motions of the expected concert protocol. The Irish genuinely appreciated U2's commitment to home, and there was a national awareness of how much they had done not only for music but the country as a whole. The Irish were grateful and proud of this band. The Elevation tour had been a return to the top of the world for U2, and here they were returning to their own. This wasn't a "sort of" homecoming; this was the real thing.

On a longer, wider history of the entire island, this place on the Boyne River was the site of a fulcrum-swinging event in Irish politics. The Protestant King William of Orange defeated the Roman Catholic King James three hundred years earlier on the very river that the stage backs on to and the majestic Slane Castle sits upon. This was also U2's first Irish gig since a more recent tragedy in the historical Protestant/Roman Catholic conflict, the Omagh bomb of 1998, when twenty-nine people lost their lives. During "Sunday Bloody Sunday," Bono, his voice cracking with emotion, read out all the names of those killed. The "no mores" in the song have always been a powerful venting of Bono's anger at the political divisions on his island, which sadly have manifested them in the death and devastation so commonplace in the eighties and early nineties. In "Sunday Bloody Sunday" he called for compromise and sent the song and the entire audience into prayer (as this whole tour had). Walking into the crowd around the heart he chanted:

U2 HAS ALWAYS BUILT AN EMOTIONAL POWERHOUSE FROM WHAT IS GOING ON AROUND THEM.

> Put your hands in the sky
> Put your hands in the air
> If you're the praying kind
> Make this song into a prayer
> Put your hands in the sky
> Put your hands in the air
> If you're the praying kind
> 'Cause we're not going back there

In addition to national history, this was a concert about the band's individual stories. In that blurb about the band's beginnings, Bono thanked each set of the band member's parents for the financial support they needed to go off to London and record their first demo. Bono's daughter, Eve, joined her father on stage to play the part of the belly dancer in

"Mysterious Ways." It added to the emotional intensity. The overwhelming emotional detonator was the recent death of Bono's father. Bob Hewson had been ill for some time, and every night on the European tour Bono caught a plane to his father's bedside where he would spend the night before flying off to the next city. On the week before the first gig at Slane, he passed away, and just two days before the concert, Bono buried his father.

The emotion of "Kite," as he dedicated it to his father, had a poignancy that it never had before or is likely to have again. Bono is often criticized for taking on the big questions, trying to change the world, and there is no doubt that was exactly what he was trying to do. What cannot be lost in his addressing of the universal is how much emphasis he put on the personal. "Kite" is about how his children look at him and he them, and later how he looks at his father and he him! At its end he simply said, "Talk to each other," and we have the wisdom of a man whose heart was still raw from loss and the realization that all he could say to his parents had been said. It was powerful advice in the micro-political in the midst of all the macro-political stuff that made up a U2 concert. The "this is not goodbye" has to be believed.

"Bullet the Blue Sky" was back to its original intention. As the song was about to begin, the words *USA*, *UK*, *France*, *Russia*, and *China* were emblazoned on the backdrop. The Edge's guitar roared into war zone turmoil. As the song neared crescendo, Bono's anger had rarely been so demented. The song ended with some sense that justice would prevail and that these nations would be brought to task for the atrocities handed down. Their doom seemed justly assured. It was September 1, and in just ten days, a cowardly and criminal response changed the New York skyline and our world forever. It was a very haunting juxtaposition.

chapter 17

PROPHETS TURN PASTORS

As another ordinary September 10 drew to a close, English singer/songwriter Clive Gregson was concluding his gig at the One Trick Pony in Grand Rapids, Michigan. For an encore he stepped away from the microphone and started into the Beatles song "Across the Universe." When it came around to the chorus, the capacity crowd joined in: "Nothing's gonna change my world ... nothing's gonna change my world ..." No one had any idea of the irony and indeed heresy of Lennon's beautiful idealism. In the morning they would wake up to their world utterly disfigured forever. The digits 9/11 were indelibly and violently imbedded into history and the souls of anyone near television sets for the month that followed. U2's "Sunday Bloody Sunday" soon came to mind when they talked about the Belfast troubles as blurring fact and fiction and TV and reality.

In the days, weeks, and months that followed, U2's songs would take on meanings that were never dreamed of at the time they were written. Bono recalled in an interview with *Rolling Stone,* "I got a call from Ali, my wife, the other day. She was just trying to get rid of stuff at home and found a videotape of us on the MTV Video Music Awards a few years ago in New York doing the song 'Please.' She said she thought it was one of our worst performances, but told me to go back and listen to the song. I put it on, and I couldn't believe what I heard."[1] It is frighteningly haunting with talk of streets capsizing, shards of glass falling like rain, and even gets the month right—September.

U2's entire album *All That You Can't Leave Behind* takes on a whole new meaning when you listen to it in light of 9/11. Yet meanings had been changing even before it. During the Elevation tour, Bono spoke about his dying father before "Kite." He told Niall Stokes from *Hot Press*, "I have a verse about taking the kids up on Killiney Hill with a kite. Then I realized, I went back in my head, and I remembered being in Rush or Skerries, one incident where exactly the same thing happened. We used to have a caravan, and I sort of felt the goodbye aspect of the song was not from me to him, but from him to me. That's the thing about songwriting—you're the last to know what you're on about."[2]

The year had begun with the death of Joey Ramone. In the last days of his life, he was listening to "In a Little While." As U2 dedicated it to him in the days after his death, a close look at the lyrics brought to the song something that was hidden from view. The "home" in the song was again a reference to the place beyond Bono's Killiney refuge. The arms that he crawled home to were beyond the arms of Ali. In a Sean O'Hagan interview with Bono a while before *All That You Can't Leave Behind* came out, he was singing the chorus as, "In a little while, Lord." On the final recording the "Lord" was dropped, but in some ways Ramone's death brought back the sense of "Lord," if not the word itself. Bono said during the tour that Joey "turned this song about a hangover into a gospel song." Maybe the truth was that he redeemed it to what it originally was.

Where *All That You Can't Leave Behind* really took on new meaning and, in many senses, new responsibilities was post-9/11. As the enormity of the events of that day dawned, the world realized that it had lost thousands of her children in the World Trade Center, and then we realized that we had lost even more. We no longer had anywhere to hide from the madmen. As hope and any kind of certainty lay forever scarred, who would bring any words of wisdom or strength? Where would the priests and pastors appear from in a world that had rejected its spiritual center during modernity and felt nihilistic in the midst of postmodernity?

This was not a generation that looked for comfort from the men in clerical collars. As the world looked to the screen or speakers for comfort of any sort, *All That You Can't Leave Behind* took on an eerie feeling of having been written for such a time as this. A whole generation was stuck in a moment that we were finding no way out of. There was even a song called "New York" that many had felt sat out of kilter with the rest of the album. Now it was center stage. U2 played in that city as they took the message to the very heart of the hurt. Bono, again to Naill Stokes in an interview with *Hot Press*, explained it, "A lot of the themes and the moods of *All That You Can't Leave Behind* seemed to just make more sense. I don't think they changed. The obvious stuff like 'New York' or a song about depression like 'Stuck in a Moment You Can't Get Out Of' or 'Kite'—songs about letting go of people you don't want to let go of, all of that seemed to really connect."[3]

So indeed would "Walk On" as it was transmitted via satellite on the Telethon for the Heroes. Beginning it with a naked vocal of Bono doing the first verse of "Peace on Earth" and then going into the new U2 anthem, as it built to its worshipful climax, the pastor and priest upped the spiritual ante and led the world from mourning into worship. As the band finished in what had become the customary way of the tour with "hallelujahs," the absurdity of giving thanks during the deepest of tragedies and most acute pain and hurt seemed to bring biblical comfort. This was the song that released most tears and touched most souls with the lightest touches of healing. The holy man had visited the mourning home to bring God to us and point us to Him. The prophets turned pastors and priests.

In interviews following, Bono was given more and more column inches to bring words of pastoral care and even challenge. He spoke of how Eugene Peterson's paraphrases of the New Testament and Old Testament books of wisdom gave sustenance to see him through. He defended faith, not only Christianity but other faiths as well, in a world that blamed all belief as the cause not the solution. He hoped for a new beginning in 2002 for himself, his family, the band, and the world, especially those countries still looking for Jubilee.

There was a real spiritual depth charge when Bono explained his prayer for his dying father and the lesson he learned. He spoke to both *Rolling Stone* and *Hot Press* about how he had prayed that his father would have dignity in death, but realized that death, like birth, was without dignity and that what he really should have been praying for was humility. In *Rolling Stone* he concluded that maybe humility is the eye by which we get through the needle. In *Hot Press* he elaborated that he thought dignity might be a human construct next door to pride, or worse to vanity. Humility might be the best thing to have before your Maker. This priest took no prisoners.

The meeting with his Maker would be on Bono's mind for quite a time to come. Three years later on Jonathan Ross' television show, Ross was looking for a bit of gossip from backstage at the Live Aid gig of 1985. With so many stars confined into such a small place, like some Celebrity Big Brother, Ross was all a-grin with the possibility of a juicy story. Bono talked about Pete Townshend and how U2 was always big fans of The Who and how being in the same room as his hero, he nervously squeezed out a question: "Are you nervous?" Townshend replied, "Don't be stupid. I'm nervous when I meet my Maker."[4] In the middle of a laid-back and often humorous TV magazine show, Bono was throwing out thoughts on the judgment day.

September 11 did seem a kind of judgment day in an apocalyptic sense. America was in shock and mourning. Rock concerts were cancelled. It was no time for celebration or partying. U2 had another leg of the Elevation tour planned. What should they do? If U2 was about celebration and partying, then they would have had the sensitivity to forget the tour. But U2 was about much more than that. The goal was indeed soul, and there were souls in need of healing. U2 was confident enough to believe that they had something that might be of help for this particular moment. So they put tickets on sale, and on October 10 they were back on U.S. stages. Bono told *Rolling Stone* that he felt "incredible and humbled to be on tour in the U.S. at this time." For the band it was a message to the world that they would not be frightened off. There was also a belief that music could change things. Songs reinterpreted in the light of the event was one thing, but how would the band reinterpret those songs in the live setting to move from prophetically raging against American arms in the summer to throwing their arms around that same country with pastoral compassion in the fall?

There is no doubt that on the stage at that first gig at Notre Dame University in South Bend, Indiana, Bono's approach was particularly cautious. In the only gig on the entire Elevation jaunt that did not begin with "Elevation," the band looked nervous and uncertain as they came on stage ... Bono led a few repetitive lines of "the heart is a bloom and shoots up through stony ground" before "Beautiful Day" finally kicked in, though there was no great kick. It was the opening prayer for this leg of the tour. The band was indeed on the stoniest ground on earth. American streets are rough terrain, and many of the nation's loved ones had just been buried beneath it. What the prayer became was that the heart is eternal and could burst through to bloom again.

Bono often walked around in sober steps, like a priest entering the wake. He was gentle in his eye contact. He looked with sympathy and sadness. He was a man who wanted to say, "Sorry for your trouble," to an entire nation and felt the entire nation needed the comfort. There were more eyes raised to heaven in search of belief, more heads in hands of disbelief. "Until the End of the World" came across as a battle of good and evil, and "New Year's Day" was about new birth, the heart in bloom, breaking through to live in hope of a brand new time. America and the world needed to be born again.

A cover of the Three Degrees' "When Will I See You Again" with its waiting and suffering took on new spiritual depth and power as it introduced "Stuck in a Moment." Faltering in emotion, Bono's voice broke. There was recognition of the plight and hopefulness of the time passing. At the end Bono said, "Wow," as the crowd cheered. He looked pensive, deep in a poignant moment, and for once, Bono was speechless. As he was about to make a comment, he thought better of it and asked The Edge to start "What's Going On." This is the Marvin Gaye song that Bono had recorded with a plethora of artists in order to raise money for the AIDS pandemic.

"What's Going On" was a sharp left turn for Gaye, moving away from his romantic Motown terrain to eyeball the Vietnam War. *Rolling Stone* would name it the number four greatest song of all time and describe it as "an exquisite plea for peace on earth, sung by a man at height of crisis."[5] Gaye was in marital and artistic crisis as well as dealing with the crisis in the nation. Smokey Robinson told *Rolling Stone* that Gaye had told him God had given him that song. It was perfect for U2: political, spiritual, and personal. With too many people dying and crying and a conclusion of war not being the answer, it was another song that hauntingly could have been written for the time. U2 used it well as an introduction to "New York."

"New York" was a beast of a song. It already had a few heads, and another ascended out of Ground Zero on that Tuesday morning. Originally, this was a song about a man sorting out life's priorities. Its placement in the first leg of the Elevation tour between "Gone" and "I Will Follow" bore this out. It is a song about the speed and madness of the city. God eventually seems to turn up and, like the lover does in Song of Songs, invites him to "come away." Only Bono could replace the desert with New York as a place of spiritual contemplation; it summed up his entire being.

Bono nearly changed the "just got a place in New York" line as it was too consumerist, but that would have left out a vital spoke in the spinning wheel of his dilemma. The line rose like a phoenix from the debris of the World Trade Center with important connotations. The fact that he bought a place in New York was now not a wealthy boast, but an action that made Bono one of the mourners. He was one of them. It was a statement of pride. This is my city. These are my people. I want to celebrate the wonder of a city that others could dare try to destroy. Against their violent hate, I stand strong and proclaim my love as an act of surrender. There would be a paraphrase, "In New York you can't forget just how strong the city's will."

ONCE AGAIN, U2 DID THE EMOTIONAL—NOT FOR SHOW, BUT FOR MINISTRY.

"New York" is the song that changed most post-9/11. There was a specific change in lyrics to mention September's and summer's love turning to winter's rain, and the lifeboats mentioned were no longer a personal carrier for Bono, but invoked thoughts of real panic-stricken emergency and the new New York heroes, the fire fighters who gave their lives to try to save lives. The earlier mention of cell phones also became more poignant, no longer a negative image for a world where all communication has to be frantic and immediate, but a means to reach those who we love and find out if they are alright or even send a last message of love before we jump from the ninety-third floor. The lines of diversity between races, religions, religious nuts, and political fanatics are given a new take, too. It is no place now for the fanatics, but still a place for abounding tolerance.

By the time they reached New York, the hesitancy of South Bend had been left behind, and they were in full flow again, aware that they were indeed bringing something soothing to a nation in raw grief. "What's Going On" and "New York" were pushed back toward the end of the set. They followed "Bullet the Blue Sky," which was dropped for the first Notre Dame concert but returned, altered to remove the rage but to retain the provocation. America had been attacked and badly injured, so the pastor stopped pointing fingers, but in the embrace there were still the warnings of revenge and war and their continued, if not increased, futility.

But it was "One" that took center stage in New York. It had been muscling up the entire second leg. It intrinsically linked Bono's preaching about how his passionate Third World debt campaign and desire to eliminate poverty to the events of the previous weeks. He had been likening the religious fanatics who hijacked the planes to the IRA terrorists of the seventies and eighties in Ireland. Just like U2 being Irish did not mean they were terrorists, so we should not look at every Muslim as a killer. "One" moved from some heartbreaking love song to a song of world peace of the carrier and the carried, everyone together getting us out of this moment and walking on.

As they sang "One" in New York, the names of the 9/11 victims scrolled across the big screens in an emotional realization that these were not statistics but human beings who lived right here in this city. He ended with a conversation with God, "Did you hear them coming, Lord," a perfect lead-in to "Walk On" with its place in the waiting room between earth and heaven. At the end of the third night at Madison Square Garden, fifty firemen walked on stage to receive applause from their fellow New Yorkers. Once again, U2 did the emotional—not for show, but for ministry.

Bono told Niall Stokes that though music changes shape to fit events such as 9/11, "Oddly enough our music meant the same thing; it's just that the events brought the subject matter closer into focus. And a lot of the themes and the moods of *All That You Can't Leave Behind* seemed to make more sense."[6] How true. *All That You Can't Leave Behind* was about leaving and leaving behind. It was about preparing for that journey between here and there. U2 was in no earth-to-earth journey on these songs. Eternity and our mortality were being addressed as few artists ever have addressed them before. That the world should have to stare the issues raised in the songs face to face so quickly was the astounding thing.

There were immediate and long-term reasons why U2 should have been designed for such a time as this. Firstly and most obviously, Bono had a rehearsal of this mourning process at the tail end of the previous leg of Elevation. Indeed, his father's illness was a factor influencing the songwriting process, Michael Hutchence's death too. After his father's passing, rather than postponing gigs in England and Ireland, Bono decided that the songs were going to be the balm to go through his grief. In some ways they had written a check that he would now have to see whether they could cash. Having experienced the soothing in his own grieving, particularly at the first Slane Castle show a few days after his dad's funeral, Bono was able to do the same for others, for a nation, for the world. Paul wrote something about this to the church in Corinth when he said, "Praise be to the God ... of all comfort, who comforts us in all our troubles, so that we can comfort those in any trouble with the comfort we ourselves have received from God" (2 Cor. 1:3-4).

There is no doubt that Bono had been prepared to be the pastor of the mourning. He had spoken about the power of the songs in his own healing process during his father's illness and particularly after his death. It was at Slane Castle before 9/11 that U2 had added "When Will I See You Again" to the set. It was a sentiment and theological idea that Bono would bring into the Telethon version of "Walk On." It was that Christian belief in resurrection. It was language that would sit very comfortably at a graveside: "We are not those who die without a hope."

U2's music had always been suffused with the eternal, hopefulness, and born again-ness. Whether it was a tragedy brought about by evil people like those who planted bombs in Northern Ireland or flew hijacked planes into the World Trade Center; whether it was the unjust laws of trade or the patent control on drugs for those suffering the HIV/AIDS pandemic; whether it was just their own dilemmas of faith or how to live their lives in the extraordinary place where fate had thrown them into, with U2 there was always hope and transcendence and depth and resurrection.

As well as the transcendent faith in the Jesus of Christianity, and of heaven as a place beyond this life, U2 had been about what goes on here on earth. Their heads might often have been in the sky, but their feet were always very much in the mud. They realized their fallen state, never hiding from it, but exposing it and touching it. But they also have had a passion for love, for change, and for the God who can bring it. "Sunday Bloody Sunday" was depressing in its description of trouble years before in Belfast, yet there was always redemption in the victory Jesus won and the "no more" was not a cry that we could not take any more as much as a belief that a day would come when there would not be any more to take. It was a chant in the Christian prayerful believing sense. This undaunted confidence became more vital than ever during this leg of Elevation.

U2 MAY HAVE OFTEN HAD THEIR HEADS IN THE SKY, BUT THEIR FEET WERE ALWAYS VERY MUCH IN THE MUD.

Then there was the old traditional Irish wake. This is a unique way of mixing the celebration of a life and the thanksgiving of it with the sadness and mournfulness of saying goodbye. There is even an old Irish saying: "Sing a song at a wake and shed a tear when a child is born." Not that there was a frivolous party going on during the later part of Elevation, but the idea that there could be cheerful smile-filled groove happening alongside lament was not alien to an Irish band. The names of the victims of 9/11 rising from the stage in the same space and time as unabashed joyousness was not disrespectful, but a vital part in a genuine grieving process.

If some were reached during the tour, then the entire nation was given an invitation to the wake on Super Bowl Sunday. The first achievement of this night was to create the buzz of a concert in three songs. As a result of the brevity of the performance, they pumped all of the celebrating into one song, "Beautiful Day," before turning to lament in the mournful "MLK" as the names rose into the Louisiana sky. Then it was the hopeful yearning of a place where the streets would have no name. This was a microcosm of the tour. Bono made a lot of America being a soul nation during "Beautiful Day," and here into the heart of it, U2 pastored the flock. It was never the intention when the tour set out almost exactly a year previously, but it had been effectively achieved from the only band who could possibly have reached far enough inside to deal with the hurt of so many.

chapter 18

TONIGHT THANK GOD IT'S THEM INSTEAD OF YOU

There is a lot of pressure on a successful rock band to come up with a great album, especially when they have already made a great album. When you have been making great albums for twenty years and are not interested in going out to pasture by simply touring the back catalog, the pressure is really on. You don't need distractions. Larry, Adam, and The Edge would sometimes be exasperated by the needless phone calls that dragged their singer, chief wordsmith, and melody maker from the recording booth. It is hard to put a ban on receiving calls from the pope. Tony Blair maybe, but Nelson Mandela?

The Edge had particular difficulties with his mate's friendship with George W. Bush. The Edge is one of the politically quiet three in U2, but the T-shirt he donned for a photo shoot that appeared on the cover of *Hot Press* might have been his subliminal message: JONAH 1:XV. The verse, "Then they took Jonah and threw him overboard, and the raging sea grew calm" is either a red herring or likening Bush to Jonah. Jonah had purposely disobeyed God and gotten a ship he was traveling on into real trouble. His sin had caused everyone to become involved in the storm of his consequences. When they got rid of him, peace returned. So the Zen Presbyterian remained silent and spoke through his T-shirt.

The Edge asked Bono not to be photographed with Bush, but there was a photograph. The President of the United States of America walking side by side with the biggest rock star on the planet. This particular president was not popular with the rock 'n' roll fraternity. On the eve of Bush's re-election, Bruce Springsteen, REM, Pearl Jam, Dave Matthews, the Dixie Chicks, and many others on a smaller scale took to the stages of America to affect the vote. They failed, which in itself has to throw up many questions about the power of rock music to change the world, but that is for another day. For this particular rock star, it was quite a risk to be photographed seeming so chummy with the president who invaded Iraq.

Bono spoke of it in his interview with Alastair Campbell on U.K.'s Channel 5 in late October 2004: "I mean the humor of it doesn't pass me by, as I think you saw. And by the way, as I'm walking there with the leader of the free world, and he sees he's just about to go into Afghanistan. I'm doing the V sign. He goes, 'You know that's the front page, don't you?' And I said, 'Why do you think I do it?"[1] Bono was doing the peace sign alongside the commander in chief.

Larry said Bono would "have lunch with the devil himself if it gets him what he needs."[2] In the whirlwind running around to economic summits, political platforms, television studios, and church pulpits, it is hard to believe that somewhere along the line he hasn't indeed come face to face with the devil himself. During the most divisive, controversial, and vocal presidential election of all time in November 2004, Bono stayed clear of any electioneering or critique of either candidate. He felt he needed to be more diplomatic. He was going to have to work with whomever won the race for the White House, and his commitment to those whom he claims do not get a vote has been strong and uncompromising. If he did not compromise on his views on the president, he would be compromising on the lives of those he was standing alongside: "I will have to work with either of them, and I'm not working on my own account. I'm representing Agnes, I'm representing people who can't get in ..."[3]

When the entire band made a rare appearance on the sofa of BBC television's *Friday Night with Jonathan Ross* in November 2004, they jousted with Bono about his extracurricular activities but ended by applauding him for his successes. Bono was far from repentant about disrupting recording sessions and pledged to spend the rest of his life trying to bring an end to world poverty. He wanted the current generation to be "remembered for something other than the Internet." It should be "the first generation to eradicate extreme poverty," he said. "I want to spend the rest of my life doing that."[4]

It was the month that Band Aid 20's version of "Do They Know It's Christmas Time" was released. Twenty years after the charity phenomenon that was Band Aid, pop stars of 2004 gathered to set aside egos and try to make sure that millions of lives would be saved in the famine and war zones across the world. Once again, it was quite a menagerie of high-flying chart-makers. Robbie Williams, Coldplay's Chris Martin, Dido, Ms Dynamite, Dizzee Rascal, Keane's Tom Chaplin, Joss Stone, Busted, and the Sugarbabes—all these darlings of British pop shared lines, and even more were dragged in for the soaring anthemic chorus, "Feed the world."

Some of the entourage were not even born when the song was first recorded; Joss Stone even admitted that she had never heard of the instigator of it all, Sir Bob Geldof. Only one of the class of '84 was still at the microphone two decades later. It was a symbol of the unprecedented staying power of U2 that Bono was back to re-record "that line." In the documentaries that surrounded the release of Band Aid 20, Bono spoke of his discomfort with the "God" line of the song. "Tonight thank God, it's them instead of you" jarred with its callous selfishness. It came across as a little unseemly on a charity record. Bono's hesitancy was understandable.

Yet, it was the most provocatively prophetic line in the entire song. It packed the punch. Here we were in the comfortable, decadent West and instead of being embarrassed about it, we were just glad that it was not us who were dying of extreme disease-ridden famine on our television news. This line asks serious questions of even the grace that many Christians say before meals. There is a bland disregard for the disturbing conclusion of a prayer that thanks God for supplying all our needs if there are forty-thousand children a day dying from hunger. Are we suggesting that God is withholding from some? Or could it be that the grace prayer should be recognized as much more universal? God has supplied our needs, and it is our withholding and hording that leaves African children without the Lord's ample supply. This line certainly throws all kinds of messy questions and demands responses. A rich rock star having to sing it may have left Bono uneasy, but charity should never be about easy, thoughtless solutions.

For Bono, Bob Geldof, the co-writer of the song and impresario of the Band Aid charity, which would eventually lead to Live Aid, had "changed my life, ruined it if I think about it, it sent me off on this incredible adventure."[5] The two have in recent years become partners in campaigning to world leaders and went together to meet the pope. Bono credits Geldof for teaching him the importance of "being focused, angry, persistent." He also sees himself as the diplomat of the two. Geldof wades in with voices raised in expletives. Of Bono, Geldof said, "He's charming, he's persuasive, and the politicians can go home to their daughters and say, 'I had a meeting with Bono today.'"[6]

Geldof has always insisted that he is an atheist. When they visited the pope, Geldof asked if the pontiff knew of his unbelief. Bono turned to his fellow Dubliner and told him he was as close to God as anyone he knew. Geldof is indeed a scruffy bundle of contradictions. When the pope gave the two rock stars a set of Rosary beads each, the atheist asked for an extra set. He is foul mouthed, but defends the institution of marriage. He is a melancholic soul rarely recognizing any joy within his life, yet he is a man who has brought a great deal of hope to millions of people and love to his four daughters. His actions literally changed people's lives. Before the new generation of pop stars recorded the Band Aid single, they were introduced to a young woman who was a dying child in some of the 1984 Ethiopian famine footage. She was now an agriculture graduate. Bob Geldof saved her life.

The mention of his daughters is another remarkable story echoing the Hosea story of the Old Testament. Geldof lost his wife—the face of British TV in the eighties, Paula Yates—to INXS singer Michael Hutchence. He was devastated. Some years later it became the focus of his fourth solo album, *Sex, Love and Death*. Hutchence and Yates had a daughter, Tiger Lily, but both then died—Hutchence on a suspected suicide and Yates in a drug overdose. Geldof, who had every right to hate the offspring of his wife's adultery that caused him physical, mental, and emotional pain, took the girl in and made her part of his family; he loves her like a daughter.

Bono was the first to recognize the obnoxiousness of his and Geldof's position. As he introduced his fellow travelers on the Heart of America Tour in his *Diary from the Road*, he concluded, "And finally, me that most awful of inventions, a Rock Star with a Cause."[7] The press too have been quick to have a go at him for his do-gooding, telling him to stick to the music. Condemning someone for trying to save lives and help others is a remarkable indictment on third-millennium priorities. It is remarkable how human beings can be so belligerent about people trying to do good. Let us lambaste people who are trying to feed the hungry or fight for drugs for the dying. When did it become a crime for someone, no matter how successful or rich he or she is, to love their neighbor? What kind of society reads such things or believes such things or employs people who write such things? How far from the hippy dream has music moved when it is more useful to make a number-one single than keep people alive? Cheap shots at someone like Bono for being more interested in giving his time and rock star privilege for the benefit of others in order to sell magazines or newspapers would seem much more offensive.

It is time for people in general and journalists in particular to finally recognize that Bono is now as much a political activist as he is a rock star.

One might be how he gets paid, but that does not confine his identity. In the time between the Elevation tour and the release of *How to Dismantle an Atomic Bomb*, Bono gave all of his time to a plethora of causes, speaking at summits, party conferences, and doing a tour of television talk shows as well as founding DATA, an organization committed to informing the public and governments about "Debt, AIDS, Trade in Africa." This nonprofit is about advocacy, not sending aid. It works in partnership with relief agencies but has a clear agenda to convince politicians and the general public that poverty in Africa is vital not just because it is the compassionate response, but because it is also for the benefit of the West, particularly America.

Bono has not only been playing the political speaker around these subjects. He has put his money and his initiative where his mouth has been. DATA is not about raising money. The organization is bankrolled by Bono, Bobby Shriver, and Bill Gates. What DATA asks of the public is that they stand up and be counted in as many political ways as possible to bring the politicians to book for the responsibility that they have. What it gives is information, encouragement, and support to individuals and causes. As its website *www.data.org* states, "DATA aims to raise awareness about and spark response to the crises swamping Africa: unpayable Debts, uncontrolled spread of AIDS, and unfair Trade rules which keep Africans poor."[8] It is Bono's major concerns and his love for Africa rolled into one organization.

The website makes it clear why Africa is the focus of its attention: "Sub-Saharan Africa, the part of the continent south of the Sahara Desert, is also the world's poorest place. Seventy percent of its people live on less than $2 a day; 200 million go hungry every day. This year at least 1 million Africans, most of them young children, will die of malaria and 2 million will die of AIDS."[9] Bono has perhaps a more subjective reason. He talks frequently in speeches and television interviews about a pivotal moment in his life during his post-Live Aid time in Ethiopia. On his and Ali's last day there, a man offered him his son and asked if he would take him home and give him a better life. Of course, he didn't, but maybe in another way he did. That child has traveled in Bono's mind and heart and soul ever since, and once he involved himself in Jubilee 2000, there was no way he could stop. Speaking at the British Labor Party Conference in 2004, he told the party in government: "Africa is a magical place. And anybody who ever gave anything there got a lot more back. A shining, shining continent with beautiful royal faces ... Ethiopia not just blew my mind, it opened my mind."[10]

The three-pronged attack of DATA is strategic. All three are bound up together. Poverty is a plowed and fertile field waiting to harvest HIV/AIDS. The crippling debts that African government is paying back to Western governments lead to the poverty, but it is also vital that we do not sort the crisis out with charity or simply unilateral intervention. The African people yearn to be self sufficient, but trade laws prevent them from being able to compete with subsidized competition worldwide. DATA fights all three problems for the one solution that will result in parents never again having to push their children on Westerners to give their loved ones a hopeful life.

Sub-Saharan African countries pay $30 million per day in debt. The Jubilee 2000 campaign made some inroads into the debilitation. The richest countries promised to cut $100 billion of poor countries' debts if those countries could prove that they were committed to fighting corruption and poverty and investing in the health and education of their people. Twenty-three African countries have received some relief. The fourteen countries that have completed the program have received $29 billion and have been putting that money into debt relief. Yet the countries affected still owe $293 billion, and the 2005 Make Poverty History campaign is keeping the pressure on countries like the United States, the U.K., France, and Germany as well as the World Bank and the International Monetary Fund.

In addition to debt relief, these countries need a fairer system of trade so that they can compete with rich nations and become self sufficient. Rich countries subsidize their agricultural sectors by $100 billion per day, and along with import duties and quotas, the African countries, with 12 percent of the world's population, are getting only a 2 percent share of world trade.

Practical action is also coming out of the Hewsons' seaside home in Dublin. Bono's wife Ali is launching a new line in Fair Trade fashion. Already patron of the Chernobyl Children's Project and international fashion shows that raise thousands of dollars for charity, Ali has been working alongside New York designer Rogan Gregory to bring competition to the high street fashion designer labels aiming to bring fairer wages to the actual workers and closing down the sweatshops. The aim is street fashion with a story that doesn't make us guilty of greedy exploitation and a style that is deeper than the outward appearance. Wearing a pair of her Edun jeans at a book launch in Dublin, Ali said, "These jeans are just as nice as any designer pair of jeans, and yet there is an added bonus of knowing that they are Fair Trade. And there's a whole collection to choose from."[11]

"THE REVOLUTION IS HAPPENING IN YOUR HOUSE, IN YOUR PURSE, IN YOUR WALLET ... SHOPPING IS POLITICS." —ALI HEWSON

It is scandalous that in trying to switch America on to justice issues like debt relief, HIV/AIDS, and trade issues, both Bono and Ali have had to prove what advantage it would be to America rather than the good idea of ridding the world of poverty, injustice, and millions of senseless deaths. In the 2005 Making Poverty History campaign, Bono showed how good it would be to America's security as well as the advantages for trade. In the concept of Edun, one of the aims was to prove that the practice could be profitable so that other companies, whose bottom line is increasing profits, might see the benefits. This is the vomit of the modern malaise of selfishly getting more with no moral or ethical conscience to give.

The astute wisdom of Bono and his team at DATA, headed up by Jamie Drummond who first involved Bono in the Jubilee 2000 project, is prepared to speak to the selfish heart. As Bono told *Time* magazine, in an edition where he graced the cover underneath the headline "CAN BONO SAVE

THE WORLD": "We don't argue compassion. We put it in the most crass terms possible; we argue that it is a financial and security issue for America ... There are potentially ten Afghanistans in Africa, and it is cheaper by a factor of one hundred to prevent the fires from happening than to put them out,"[12] meaning it's cheaper to prevent terrorist cells from forming due to poverty than to destroy a country after the fact. In Jesus' parable of the Good Samaritan, it cost the aid giver, and he was generous in his personal cost to see his traditional enemy healed. Bono might have used the Bible to open the ears of the conservative Republican evangelicals, but he knew too well that it was not the sacrificial demands of Scripture but selfish benefits that would move America.

Where Ali, in particular, and Fair Trade, in general, hit the nail on the head was in everyday actions, not in the intellectual or economic ether. For Ali there was an everyday dilemma. As a mother she didn't want to think that another mother's child was exploited in making her children's clothes. She didn't want to think that she or her children wore the stories of injustice. Companies who leave factories and the souls of their workers desolate to set up elsewhere in order to save a few cents per T-shirt were not something she wanted to support. Clothes that say that people in the West walked over the poor to feed their greed might look good, but they should feel bad.

The whole of Africa had 6 percent of world trade in 1980, and by 2002 that had dropped to 2 percent. Increasing Africa's trade possibilities and giving jobs to the people of that continent are more lasting ways to make poverty history than debt relief and charity, though we should never give up on those. African writer Ben Okri wrote, "Stories are the secret reservoir of values: change the stories individuals live by and tell themselves, and you change the individuals and nations." Wearing clothes with positive and life-changing stories could be infectious.

In the book edition of *How to Dismantle an Atomic Bomb*, Bono spelled it out, "Shopping is politics. You vote every time you spend money."[14] He pointed out that, of course, trade is good BUT only when it is fair. Ali echoed her husband, who I suspect might have been echoing her all along: "The revolution is happening in your house, in your purse, in your wallet, how you spend your money ... shopping is politics."[15]

The United Kingdom has been trailblazing in the Fair Trade market. There was a 50 percent increase in sales in 2004 alone. The number of Fair Trade-certified products rose from 150 in 2003 to 834. Café Direct, the Fair Trade marked coffee, now has 19 percent of the gourmet coffee market. It has only been a decade since charities like Christian Aid encouraged people to campaign in their local supermarkets to have Fair Trade coffee on the shelves. It seemed such a small token of activism, and yet today all major chains carry various Fair Trade products, and the co-op's own chocolate brand, for example, is totally Fair Trade. America is a long way behind with few people knowing anything about Fair Trade, never mind the opportunity in their locality to buy it.

HIV/AIDS is a pandemic in Sub-Saharan Africa. Every day 6,300 die from HIV/AIDS and another 8,500 become infected as well as 1,400 babies becoming infected by childbirth or their mother's milk. The virus has already taken 17 million lives, and 25 million are infected. This is literally taking out generations of people, the number of people affected is even far greater in number than those infected. Poverty breeds HIV/AIDS. Education is vital to stemming the tide. Countries like Uganda have proven that there can be a halt to the ever-growing statistics through good education and awareness campaigns.

Drugs that are easily available in the West have been kept from those dying. The impact of ARV (anti-retroviral drugs) has been powerful; where the drugs have been available, people at death's door find themselves back to work within months. The prices of these drugs have decreased in recent years, and 700,000 people now have access, which is a step forward, but another 5.3 million people are in need of them.

The *Time* magazine article suggested that Bono, since joining the Jubilee 2000 campaign, "has molded himself into a shrewd, dedicated political advocate, transforming himself into the most secular of saints, becoming a worldwide symbol of rock 'n' roll activism."[16] Secular saint is not really accurate. Bono has always brought to his argument a deeply biblical *raison d'être*. He has spoken about the contract there should be to "love your neighbor" as Jesus commanded. He has likened the HIV/AIDS crisis to leprosy and challenged a Christlike response. He also said history would judge us for watching Africa go up in flames and added if history judges us hard, then God would judge us even harder.

"WE HAVE THE CASH, WE HAVE THE DRUGS, WE HAVE THE SCIENCE—BUT DO WE HAVE THE WILL TO MAKE POVERTY HISTORY?" —BONO

One place where Bono got to wear all his hats on his head on the same day was the 46664 concert that took place at Green Point Stadium in Cape Town, South Africa, in November 2003 to launch a new initiative to help raise global awareness of AIDS/HIV endorsed by Nelson Mandela. 46664 aimed to highlight the emergency of AIDS/HIV through unique live events and music related initiatives. 46664 was Nelson Mandela's prison number for the eighteen years out of his twenty-seven in captivity that he spent on Robben Island, just off shore from the stadium where the gig took place. The campaign was launched with a four-and-a-half-hour concert featuring Eurythmics guitarist and songwriter Dave Stewart who had the original idea, Queen, Annie Lennox, Beyonce, Ms Dynamite, The Edge, and Bono in a variety of collaborations.

Where 46664 differed from other concerts of its type was that this was not a gig-fest where the best-selling acts of the day are each given their fifteen minutes of charity. This was more perfectly planned. The bill was cleverly thought through with the old players alongside the younger chart-toppers and the Africans alongside the Westerners and Jamaicans and a few South

Africans thrown in to bring the whole thing back home! Once the bill was set down, there were songs written for the event, fascinating collaborations, and intriguing cross-fertilization of genres. The Soweto Gospel Choir deserves a special mention with their constant presence, but particularly their "Bohemian Rhapsody."

Bono took lead vocals for "46664 (Long Walk to Freedom)," which was the last song that Clash main man Joe Strummer wrote before his untimely death. It was co-written with Bono and Dave Stewart and was one of the two most powerful emotional moments of the concert. As Bono got the crowd in a sing-along groove of the "long walk to freedom" refrain, Mandela himself, right on cue, took faltering steps, with the aid of a stick, across the stage to the podium. It was a beautiful soundtrack to an inspired walk. This was a concert of victorious celebration as well as tragedy and challenge. It was a fully realized follow-up to the Mandela concerts at Wembley in 1988 and 1990 when rock music joined with political lobbies to free Mandela and the entire black population of South Africa. Here we all are almost a decade after democracy had been won. To see the reality of such an achievement helped empower the belief needed that since apartheid had been vanquished, we could do the same to the next great enemy of this beautiful people—HIV/AIDS. When Mandela began his speech to a mixed-race Cape Town crowd with "Comrades and friends," there was a tingle in the soul.

Which takes us to that other eye-filling moment of the night. One of the first songs that caught my attention and sent me looking to what was going on in South Africa was Peter Gabriel's tribute to Stephen Biko, who was killed in police custody in 1977. Gabriel introduced the song "Biko" by saying that it had been a long time coming, but at last he could sing it for the first time in the land it was written about. Twenty-five years later history was being tied up—a reminder how far the forty-thousand people gathered have come.

As well as the political, the air was rife with the spiritual. From the outset Bob Geldof described what was to come as everybody's "Redemption Song" with a Bob Marley cover. Jamaican Abdel Wright took up the mantle of his fellow countryman, Marley, charging the Church for using the name of Christ for hypocrisy. Andrea Corr's vocal to Brian May's acoustic on "Is This the World We Created" was hymn-like. During "Amandla" this young boy called Andrew Bonsu prayed that, in the name of Jesus, we would overcome all that the devil has planned for the world ... it is almost like Church. Bono and Beyonce, those with a more than vocal Christian faith, were giving the Amen a whole lot of Dixie behind him.

The concert was consequently released on three CDs and a DVD. The DVD added short documentary films about HIV/AIDS and the making of the concert, and there were twelve one-minute movies done by artists. The message was too crucial not to be overemphasized. When you see Annie Lennox meeting Mandela with 17 MILLION DEAD on her T-shirt, the reality hits home. These musicians were giving us the inspiration, the launch pad to make the difference. At the end of the horrific tale of Gabriel's "Biko," he finished with the words, "and as always the rest is up to you ..." It is only the people's response that Bono has ever questioned. He thoroughly believes that it is possible to end the plight of Africa. He concluded his speech to the British Labor Party Conference, "We are the first generation that can look extreme and stupid poverty in the eye, look across the water to Africa and elsewhere, and say this and mean it: we have the cash, we have the drugs, we have the science—but do we have the will? Do we have the will to make poverty history?"

chapter 19

AMERICAN PRAYER

It was never ambiguous in the intonation. When Bono said that "religious people are often the most judgmental" in his introduction to "American Prayer," he was not pointing a finger at the Church. Instead, he was speaking for himself and his co-singer Beyonce. Written especially for the 46664 concert in Cape Town, the song is a call for the Church to finish what Jesus started. Not just pray prayers, but build another world where the prayers of the people of America might actually be seen across the world. It is about children screaming that they need to see the reality of the pietistic disciplines of the Church. The healing, the meaning, and the belief of these prayers are a lifeline to those dying in Sub-Saharan Africa, which is what the concert was all about. "It's time for the Church to open her doors and become a sanctuary ... if God loves you ... what's the problem?"

For the best part of two decades, U2 has felt uncomfortable around the Church. Bono said, "I'm not often so comfortable in church. It feels pious and so unlike the Christ that I read about in the Scriptures."[1] He reckoned that he saw faith from a very different perspective than the average Church member and that was a source of frustration. "To some people the church is their ticket to respectability, a certain bourgeois point of view, a safety net for when they go to bed. My idea of Christianity is no safety net, a scathing attack on bourgeois values, and a risk to respectability."[2] This respectability is what has caused the Church to shun those suffering from HIV/AIDS. Bono finds this hard to equate with his view of Jesus as the one who set respectability aside to befriend the leper.

"I'M NOT OFTEN SO COMFORTABLE IN CHURCH. IT FEELS PIOUS AND SO UNLIKE THE CHRIST THAT I READ ABOUT IN THE SCRIPTURES." —BONO

Bono often said that growing up in Ireland he had seen religion sometimes being the enemy of God. The Church though was a place of power and, if restored to its original purposes, a place of loving welcome to the outsider. In 2002 Bono took a leap back into the faith community. The reason for his gesture was not to explain the last twenty years of his art to those who spent too much time wondering. It was a sign of his commitment to AIDS that he would throw all his hitherto caution to the wind and race headlong into places where he had been consciously avoiding for so long. It would seem that George W. Bush was the man who suggested that Bono go and build support among the faith community. In December 2002 he joined the Heart of America tour that took in seven states in seven days and had Bono in church pulpits and speaking at Wheaton College as well as meeting with any group of influential Christians he could, like Franklin Graham, son and heir to the world's most famous evangelist Billy, and Bill Hybels, who heads up the evangelical megachurch at Willow Creek in Chicago, Illinois.

In his diaries from the road published on DATA's website, Bono recalled how at Willow Creek, "Reverend Hybels and his wife, Lynne, sit me down and lift me up at the same time."[3] Hybels would say of the same meeting, "After a two-hour private meeting in my office, I came away convinced that Bono's faith is genuine, his vision to relieve the tragic suffering in Africa is God-honoring, and his prophetic challenge to the U.S. Church must be taken seriously."[4] Bono was also lifted up by his time at Wheaton College, "I really loved this crowd. These are the loudest Christians in the world ... normally I am not comfortable with Church people, they're pious, they're judgmental. These young students gave me hope."[5] It has been a long time since Bono inhabited the Church world to such an extent, and he was becoming aware that it was not all living up to the generalizations he and the wider public labeled it. In addition to a realignment of his own bias, he was also becoming an advocate to the world that he had found good things in the evangelical heartland.

Chicago journalist Cathleen Falsani traveled with the entourage and wrote the cover story for *Christianity Today*. She talked about Bono throwing the gauntlet down, wherever he got the opportunity, passionate not only about AIDS but also about living his life to the full. He recalled one pastor's recent advice: "Stop asking God to bless what you're doing. Find out what God's doing. It's already blessed." "That's what I want," Bono said. "I want to align my life with that."[6]

His belief is strongest when it comes to God's compassion for those suffering the AIDS pandemic. His challenge to his little time in the history of the world is, "This generation will be remembered for three things: the Internet, the war on terror, and how we let an entire continent go up in flames while we stood around with watering cans. Or not."[7] Should we be praying for God to intervene? He has another twist on that. He believes that "God is on His knees to the Church on this one. God Almighty is on His knees to us, begging us to turn around the supertanker of indifference on the subject of AIDS."[8]

Bono's first encroachment into institutional Christendom was on a big screen at Christian music festivals all over the United States in the summer of 2002. The first time the video message was relayed to Christian music fans was at Creation East in Mount Union, Pennsylvania. His script was later published in *The aWAKE Project: Uniting Against the African AIDS Crisis* (W Publishing Group). It was Bono's usual formula of statistics, scripture, and challenge.

> Today—in the next twenty-four hours—5,500 Africans will die of AIDS. Today in childbirth 1,400 African mothers will pass on HIV to their newborns. If this isn't an emergency, what is? In the Scriptures we are not advised to love our neighbor, we are commanded. The Church needs to lead the way here, not drag its heels. The government needs guidance. We discuss; we debate; we put our hands in our pockets. We are generous even.
>
> But, I tell you, God is not looking for alms; God is looking for action. He is not just looking for our loose change—He's looking for a tighter contract between us and our neighbor.
>
> I should be preaching to the converted here. There are 2,300 verses of Scripture pertaining to the poor. History will judge us on how we deal with this crisis. God will judge us even harder.[9]

Bono's time among the converted led to an invite from musicians in Nashville to come and meet them as a motivator and inspirer. Contemporary Christian artists had been involved in development projects, with many artists endorsing Compassion International for many years, but it was rarely central to the purposes of most artists. As DATA investigated ways to infiltrate the Christian community, the music industry was an obvious route to take. Someone tipped off Charlie Peacock, a musician who had actually been a stable mate of U2 at Island Records for a short period in the eighties, and Jay Swartzendruber, at that time publicist with Gotee Records but editor at *CCM* magazine, and they invited Bono to meet the fraternity.

Care was taken as to who would be invited, and an interest in Africa was a prerequisite. Eventually in late December 2002 at the tail end of the Heart of America tour, Bono was sharing a room in Peacock's home with the likes of dc Talk, Switchfoot, Jars of Clay, Sixpence None the Richer, Steve Taylor, and Michael W. Smith. It's hard to envision what Bono knew of this little subculture before he headed into the heart of it.

The response was strong, though it was unlikely that Bono could fail among a bunch of people who had probably idolized him from afar. Jon Foreman, the lead singer of Switchfoot—whose album *The Beautiful Letdown* would sell 2 million copies—said after the meeting:

> I would not have dropped everything and booked a ticket at the last minute to hear a social worker discuss the problems in Africa. I probably wouldn't have attended the same sort of meeting in my hometown ... I am a selfish, star-struck, rich, American, Anglo-Saxon fan of Bono. Bono came to work. He took a couple hours to talk to a bunch of fans to tell them to use their clout to change the world ... To feed the poor, to clothe the homeless, to heal the sick, to preach the good news of the kingdom of heaven. Sounds like an odd headline: "Bono Comes to Nashville to Convert the Christian Music Industry." I was convicted. Guilty.[10]

Dan Haseltine from Jars of Clay also spoke of the challenge and inspiration to get active:

> U2 has been a model of sorts. They have been a good example of people living lives in the reality of the Gospel. Lives that spend more time doing than explaining. More time actually loving than analyzing what love might look like. That is Jars of Clay's focus as well. We choose to write songs about life ... prophetic in nature rather than as Bono put it, "making commercials for God." Worship is in the "doing" even more than the "talking."[11]

Jars of Clay indeed did get active. They had already planned a trip to Africa not long after the mini summit of musicians. Coming home from Malawi, Zimbabwe, and South Africa, they set up Blood:Water Mission, a foundation dedicated to finding clean water and clean blood for Africans struggling with HIV and AIDS. In the summer of 2004 they were back in South Africa doing three concerts in Cape Town, Durban, and Johannesburg to raise funds for local projects.

During these concerts, singer Dan Haseltine told the crowd, "There is a great worship movement happening where we're from in America!" Cheers arose from the crowd. "I imagine there is one happening here in South Africa!" Even louder cheers. "Well, we are waiting ..." Haseltine paused and changed the mood. "Because if this truly is a movement of God, then it will come down from the worship into real action on social issues. It hasn't happened yet ... but if it is really of God, it will happen ... so we are still waiting ... " The cheers were subdued by the challenge. Haseltine knew that this concert, like every other concert, like the general spirit of Christendom, was a spiritual pat-on-the-back, warm-and-fuzzy experience for many without any trace of the cross-carrying Jesus that the entire thing was meant to represent.

Yet there was a genuine hopefulness among many Christian artists that a change was coming and that worship would give way to the things that Jesus most cared about—the marginalized. Michael W. Smith, during whose live set Bono's video message at Creation had first been played, is Mr. Contemporary Christian Music. He is nice from hairstyle to trousers to melody and vocal. In the Encyclopedia of Contemporary Christian Music, Mark Allan Powell said he "is generally considered to be the prettiest boy in Christian music—in terms of physical appearance and sometimes with regard to musical output as well," going on to liken him to Barry Manilow.[12] Everything is pristine and theologically squeaky and on the Republican side of Christianity. He has a "W" as a middle initial, and, as coincidence would have it, the "W" in the White House calls him "the real Dubya." They have been friends for years. Smith even sang immediately before Bush's speech at the Republican Convention in 2004. He seems the last person, in a subculture that for years U2 has been trying to avoid, who would be invited to play with U2. Yet in 2004 Michael W. Smith did just that—playing B3 organ on a yet-to-be-released song "North Star," about the strong rock of faith that was Johnny Cash. He is thanked on the sleeve of *How to Dismantle an Atomic Bomb* for his help with the DATA project. In May 2004 he helped Bono launch The One campaign.

Late in 2004 Smith released a new album, *Healing Rain.* After two very successful worship albums into a marketplace flooded with such ventures, this was Smith's first song-based album of the new millennium. Two songs in particular suggest that Bono had been of great benefit. With a sound reminiscent of Springsteen's "Streets of Philadelphia" blending into a Men at Work eighties' hit "Down Under" chorus, "We Can't Wait Any Longer" is a rare thing—a Christian protest song, a declaration of injustice, and a call to act now. The use of the Uganda Children's Choir does not make it schmaltzy as it could have done, but adds even more poignancy as the children plead in Swahili for somebody to hear them crying and to save them.

"U2 HAS BEEN A GOOD EXAMPLE OF PEOPLE LIVING LIVES IN THE REALITY OF THE GOSPEL." —DAN HASELTINE

Smith talks about waking up from slumber and the need to shake and wake "it" up. The suggestion is strong that this is a song about the Church's indifference; Bono's campaigning is making its mark. Smith said, "That song was inspired by my work with Bono and DATA. He's doing a great work. I believe we can't simply turn a blind eye to 6,500 to 7,000 kids who die every day [of AIDS] without doing anything about it. It's my challenge for people to become proactive in some way—call your congressman, call your senator, support the AIDS initiative, whatever—just get involved somehow. Do something." To *CCM* magazine he spoke of his own need to go to Africa: "I'm speaking and trying to wake America up, but it's still not enough for me. I need to go to Africa. I don't need to just pour my money into it. It's easy to give money. Just write a check all day and feel good. That's what a lot of people do. But we've got to get our hands dirty."[13]

Another song on the album was inspired by the title *How to Dismantle an Atomic Bomb*. Smith was the first person to go public with a little anecdote now in common circulation where Bono asked if he knew how to dismantle an atomic bomb. No. Bono's answer was "love, love, love." Bono's words, along with a viewing of Mel Gibson's *The Passion of the Christ,* inspired the other great song on Smith's album, "I Am Love." Co-written with a new discovery on the Christian scene, Taylor Sorenson, this is a powerful evocation of God's love for humanity, big, bold, strong, and sensitive enough to dismantle whatever.

"In the name of love" is a well-known U2 phrase that has had stadiums across the world high on excitement for twenty years. It was the title chosen for a tribute album of U2 covers. It had the added ingredient of being a fundraiser for AIDS charities. Artists United for Africa was a cooperative of Christian artists who made an album of U2 songs to raise money for AIDS projects. It was a gesture that suggested a couple of things: that U2's underground influence on the majority of Christian acts was now being publicly recognized and that Bono's preaching about AIDS was getting through. The more cynical might have seen another industry angle. The vast majority of Christian radio stations had a ban on U2. U2 was not quite kosher. Their Christian standing was dubious, and their lifestyle was no role model. Even more bizarre than the judgmental exclusion was the perverted quirk that their songs could be played by other artists. This was an astounding scenario in the mindset of evangelical Christianity where absolutism was held against what was perceived as the existentialist, secular, postmodern, anti-Christian philosophy of relativism. The conclusion is that truth is not in the words, but in who sings the words. Now that is stranger than fiction.

At its most cynical, a tribute album would at least allow more U2 songs remade by clean-cut boys and girls, to be played on radio. Christendom likes a certain amount of the coolness of U2 without any of the risk. Most of these artists have been in some ways influenced by the sound or spirit of U2. Christians growing up and becoming musicians in the Dublin band's twenty-year reign were shaped by their songs. That they would eventually cover these songs whose theology they could embrace seems obvious. That they should do it now when Bono had been meeting in underground catacombs with the movers and shakers of the contemporary Christian music industry seems to be even more obvious. At the same time the Church had been reassessing the soundness of U2's faith and, tentatively, as conservatives are not renowned for their acceleration, sprinkling a little more grace and affirmation than the judgment and damnation of the past. Bono's call was that they do something about Fair Trade, debt, and HIV/AIDS, and here was a tangible response.

Another product that raised funds for AIDS and connected the Christian subculture to U2 was a book of sermons. *Get Up Off Your Knees: Preaching the U2 Catalogue* showed that for some years a variety of clergymen and Church leaders had been aware of U2's spiritual power and poignancy. Compiled by two Episcopalian clergy, Raewynne J. Whiteley and Beth Maynard, it reveals how preachers and teachers from a wide range of theological positions have been using U2's lyrics in sermons. Of course, they could be using their knowledge of U2 to bring something cool to their scriptural pontification and draw in some cynical young people. The depth of U2 analysis and biblical content in this book betrayed a deeper truth. U2 had been taking theological concepts into the public marketplace all along.

The foreword was written by Eugene Peterson. Peterson has been a reluctant player in the U2 and Christianity connection for a while. He was a Presbyterian minister in Maryland for nearly thirty years before he became Professor of Spiritual Theology at Regent College in Vancouver, British Columbia. After five years there, he maintains a strong relationship with that college but has retired to Montana to continue his writing career.

Peterson was therefore on the U2 radar, but stuck out in Montana, he has never been bothered to take all the flights necessary to meet up with the band. Even though he once raced against the first man to break the four-minute mile, Roger Bannister, he is most famous for his paraphrase of the Bible—The Message. Bono took to The Message a few years ago and has talked about it openly in the press, eventually endorsing it on its back jacket.

In *Get Up Off Your Knees,* Peterson wrote perhaps U2's strongest endorsement to the Christian Church. His conclusion was that U2 is indeed a prophetic voice, saying, "God the Holy Spirit has used prophets, biblical and contemporary, to separate people from the lies and illusions to which they've become accustomed ... prophets train us in discerning the difference between the ways of the world and the ways of the Gospel, keeping us present to the presence of God."[14] His interpretation of why the Church has been slow to embrace U2 is that, "Prophetic voices that challenge the people of God to live 'in accordance with the scriptures,' scriptures that are especially vocal about care for the poor, the suffering, and the disreputable have never received cordial treatment from people who use religion to cocoon themselves from reality."[15]

Uncordial treatment was in evidence in *Christianity Today* in March 2003. Cathleen Falsani's insightful article on the Heart of America tour was laced with anecdotes about Bono's clearly articulated faith. She wrote about how he told her, "That there's a force of love and logic behind the universe is overwhelming to start with, if you believe it, but the idea that that same love and logic would choose to describe itself as a baby born in s--- and straw and poverty is genius. And brings me to my knees, literally."[16] Her article and Bono's face on the cover of such a benchmark of evangelicalism should have completed the bridge. Yet her article was negated to a great extent by an attacking editorial in the same issue. To put Bono on the front cover of the magazine, that no doubt would be a good sales angle, and then to knife him in the soul with a tirade of narrow-minded judgment revealed the suspicion that remained against all things U2.

The accusation was that Bono had a thin ecclesiology. In other words, Bono was not a card-carrying evangelical, so his biblical mandate could therefore be dismissed. "Bono has declined to speak with American evangelicals' mass media for years, and we're thankful that the urgency of his cause has changed that ... but Bono's excursion into American evangelicalism was missing one crucial element: a sense that he felt much respect for the evangelical culture he was lecturing."[17] This again veered toward a relativist view of God's Word. If someone who evangelicals feel has ticked all the boxes of acceptance, then it was authentic. If, as in Bono's case, the prophet was out on the fringes, then he could be dismissed. Ironically, that was where most of the biblical prophets and certainly Jesus Christ Himself stood. The editor also defined ecclesiology as cooperating with the Christian media and being visually a member of some established Church group that he or she could investigate and write an analysis of. It assumed U2 had no spiritual family or support or fellowship. It was full of assumptions.

The editor committed a hypocritical error when he or she pointed the finger at U2's use of money, suggesting they squandered cash in their nineties concert tours while the Church pumped aid toward relief. So Bono could not critique the Church, but he or she who wrote editorial could critique Bono. What did he or she know about Bono and U2's giving to charity or benevolent investment? The punch line, though, was extraordinary and yet maybe predictable from a Church still captive to modernist formulas and systems: "Bono has said repeatedly that Christianity without an element of social justice is empty. We agree. But a Christian's pleading for social justice without worshipping God regularly within the community of the Church is little more than activism for its own sake."[18] To say that helping others was empty or meaningless if the person doesn't attend Church regularly was at best untrue and at worst theologically dangerous. Thankfully, it was not meaningless to those who received the help or the giver who Jesus said would be sheep on the road to heaven, and there were no clauses about the need for Church records to confirm the reward.

The editor was no lone ranger. There is something within the evangelical psyche that is naturally suspicious. For every little group of believers delving into the lyrics of new U2 albums like Bible studies, there is another group who is equally interested in being a judge and jury, obsessed to damn them as definitely not Christians at all. It is a bizarre pastime and hints at a dark side at the heart of the human psyche but perhaps accentuated in evangelical communities. It has remnants of the Pharisees' desire to self-righteously judge, demand conformity, and exclude. There is a determination to castigate and damn and do it with a fervent glee. There is a lack of gentleness and grace. At times there is a frightening viciousness.

It is understandable that mainstream evangelicalism will misinterpret or be uncomfortable with some of U2's words and actions. Bono used the F-word in receiving a Golden Globe Award. America's Federal Communications Commission investigated Parents Television Council's complaint but ruled that in this context it was not offensive because it "did not describe sexual or excretory organs or activities." Bono later spoke about how in Dublin that is everyday usage. It is; indeed it is almost poetic the way that particular accent says the word, and there are many offshoots from it that have become like punctuation marks in everyday speak. It may have been a cultural error of discernment, but really he should have known better.

Perhaps as a response to the accusation and to the fuss over Janet Jackson's breast coming into display at the 2004 Super Bowl, he acted out some sexual suggestiveness on top of a female member of the audience when the band played on the Letterman show. Bono has the same adrenaline rushes as any rock star, and he has found himself in pretty lewd situations. Christians hung up on respectable behavioral patterns have gotten upset. Bono is this dichotomy of being a rock star with a massive ego and yet a caring philanthropist who takes pleasure in ridiculing the egocentric rock star! He confessed to *Spin* magazine, "I've watched myself being interviewed on TV, and I've just thought to myself, 'What an a--hole!'"[19] At least he is aware.

Bono, Larry, and The Edge are not in the slightest interested in whether the evangelical Church accepts them or not. The "U2 apologetic" strand of this book would not be of the first bit of interest to them. They are only too aware that it is God who judges and it is God who offers grace. They have no interest in what the evangelical subculture thinks about them at any level. When they are speaking publicly, as Bono is more and more, about God and scripture and how to live by that scripture, they are not carefully choosing their words to gain enough marks to pass some skeptic evangelical's examination. They are working within bigger contexts, taking what they really believe to the world beyond the Christian ghetto, and to reach that world they are happy to be misunderstood by the evangelical doubters who live in their absence-of-doubt world! Their faith is bigger, their vocation is bigger, and their God is bigger. They are secure enough to be able to live outside the conformity.

chapter 20

IT COULD BE ABOUT GOD

Adam said, "It might be about God,"[1] and though he was speaking about the song "All Because of You" specifically, it was an articulate phrase to describe the entire album. When the band sat down to write the songs for *How to Dismantle an Atomic Bomb*, there was a lot to catch up on. There was the death of Bono's father and the birth of his fourth child. There was 9/11 and wars in Afghanistan and Iraq that had divided the world outside of America, and America itself. They had used songs already written to deal with such things, but how would these events affect the next album? After it was released, The Edge shared his surprise: "I thought actually this would be a more political album. I think Bono did, too. I'm amazed at how personal it is. It's not a manifesto. It's about what matters. It's an honest snapshot of where we're at."[2]

The first single, "Vertigo," was a sonic explosion of spiritual shrapnel pummeling the soul with every line. It was dizzy with the temptations of choices. It was not a new theme for Bono, who got lost in New York's pleasurable alternatives on the last album. Even for the man of faith, sure of his salvation, it was a world a-swirl with options, and most of them not good. The mind can be led astray down all kinds of unhelpful alleyways. Then in the darker, quieter shadow-casting shift of pace and sound level, the devil gets his say, and an inviting say it is, too. In the Gospel of Matthew it is recorded that Jesus went out into the desert for forty days and nights. At various times Satan came to tempt Him with options to His destiny, vocation, and Messianic mission. At one point he took Jesus to a very high mountain and showed him all the kingdoms of the world and their splendor. "If you worship me, it will all be yours" (Luke 4:7). Bono coupled this idea with another of the devil's tactics in the Garden of Eden, where he told Eve that she would surely not die if she ate from the Tree of the Knowledge of Good and Evil. In "Vertigo," make a deal with the devil and you get absolutely everything and no one gets hurt ... tempting.

In his book *The Unbearable Lightness of Being*, the Czechoslovakian author Milan Kundera wrote, "Anyone whose goal is 'something higher' must expect someday to suffer vertigo. What is vertigo? Fear of falling? No, vertigo is something other than fear of falling. It is the voice of the emptiness below us which tempts and lures us, it is the desire to fall, against which, terrified, we defend ourselves."[3] U2 lives their lives in the very heart of such temptations. What other place is so filled with hedonism, drugs, sex, and whatever else money can buy? When you are centered on something spiritual, it throws constant dilemmas at the soul, and most of it is hardball.

Bono explained:

> It's a dizzy feeling, vertigo, a sort of sick feeling, when you get up to the top of something, and there's only one way to go—that's not a dictionary definition, that's mine. And in my head I create a club, called Vertigo, with all these people in it, and the music is just not the music you want to hear, the people are not the people you want to be with. And then you just see somebody, she's got

> a cross round her neck, and you kind of focus on it because you can't focus on anything else, and you find a little, tiny fragment of salvation there.[4]

That is another beautifully subtle image of Jesus as Messiah. Another songwriter with a Christian pilgrimage, Peter Case, often dropped Jesus into storylines of songs and said that his purpose was to have audiences taken by surprise, not expecting to find Him there. From a cross around some scarlet-nailed groover's pretty little neck, Bono glimpses the image that reminds him what really matters in the spin of the dance floor. God teaches him, and what is he taught? How to kneel.

Kneeling is a recurring image in the U2 canon. There is the advice in "Mysterious Ways" that if you want to reach up and touch the heavens, then you'd have to get down on your knees. The fundamentalist religious fanatics of "Please" are told to get up off their knees. In "Love and Peace or Else" the singer is not so comfortable on his knees. There is challenge to the humility that surrender to God brings. It is not easy to follow Jesus. It messes with your decisions and choices. It throws a multitude of complications into a life that could be all things fun. "City of Blinding Lights" ends with a lingering twist in the tale that blessings are not just for those who pray ... "luckily."

There is another "on your knees" link to the album's second track. "Miracle Drug" is a song based around the life and disability of Christopher Nolan, a school colleague of the band. After a difficult birth, the motor center of his brain was so damaged that he could not coordinate his limbs. His voice was so distorted that it was unintelligible. When he was eleven, he was given a new miracle drug called Lioresal, which relaxed his muscles so that he could move his neck ever so slightly. He was given a unicorn stick that was strapped to his forehead and allowed him to type. The family was aware that Nolan's mind was probably not as tattered as the rest of his body. They knew he was making an effort to read. However, the tiniest movement of his neck revealed a genius who had been captive in a dysfunctional body for years. He started to write, and poetry started to flow. He was fifteen when his first book, *Dam-Burst of Dreams,* was published.

Bono had been drawn to Nolan through school. Nolan arrived at Mount Temple around the end of U2's time there. That he became a great Irish writer who won the Whitbread Book of the Year in 1987 also endeared Bono. Yet there were a couple of crucial aspects to his story that caused Nolan to end up in a song. The first was that when he finally got the chance to write, Nolan didn't rage at God but wrote his first poem, "I Learn to Bow." Bono was impressed with the attitude of a frustrated genius unable to communicate who saw being able to move his neck ever so slightly as the greatest blessing of life. Being angry with God seems a more natural response than to bow in worship. Bono was fascinated at such humility. Interestingly, in Nolan's third poem, "Ambitions," he wrote about "pills you find as lasting prayer/An irate person may possibly/have faith instead of despair."[5]

"I'M AMAZED AT HOW PERSONAL THIS ALBUM IS. IT'S AN HONEST SNAPSHOT OF WHERE WE'RE AT." —THE EDGE

Like many U2 songs, "Miracle Drug" is about more than what the song is about. Bono reflected on a story like Christy Nolan's, and it sent him off in contemplation and into other ideas and lessons. "Miracle Drug" is also a prayer for the pills that might defeat HIV/AIDS. In many ways the song is about believing even when there seems no reason to believe. Nolan's mother spoke to him and read to him and stimulated his mind, having absolutely no idea that there would be any miraculous end to the story. There must have been times when she wondered whether she was wasting her time and when family and friends told her she was. Yet she believed and hoped against all the odds. Nolan's mother gave Bono strength in inspiration. American Christian leader and political activist Jim Wallis wrote about such a hope in his book *The Soul of Politics*. He said, "Hope believed is history in the process of being changed." He continued: "Hope is believing in spite of the evidence and watching the evidence change."[6] Bono saw such hope in Nolan's story and prayed for the same in Africa.

In this song there is faith going out to the miracles of medicine. There is the idea that failure is not when you seem to be getting nowhere, but when you quit trying. Again there is a quote from the Gospels. Jesus told the disciples that come Judgment Day those who saw Him as a stranger and invited Him in would go to heaven. They asked when they saw Him as a stranger, and Jesus responded by saying that what they had done for the least of His brothers, they had done to Him. The treatment of the alien or stranger is a major concern to God throughout the Bible. He is all about the refugee. The children of Israel were refugees as they fled Egypt, where they were aliens, and were brought by God to the Promised Land. Jesus himself fled in the arms of Mary and Joseph to escape Herod's death squads—the darker, more menacing side of the Christmas story. The stranger here could be Nolan, who probably was strange to everyone before and after he started to write. It could also be the marginalized dying without drugs in the southern states of Africa. U2's homeland was also in the midst of its own racist struggles at the beginning of the third millennium. Asylum seekers and immigrants were being attacked and made to feel unwelcome by government policies and a large section of the population, too.

It was not going to be *if*, but *how* and *how much* Bono's dad's death would be addressed on *Atomic Bomb*. The answer is in the song "Sometimes You Can't Make It on Your Own" and the album's other big ballad "One Step Closer." The former became the band's second single in the U.K. and Ireland and is very much the album's "Stuck in a Moment ..." type cut. Bono wrote it before his dad's death about their precarious relationship. Bono sang it at the funeral. The man is still alive in Bono himself. A rock star who grew up on punk can only have the opera in him through his father. From the subjective need of one another in a parent-child relationship that didn't always outwardly show affection and love, Bono reminds us all of the objective truth that we are not islands, no matter what

Paul Simon sings, and we are dependent on one another.

If "Sometimes You Can't Make It on Your Own" is primarily about Bono's perspective, then "One Step Closer" is more about his dad. It seems that it was during yet another philosophical and theological debate with one of the Gallagher brothers from Oasis that drew out the title. As Bono shared about his dad having a crisis of faith just before he died, Gallagher added, "Well, he's one step closer to knowing now." There is the echo of an old Bruce Cockburn song "Closer to the Light" written about singer/songwriter and producer Mark Heard, who died tragically after a performance at Cornerstone, a Christian music festival, in 1992. Having used Cockburn's lyrics consciously in the past, he might be using them subconsciously here; both songs are very similar in content.

There is a rhythmic disturbance with "Love and Peace or Else," a song full of proverbial nuggets that throws the listener and tosses him about. There are echoes of early seventies glam rock, T. Rex in particular. The song is about finding love and peace in the midst of a world in turmoil. It is personal love and peace in the heart, and political love and peace in the world. It is what we need, and if we don't find it, we are in trouble. There are hints, some bigger than others, about the things that stand in the way of the love and peace, the removal of which can set us free. With regard to the personal, Bono goes on about his wealth again. It—like our lives and political allegiances, conquering ambitions, and power trips either personal or national—needs to be laid down. The treasure could become a jealous lover, which is not needed in life's real goals—peace and love. Here he echoes the teaching of Jesus, who warned against trying to serve God and money. For the Christian, God is the source of love and peace that the world cannot understand.

God is also the reason to lay down your guns. Here specifically it is those who claim the fatherhood of God who are being encouraged to surrender their weapons. Children of Abraham and Zion can only be about Israel and Palestine. Bono has been intrigued by those faiths that claim the same ancestry as his own. He spoke to Stuart Clark from *Hot Press* about a festival in the Middle East to help with the peace effort there. "The only idea I had and one they'll be pursuing is a Festival of Abraham, which will celebrate the three traditions that call Abraham their father."[7] He spoke, too, of a building in Europe called the Eye of Abraham, which would house Jewish, Muslim, and Christian worship so that people could investigate each other and learn their differences but also the roots that they hold in common.

The reference to "the troops hitting the ground" seems to be about the Iraqi war, which Bono had been fairly quiet about as a result of his other campaigning. The sense of God's involvement in the delivery of the peace and love and the professed faith of President Bush, who has engaged with Bono on the things of faith, is what causes the song to end with the "Where is the love?" question. Where is the upside-down Christlikeness of the president's response to 9/11? What about love thy neighbor? Where is the love?

The next song, "City of Blinding Lights," is about growing up. It is about innocence being lost for the first time in the big cities of London or New York. It is the spiritual pilgrim maturing in his faith and taking on the world. He is older, he is wiser, he has more doubts. Time is moving and changing things, but Bono wants to hold onto the boy inside the man. This is a reference to both *Boy* as an album and the spiritual child within. Jesus said, "I tell you the truth, anyone who will not receive the kingdom of God like a little child will never enter it" (Luke 18:17). He is talking about naiveté, innocence, and imagination—childlikeness. Yet Jesus was not suggesting we stay childish. The song brings us back around to prayer. Some pray for blessings. Some steal blessings. God allows the rain to fall on the crooked and the just, which means blessings do not only come to the religiously disciplined ... luckily.

In his introduction to the song on the band's official website, *www.U2.com*, Bono tells a story that he has been sharing with journalists about an Anton Corbijn photographic exhibition. He said:

I saw this photograph—I guess I would have been twenty, twenty-one—getting into a helicopter, the first time I'd ever been in a helicopter, first or second video we made, and it was New Year's Day, and we're just about to take off. And I saw this face, and the face was so open and so empty of complications and so the naiveté was there and it was so powerful, and this Dutch journalist came up and said, "Bono, what would you say now to this Bono back then, have you anything you would say?" And I was trying to think what I would say, and it kind of just came out of my mouth, I said, "I'd tell him he's absolutely right, stop second-guessing yourself." Back then I didn't know how powerful that naiveté was, I didn't know how powerful that innocence was, so I was trying to rid myself from it, I was trying to set fire to myself and get rid of this, become a more worldly person, become a man of the world, and, of course, the less you know, the more you know, sometimes the less you feel and really understand. So "City of Blinding Lights" came right out of that moment for me, it's a story of innocence and experience, and the chorus is set in one of the greatest moments for me ever on the stage when we were the first band to play New York City, after 9/11, and we turned on the lights during one song, and I just saw twenty thousand people, their eyes wide open and tears just rolling down their faces, and it was an amazing moment for me, musically, and I just shouted out, "Oh you just look so beautiful tonight." And so that's become this song.

Speaking about "All Because of You," Adam told *Blender* that "it could be about God." It could be about all kinds of people. It could be Bono's dad again. It could be his wife, Ali. Who made him who he is? And that is who the "I am" line is about. Isn't it? If you take the clues elsewhere on the record and in the book that accompanies it, then Adam might be on the money. "I am" is the phrase that God used for Himself when He spoke out of a burning bush to Moses in the wilderness. Moses was not so sure about taking on his adopted grandfather, the pharaoh, who had oppressed the children of Israel so cruelly. He was also unsure about how the Israelites would receive him, so he asked God, "Who will I say sent me?" God replied, "I am who I am. This is what you are to say to the Israelites: 'I AM has sent me to you'" (Exod. 3:14). Jesus used the phrase to hint at His true identity and to goad the Pharisees, to whom the names for God were sacred. Another such name was Yahweh, so for Bono to use "I am" so powerfully on the same album as "Yahweh" seems a little coincidental. He also evoked another name for God, Jehovah, during "Mysterious Ways" on the Elevation tour. There is a clue to this in the book that comes with the album, which hints that an original lyric might have been: "Take off your shoes/Who are you, said Moses to the burning bush/I am the great I am/All because of you/All because of you."[9]

There are, of course, hints in the song itself. Calling yourself a child of grace claims some inheritance to God's shaping. Elsewhere Bono is aware of the cracks in his life and that whoever this person is who makes him who he is could make him perfect again. The Christian theology of sanctification is that God works and shapes until we are made perfect in Christ on the other side of this life. Being born when you are already alive has Bono off onto another recurring thread through U2's work. It has already been mentioned in "Love and Peace or Else." In a verse of that song, there is the juxtaposition of Bono's experience with the death of his father and the birth of his son. It finds Bono hoping that everyone will get to leave as we arrived, all wrinkly but with "a brand new heart."

"Born again" is a phrase used by Jesus to describe to a Pharisee named Nicodemus what needs to happen in the process of our conversion to the ways of God. In recent history the more fundamentalist corners of American Christianity have taken ownership of the phrase, and it has become synonymous with a right-wing conservative political perspective. Bono explained his feelings in some detail to *Mother Jones* magazine in 1989:

> I never really accepted the whole "born again" tag. It's a great term, had it not been so abused. I accepted it on one level, in that I loved the idea of being reborn ... I think people should be reborn

> every *day*, man! You know, every day again and again and again! At twenty years old, this idea of "surrender every day," this idea of "dying to oneself" ... was so exciting! Then I came to America in 1981, the land of milk and the .357 Magnum. It blew my mind that this word "reborn" meant nothing.[10]

Bono, however, was not going to allow the truth of the concept to be lost in the misuse and abuse of the term. The "born again and again and again" ... actually becomes a line in the song "Mercy," which was eventually left off the album.

The marriage of Bono and Ali is a wonder of rock history. It should be said that Larry is with the same childhood sweetheart for nearly as long, but that is a very private affair. Bono and Ali have baffled the celebrity press for a long time. They have held family values in the midst of the madness of a rock star lifestyle. In the press around this album's release there was a little concentration on Bono's family. The tabloids had "Six in a Bed" headlines that had nothing to do with supermodels but about the bigger bed Bono and Ali had to buy to fit their whole family into their sleeping arrangements. He told the Irish tabloid *Sunday World*, "Ali is the most extraordinary woman. I still can't figure her out. I still feel I don't know her. She's a very mysterious woman and she's very independent."[11] Hence, the mysterious distance of a man and a woman.

What "A Man and a Woman" does nail is the Hollywood lie of romance. In the world that revolves around Bono, cataloged best by gossip columns of the celebrity glossy magazines, marriages fall apart in just a couple of years, a few months, and in quite literally, in Nicholas Cage and Lisa Marie Presley's case, a few days. Prenuptial agreements are more vital than the vows. No one seems to intend to keep them. They have become no more than some romantic day out. "A Man and a Woman" challenges the core of such shallowness. Bono declares that he could not risk love for romance. In "Miracle Drug" he says that he's had enough of romantic love, and here he is saying that there is something deeper, more important, and much more satisfying. Bono admits it is a personal song, but it is also a raging antidote to all the examples of love that his peers pump into the minds of teenagers and those much older than that.

The song that most obviously marries Bono's African campaigning and his art is "Crumbs from Your Table." It is a very close relation of "American Prayer," which he sang with Beyonce at the 46664 concert in Cape Town at the end of 2003. Both songs were written inside the walls of the Church. Bono was initially a little frustrated: "I was kind of angry—angry at the Church as well because the Church was very slow to respond to the AIDS emergency, very judgmental about people with AIDS. (They have since changed their position, and I'm very impressed; they're all starting to wake up and realize that AIDS is leprosy, you know, just read your Gospels and figure it out.)"[12]

"POSSESSIONS ARE A WAY OF TURNING MONEY INTO PROBLEMS. I DON'T HAVE ANYTHING THAT I'D MISS IF IT GOT STOLEN." —THE EDGE

These are songs about belief becoming flesh. The beliefs people have in their heads and speak with their mouths are no good to the hungry, the exploited, and the diseased. In "Crumbs from Your Table" there is an ironic truth where Churches who do signs and wonders and miracles are being asked for something far more ordinary. The irony is that some Church groups are straining every spiritual sinew to convince the world of their authenticity by conjuring miraculous healings and extraordinary manifestations, while the miracle that the poor need is the ordinary sharing and justice of very everyday things. There is a travesty of justice in the modern world that where you are born and live should affect whether you live or die. AIDS is not a charity issue but a justice issue. It is about human rights. Why should people on African townships die for the lack of something that Westerners take for granted in the global village of 2004?

From macro-economics Bono moves to the micro-personal and cuts to the heart as he asks if we are prepared to demand rights for ourselves and yet turn a blind eye in the denial of those rights for others. It is a dire condemnation on humanity, but here Bono is turning the screw. This is not just humanity. This is the part of humanity that talks about the love of God. Such incisive preaching to the selfish West should cut deep.

An album about loved ones and events caused the band to think more about their families and led them to face the fact that Bono and The Edge's own children were reaching their teens. Indeed, it might have been a reason the band gave up their masks and irony. Eating disorders, depression, and suicide have never been more prominent among the young. The pressures on youth to look good, to have the right shape, to wear the right designer labels have never been so strong. Magazine editors, film directors, and pop video makers all scream out the message of "look like this, act like this, own this, and carry it like this." Living in the center of a celebrity world, rock stars see the heightened symptoms of what is the most chronic psychological disease of the age.

"Original of the Species" started out as a song about Bono's goddaughter, who happens to be The Edge's daughter. Bono explained, "It's just [about] watching some people, as I have, be ashamed of their bodies and particularly teenagers with, you know, eating disorders and not feeling comfortable with themselves and their sexuality."[13] The true, vulnerable, honest self is hidden behind the image that their peers will give affirmation to. This song screams to see more of who the person really is, and it doesn't want anything from them that would be less than authentic. You are amazing as God made you, so don't allow humans to desecrate your originality. You are the only you, so let us be having the real you, not the slave to fake. It is antidote to most of what pop music inculcates.

If there has already been a lot of falling on your knees, then the closing "Yahweh" is the ultimate fall-on-your-knees song; it is nothing short of a modern hymn. There are traces of Frances Ridley Havergal's eighteenth-century hymn "Take My Life and Let It Be (Consecrated Lord to Thee)" in which the English poet offers his hands, feet, silver, gold, will, and love over to God. Likewise, "Yahweh" is a giving over to God to sort out your life. Lips that judge need to be kissed. Bono said it is about Jerusalem, which is obviously the city that is to shine on a hill, but to go back to The Edge's comment that he thought this would be political and that it turned out very personal sums this song up perfectly. "Yahweh" is a song of deep commitment and allegiance, like the "Street Prayer" from the Elevation tour made song. It is also an unlikely yet powerfully poignant ending to a rock album.

And then ... for some bizarre reason in the European version of the album, they added the experimental and Eastern-flavored "Fast Cars." A detailed list of the world's technological gadgets and the societal ills that come from them, it throws the mood and disturbs the disturbing of the heart that "Yahweh" prays for. It takes away the spiritual conclusion, the altar call, the benediction, and for a band as intentional as U2, it is a strange twist in the tale. There had been much discussion about running order for the album, and when it was too long, they decided to jettison "Fast Cars" and another song "Mercy." Are they softening the spiritual blow for secular Europe whereas Americans can take the Christian concentrate without diluting? It would have made more sense as an extra track on the CD single, which it indeed became, or as a free download. It ended up on the European versions, and in America it appeared in the book edition. There were actually three versions: the CD, the CD with a DVD of interesting chat and documentary and a few live versions, and the book, which had the CD, the DVD, and a hardback book filled with jottings, drawings, and photographs by the band.

How to Dismantle an Atomic Bomb was U2's first album in the download era. "Vertigo" was number one in the download charts long before the single was released in the shops. Downloading also changes the need for the packaging. Nowadays albums are downloaded onto players with maybe five thousand other songs. Titles are not as well-known, credits are no longer given a place. For Bono, a man in his early forties, the disappearance of hard copy was an issue. The more mature record buyer remembers the twelve inches of vinyl and, more important, the gatefold sleeve, the art work, the lyrics, and the extra information to peruse while listening. Bono wanted to create something new, something to keep the old alive. He told *www.u2.com*, the official website, "It's trying to make the CD a more important object, because when the Beatles put out *Sergeant Pepper's Lonely Hearts Club Band*, it wasn't just a listening experience, it was a thing you held in your hands and opened—gatefold—and it had all these characters in it. That kind of inspired us to do something special with the packaging."[14]

In the book, as always, Bono took the majority of the words with the others falling in with art and photographs. The Declaration of Human Rights is there as well as quotes from Ghandi and Bhagavad Gita as quoted by Oppenheimer. Bono's scribblings can be hard to make out at times, and sentences turn corners and go in all kinds of directions, but they do give both an insight to the lyrics of the songs as well as an opportunity for Bono to wax lyrical and long on issues not met head-on in the songs. The plight of the poor, the politics and everyday economics of poverty are Bono's main themes. It is as though he has spent his last five years in complete contemplation of what poverty is and how it relates to us and particularly to himself.

This is not about a rich rock star giving away millions of dollars to feed the poor. There is no doubt Bono does such things but does it in private and in the absence of the media spotlight. Speaking to the *Irish Times* about the band turning down $23 million for one song in a car ad, he said that they could have used the money for charity, "But you either tell people you're giving it away—then by our definition, it is no longer charity, in the sense that the right hand shouldn't know what the left hand is doing."[15] This is another quote from Jesus in the Sermon on the Mount, where He is attacking the Pharisees for working out their prayer, fasting, and giving for the ulterior motive of enhancing their self-righteous reputation. Once more, Bono's living in very detailed ways is guided by his following of Jesus.

In the book he challenges the readers not to think a little bit of giving is their responsibility met.

Poet and rock biographer Steve Turner has been a friend of the band for many years. Bono wrote the foreword to Turner's poetry book *King of Twist*. In some ways the writings are very Turneresque. Little wordplays like, "We want more/I need more to want less."[16] These words come at the foot of the lyrics for "Ave Maria," which eventually was released as an extra track on the "Sometimes You Can't Make It on Your Own" single, but are not part of the song, though they do sum up the song's meaning, where it is not riches but how we deal with the riches that decides whether we are really rich or poor. Being among the richest rock stars in the world, U2 is open to accusations of hypocrisy in campaigning for charities while endorsing Apple iPods and selling tickets for concerts at high prices. Yet when the BBC investigative program *Liquid Assets* scrutinized their wealth, it could only speak of the band's integrity. The Edge has said, "Possessions are a way of turning money into problems. I don't have a big car collection. I don't have anything that I'd miss if it got stolen." This might be the secret to how U2 has held in check the excesses of the world they inhabit. There is more to life. There is more than this life. There is more to their art. The book, like the songs, has God all over it.

chapter 21

EVERYONE

There is something wrong with the picture. Something a little askew, a little blurred. In March 2005, U2 was welcomed into the Rock and Roll Hall of Fame, an honor confined to those who have been in the rock 'n' roll business for a minimum of twenty-five years. Days later they set out on the first leg of the Vertigo tour, which would break box-office records and prove that they were just as creative, commercially successful, and culturally crucial as when their debut album *Boy* was released in 1979. In the U.K., they had a host of nominations for the annual NME Awards in 2004. Their adversaries were Franz Ferdinand, The Killers, Kings of Leon, Snow Patrol, Keane, and Razorlight, most of whom were thrilled to become support acts on the Vertigo tour. These four men in their mid-forties seemed to be out of place in such a youthful world. Yet there they stood on their own merit, as relevant as ever and annoying critics who would prefer that fashion was quicker and more disposable. U2's longevity was unprecedented. Bruce Springsteen said in his welcoming speech at the Rock and Roll Hall of Fame that U2 was the last band for whom he could name all its members, which summed up U2's unique place—a current band that also happened to be legendary.

Springsteen was the only artist, in any way comparable, who could introduce them into the Hall of Fame. Bono had welcomed Springsteen in 1999, and interestingly that had ushered in the New Jersey Devil's return to big-time relevance as he and the E Street Band reformed for a great tour and the release of *The Rising*, which was in the same pastoral department as the last leg of U2's Elevation tour in the year after 9/11. Springsteen's speech was remarkable—brilliant in delivery, dynamic in content, hilarious in defamation, and prophetic in its spiritual edge.

The spirituality that Springsteen pontificated with some understanding and authority should not be a surprise. The course of his career has seen him move from a vitriolic hatred of his Catholic upbringing to a coming-to-terms with Christian spirituality. In the seventies he sang about Adam's curse upon us all and how we have to pay the wages of our sin but shifted to prayerful, grace-filled language in the nineties, culminating with the hopefulness of songs like "Land of Hope and Dreams" and "My City of Ruins." A month after the Hall of Fame speech, he released *Devils and Dust*, which included a song that could have been straight off a U2 album, "Jesus Was an Only Son."

It's not at all contrived to credit U2 with having a hand in Springsteen's reconciliation with that Jesus. Neil McCormick, the rock journalist and school friend of the band, wrote the book *Kill Bono*, which has an underlying thread (likely to be unconscious to the agnostic McCormick) that reveals Bono's commitment to including his faith in the way he treats people and in his conversations. In the book *Bono: In Conversation with Michka Assayas*, Bono lays out an erudite theology of his faith, which is particularly gripping in the parts where the interviewer and interviewee are spiritually sparring about whether Jesus is God. McCormick gets annoyed that Bono brings God into every conversation, and Assayas is agitated that he is always quoting scriptures. Billy Corgan and Noel Gallagher have had spiritual conversations with Bono, and there was even a press call in the U.K. where Prime Minister Tony Blair was bringing Christianity into his argument, and it seemed maybe Bono had rescued certain religious phrases from anathema to everyday speak. The impact of the unabashed nature of his Christian commitment in a world where it seems incongruous should not be underestimated.

Just two weeks after the Hall of Fame induction, the Vertigo tour began in San Diego, California, and the Hall of Fame accolade was recognized in the set list with a song cycle that closed the circle between the title track of the tour and songs from *Boy*, two and a half decades before. It was a long time since "The Electric Co.," "The Ocean," "Stories for Boys," and "An Cat Dubh" were in a U2 set list. This added another unknown quantity to the great conundrum of what to put in a U2 set list. Every time a new U2 album released to an expectant world, the time of anticipation only subsided for a brief period before there was another time of pregnant longing to see and hear how the new tunes would take on different directions. Not only that, but like a test tube where the adding of different chemicals causes different reactions and explosions, so adding the new songs to the U2 stage set can fundamentally change the interpretations of an entire catalogue.

Then there was another variant to be added: the stage and lights. Since Zoo TV took the potential of a rock show and propelled U2 into another orbit, the band had been shifting the possibilities. Elevation was a return to the less spectacular, revealing the band's primary colors; with its heart-shaped stage, the band's proximity to its audience had been redefined. What would the unique character of 2005's Vertigo be? What would the theater of U2 imaginings conjure on the stages of the world?

Willie Williams has been U2's fifth member for twenty years, responsible for designing their live shows. It can never be underestimated how vital a cog he is in their live machine. When Vertigo sent the head spinning, Williams' role had never been so important or influential. The heart was reshaped to make an "ellipse," and floor lights not only circled its circumference but were embossed in the floor of the stage itself. The impact was subtle but spectacular, and every song was given its mood and atmosphere by the genius of Williams' art.

Whether literally elevating the band in "Vertigo" with an optical illusion of the full-on red contours to the speed race along the tracks of "Elevation" to the pulse of the ECG machine declaring healthy life in "Miracle Drug" to the jitterbug stutter in "Zoo Station" and the epilepsy inducement on "The Fly," the whole auditorium was continually refigured. The back lighting was equally subtle and startling. With a huge section of the crowd seated behind the stage, Williams needed to come up with visuals that would not obstruct the view. Enter the color-shifting, bead-bulb curtains, or "factory lights" as Williams calls them, that would allow mood change and radiant color in certain songs. "Elevation," with a gentler groove musically in the first half, became a red-light district of the soul; "Sometimes You Can't Make It on Your Own" was cloaked in the blue sadness of a wake, and a ghostlike man walked as Bono strode around the ellipse. The storyline was embellished throughout with a reprise of the early nineties as Zoo TV's flashing, postmodern word bombardment reappeared during "The Fly," and fighter planes raced across "Bullet the Blue Sky." Adam and Larry's rhythm section has always held U2 tight musically, but on this tour Williams was equally on the beat making light changes with millisecond precision.

THERE IS A SENSE WITH U2 THAT THEY SEE THE REASON TO BELIEVE IN EVERY SITUATION NO MATTER HOW BLEAK, DARK, OR SEEMINGLY IMPOSSIBLE.

There is always an awareness at a U2 gig of the financial resources that this band is investing to set themselves apart from everything else. The size of their sound and spectacle is massive, and they have the money and the technology to keep dreaming it up over and over. Rarely does a concert go by that Bono doesn't thank the crowd for the money they have spent, and with a controversy surrounding the ticket sales of this tour, Larry apologized to fans who missed out because of scalpers on the band's official web page (*www.u2.com*) as well as during their speeches at the Rock and Roll Hall of Fame. Taking people's hard-earned wages and having such possibilities brings with it a serious responsibility, and U2 uses it to give back to the fans the greatest rock 'n' roll night of their lives. Yet, of course, U2 is never just about having a good time.

Scottish songwriter Ricky Ross, the soul and voice of another late eighties U.K. stadium band Deacon Blue, sings about how songs that are not about the Maker might just be for display, and U2 has built a career upon such a philosophy. To listen to their younger support bands, there was a sense that maybe the difference was not just the obvious wisdom and maturity that U2 has garnered during two and half decades but also the depth of soul underneath the songs. U2 concerts are never about just entertainment or display. They are about creating a place where belief in transcendence meets this old earth to affect transformation spiritually and socially.

There were many messages on Vertigo, many vignettes of inspiration and challenge. If Elevation was taking the people into Church—maybe some for the first time and many others for the first time in years—there was a sense on Vertigo that now that we are in Church, inhabiting a sacred space of praise and prayer, it is time to work out what that worshipping and praying had to do with the troubles of this old world and how belief might change it. Hymns, psalms, and spiritual songs, as the apostle Paul asked the church in Ephesus to sing to one another, took pre-eminence during the show. "Gloria" from *October* received a very welcome reintroduction after fifteen years. The final encore most nights was a trilogy of testifying in "All Because of You," commitment prayer in "Yahweh," and the return of "40" as a final communal psalm of belief and hope. Indeed "Gloria," with its intention of giving all that we have to God, to then asking God to take all that we have and use it for the betterment of the world in "Yahweh" wrapped the concert and their careers around that mystical connection of these Dublin boys and the God who fills the cosmos. There was the stark evidence of answered prayer when Bono shared that twenty-four years before he had asked God to "loosen his lips"; did he have any idea what he was asking?

When God loosens your lips, there comes an even more daunting responsibility. Once again, U2 used it carefully with powerful effect. On the Vertigo tour their belief became tangible. Before "Miracle Drug," Bono talked about how getting onto this stage had been a miracle and that there were many times when they did not think they would make it. He said they were going to continue to depend on miracles. He also quoted one of his friends and heroes Lou Reed, who said it takes a "busload of faith to get by." Bono said that in addition to God and each other, he had faith in science and doctors. He had faith, too, in the future and the future of the band. He then said, "God can inspire doctors and nurses; that's our prayer."

There is a sense with U2 that they see the reason to believe in every situation no matter how bleak, dark, or seemingly impossible. The belief in God and their fellow human beings is channelled into the causes they believe in. The sermon of Vertigo is about human rights. With the ecstasy of the opening numbers, the audience soared through "City of Blinding Lights," "Elevation," "Beautiful Day," "Gloria," and "Miracle Drug." Then came a shift in intention. As "Love and Peace or Else" began, Williams sent one thin red line out across the circumference. It signaled the edge, not the guitarist but the thin line of danger and precarious precipice the modern world dangles over. Here was the central thrust as the audience looked at a world divided, a war-torn, tortured, and scarred earth.

In this section the songs changed most. Songs that were specific to certain world headlines through the years all blended into one universal statement of the state of the nations. "Sunday Bloody Sunday" was not landlocked in Ireland, and Bono ignored the Irish flags waving invitations to be lifted from the crowd. "Running to Stand Still" and "Bad" were no longer huddled in drug-dealing Dublin doorways, and "Bullet the Blue Sky" lost its end-of-song, El Salvadorian, anti-American foreign policy rant. Instead, the audience found itself in the daily Middle East headlines with American soldiers returning from Iraq and people being tortured in the name of Christianity, Judaism, and Islam. Bono moved his headband over his eyes, making a blindfold with symbols of the three faiths (half moon, Star of David, and the cross) scrawled over it. He was on his knees with arms over his head in a tied-up pose, wondering how three faiths—all descended from the same father, Abraham—could be doing such barbaric things to one another and proposing mutual understanding by using the half moon as a C, the star as an X, and the cross as a T in the formation of the word CO-EXIST.

It all climaxed as smoke filled the floor, and on the screens appeared the first few articles of the Declaration of Human Rights. "Everyone," which echoed across the venue as the band kicked in, has the same rights to the same equality. It was the theme of the sermon. As "Pride (In The Name Of Love)" concluded in crescendos of accolades to Martin Luther King, Bono asked the crowd to sing for Dr. King's belief in his "dream large enough for the whole world" because he believed that "everyone is created equal in the eyes of God ... everyone is equal in the eyes of God." He repeated it with preacher's effect. Throughout the Vertigo set, the idea of ONE seeped into the conscience. Whether the "we can be as one tonight" in "Sunday Bloody Sunday" or carrying each other in "One" though "we are not the same," there was a uniting energy that was a constant. "Sometimes You Can't Make It on Your Own" was subjectively about Bono's dad, of course, but objectively it asked big questions of our need for one another.

"All Because of You," one of the second encore trilogy of songs, certainly insinuated that the "you" in the title is God, but it could be taken wider than that. In the South African tribe Xhosa, there is an idea called "Uhuntu." Bono told Cathleen Fulsani how Archbishop Tutu had introduced him to the idea: "Essentially, what it means is 'I am because we are.' And it's about the interdependence, how we need each other and we have a stake in each other. One part of the community can't thrive truly while the other part of the community is in the dirt. In tending to them, we will be better off ourselves. It's that simple. Ubuntu."[1] It was this philosophy that drove Nelson Mandela to reconcile his people with the violent criminals of the cruel white oppressor in post-apartheid South Africa. Coexistence was vital not only to the peace of the nation but to the very identity of his people. Being one with others is crucial to the wholeness of our humanity.

There was a sense that the band themselves were celebrating and flaunting their own sense of oneness. It would be wrong to play too much on a change in Adam as the reason for this, but he has been the member of the band who in the past found himself feeling isolated. In the early eighties as they did Bible studies in the back of the tour bus, he went out and lived the hedonistic lifestyle to the full. Ironically, today when the others go out for a bottle of wine together, Adam is the one who stands aloof, having rid himself of the effects of his addictions, addictions that once caused him to be unable to play in a concert. In recent days he has been the one throwing spiritual snippets out, declaring that something transcendent was happening in the venues of the Elevation tour, that "All Because of You" "could be about God," and that he was keen to play "Yahweh" live. The suspicion that Adam had caught up with Bono, The Edge, and Larry in the spiritual journey was confirmed when Michka Assayas asked if they were believers now, and Bono declared, "Yes. Adam had his own path, and it took him further out into the world. But I would say Adam is, right now, the most spiritually centered of the band."[2] As the U2 analyst wondered at the recent openness about things of faith, could Adam's enlightenment be one of the major impetuses?

In an effort to show that U2 is not only about Bono, who is in the papers every day and is one of the highest profile celebrities on the planet, each band member walked around the ellipse. Adam was more engaging with the crowd, and even Larry made it down to the ellipse for a bit of drumming on "Bullet the Blue Sky." As the four faces of U2 were projected on four screens, there was a clear distinction in the different characters. Bono was Bono, a contradiction of self deprecation and a working-class Dublin strut and swagger. Adam looked like he was of the aristocracy, exuding a great deal of what Springsteen described as sophistication. Larry was so intense and focused, suspiciously watching every move of the band he put together to see whether they will pass the test. The Edge was simply the coolest human being who ever walked the planet, never mind a stage, and this is *real* cool, not any fashion-disguised fake. When they played together, the sum was more wonderful than any of the parts could ever be in any other musical combination. The oneness they attempted to impart to the entire world was evidenced visibly; they practiced everything that they preached.

"IN U2'S MUSIC YOU HEAR THE SPIRITUALITY AS HOME AND AS QUEST. I BELIEVE THIS IS A BIG PART OF WHAT'S KEPT THEIR BAND TOGETHER ALL OF THESE YEARS." —BRUCE SPRINGSTEEN

In that Hall of Fame speech, Springsteen said he believes that oneness has been the result of the spiritual soul of the band. He said that bands might come together by accident, but they don't stay together by accident. Twenty-five years of democracy and growing together needs some explanation. Springsteen said, "In their music you hear the spirituality as home and as quest. How do you find God unless He's in your heart? In your desire? In your feet? I believe this is a big part of what's kept their band together all of these years."

One is also the name of the project created as a practical response to the show. Out of the DATA organization, Bono created a single cause that sets out a powerful target but isn't out of reach. The aim is to bring the North American audiences up-to-speed with their European counterparts, who are hurtling on toward the Making Poverty History campaign. Outside the venues, orange T-shirted volunteers encouraged fans to sign up to the campaign and sold the white wristbands so popular in Europe that people are buying on eBay. The goal is for 1 million Americans to campaign at their churches, communities, or any other level. Martin Wroe's words in the program echo the evening's theme: "Each ONE of us can make a difference. Together we can change the world."[3]

The belief that people have the power to create change is palpable in the U2 ethos. Bono has always cited John Lennon's influence in his political awareness and the sometimes naïvetè of Lennon's songs "Power to the People," "Give Peace a Chance," and "Happy X-mas (War Is Over)," and Lennon's bed-ins and other crazy stunts in the late sixties and early seventies seem to have their continuation in U2 but with much more realism, thought-out strategy, and political clout. When Bono speaks of world leaders, he always begins from a place of trust and belief in their inherent goodness and their desire to do something. As Christianity has evolved, it has often been more inclined to see the badness in humanity rather then seek out the good. The belief that humanity has fallen from its original state in relationship *with* God has often caused us to forget that humanity is made in the image *of* God.

Bono has not been distracted. He looks carefully for the goodness. In Vancouver, British Columbia, even though he'd been at odds with Paul Martin, their prime minister, in the press, he commended him, then gave out his phone number in order that he might be encouraged to do the good that Bono believed he wanted to with regard to aid. Likewise he connects to the goodness in the crowd in "Pride (In the Name of Love)" Bono pretended to pull his heart from his chest and throw it out into the crowd. It was a symbolically mimed prayer. As he sent love out to them, they would be inspired to find the love within themselves to also reach out in love. And he believed that they could make a difference. This is the same belief that Springsteen spoke about: "This has carried their faith in the great inspirational and resurrective power of rock 'n' roll. It never faltered, only a little bit. They believed in themselves, but more importantly, they believed in 'you, too.'"

Being in the middle of the greatest rock 'n' roll adrenaline rush in the world helps to energize an atmosphere of faith, hope, and love. To quote Springsteen yet again, "A great rock band searches for the same kind of combustible force that fueled the expansion of the universe after the big bang. You want the earth to shake and spit fire. You want the sky to split apart and for God to pour out." U2, though, has never been about conjuring up magic feelings. They want the signatures on the Making Poverty History petitions as people leave the venues. They want that phone call to the prime minister. They want to do more than entertain; they want to change the world.

NOTES

CHAPTER 2: DUBLIN CITY, IRELAND

1. James Henke, "U2: Here Comes the 'Next Big Thing,'" *Rolling Stone*, 19 February 1981.

2. Niall Stokes, *Into the Heart* (London: Omnibus Press, 1996), 11.

3. Greg Kot, "U2 Renewed," *Chicago Tribune* (*www.chicagotribune.com*), 2001.

4. Bill Graham, *Another Time, Another Place* (London: Mandarin Paperbacks, 1989), 24.

5. Ibid.

6. Os Guinness, *The Gravedigger File* (Hodder Christian Paperbacks, 1983), 82.

7. Howard Sounes, *Down the Highway: The Life of Bob Dylan* (London: Transworld Publishers, 2001), 323.

8. Derek Poole, "U2 Gloria in Rock 'N Roll," *Streams*, 1982.

9. Ibid.

10. John Waters, *Race of Angels* (Belfast: The Blackstaff Press, 1994), 154.

11. James Henke, "Blessed Are the Peacemakers," *Rolling Stone*, 9 June 1983.

12. Susan Black, *Bono in His Own Words* (London: Omnibus Press, 1997), 29.

CHAPTER 3: OCTOBER

1. Neil McCormick, "Autumn Fire," *October Review, (Dublin) Hot Press*, 16 October 1981.

2. B.P. Fallon, *Faraway So Close* (London: Virgin Books, 1994), 47.

3. Bill Flanagan, *U2 at the End of the World* (London: Bantam Press, 1995), 45.

4. Mark Le Page, "Bass Notes: U2's Adam Clayton on Geography, Spirituality and Rock 'n Roll," *Montreal Gazette*, 26 May 2001.

5. John Waters, *Race of Angels* (Belfast: The Blackstaff Press, 1994), 168.

6. Liam Mackey, "I Still Haven't Found What I'm Looking For," *(Dublin) Hot Press*, December 1988.

7. Bill Flanagan, *U2 at the End of the World* (London: Bantam Press, 1995), 47.

8. Olaf Tyaransen, "U2: The Final Frontier," *(Dublin) Hot Press*, 8 November 2000.

9. Steve Taylor, Youth Specialties Seminar, Atlanta, Georgia. Chapter 3:

CHAPTER 4: "SUNDAY BLOODY SUNDAY"

1. Niall Stokes and Bill Graham, "The World About Us," *(Dublin) Hot Press*, March 1987.
2. Susan McKay, *Northern Protestants: An Unsettled People* (Belfast: The Blackstaff Press, 2000), 16.
3. Liam Mackey, "I Still Haven't Found What I'm Looking For," *(Dublin) Hot Press*, December 1988.

CHAPTER 5: LIVE AID

1. Chris Heath, "U2: Band of the Year," *Rolling Stone*, 15 January 2001.
2. Tony Campolo, *Who Switched the Price Tags?* (Waco, Texas: Word Inc., 1987), 23.
3. Robert Hillman, "At Home in Dublin," *Los Angeles Times*, April 1987.
4. Liam Mackey, "I Still Haven't Found What I'm Looking For," *(Dublin) Hot Press*, December 1988.

CHAPTER 6: FOR THE REV. MARTIN LUTHER KING—SING!

1. Bill Graham, *The Complete Guide to the Music of U2* (London: Omnibus Press, 1995), 38.
2. Ibid, 41.
3. Robert Hillman, "At Home in Dublin," *Los Angeles Times*, April 1987.
4. Liam Mackey, "I Still Haven't Found What I'm Looking For," *(Dublin) Hot Press*, December 1988.
5. Danny Eccleston, "The Elastic Bono Band," *Q*, November 2000.
6. Joe Jackson, "In Search of Elvis," *Irish Times*, 1 November 1994.
7. Peter Williams and Steve Turner, *Rattle and Hum: The Official Book of the U2 Movie* (London: Pyramid Books, 1988).
8. Steve Turner, *Hungry for Heaven* (Virgin Books, 1988).
9. David Breskin, "Bono: The Rolling Stone Interview," *Rolling Stone*, 8 October 1987.
10. John Waters, *Race of Angels* (Belfast: The Blackstaff Press, 1994), 165.

CHAPTER 7: YOU KNOW I BELIEVE IT

1. Niall Stokes, *Into the Heart* (London: Omnibus Press, 1996), 62.
2. Dave Tomlinson, *The Post-Evangelical* (London: Triangle, 1995), 3.
3. Robert Hillman, "At Home in Dublin," *Los Angeles Times*, April 1987.

4. Bill Graham, *The Complete Guide to the Music of U2* (London: Omnibus Press, 1995), 61.

5. "Top 100 Albums of the Eighties," *Rolling Stone*, 16 November 1989.

6. Niall Stokes, *Into the Heart* (London: Omnibus Press, 1996), 104.

CHAPTER 8: HEARTLAND

1. Anthony DeCurtis, "Rattle and Hum Review," *Rolling Stone*, 17 November 1988.

2. Bono, "Remembering Allen," *Rolling Stone*, 29 May 1997.

CHAPTER 9: REINVENTION

1. H.R. Rookmaker, *Modern Art and the Death of a Culture* (Leicester, England: InterVarsity Press, 1970), 30.

2. Steve Jelbert, *The (London) Independent*, 5 May 2000.

3. Bill Flanagan, *U2 at the End of the World* (London: Bantam Press, 1995), 207.

4. B.P. Fallon, *Faraway So Close* (London: Virgin Books, 1994), 47-48.

5. Bob Dylan, "God on Our Side," *Times They Are a Changing*. Columbia, 1963.

6. Brendan Kennelly, *The Book of Judas* (Newcastle Upon Tyne, England: Bloodaxe Books), 10.

7. David Fricke, "U2 Finds What It's Looking For," *Rolling Stone*, 1 October 1992.

8. Bill Flanagan, *U2: Complete Songs* (1999).

CHAPTER 10: EVERYTHING YOU KNOW IS WRONG

1. *Achtung Baby*, Island Visual Arts, 1992, videocassette.

2. Bill Flanagan, *U2 at the End of the World* (London: Bantam Press, 1995), 13.

3. Neil Postman, *Amusing Ourselves to Death* (New York: Viking Penguin, 1985), 3.

4. Douglas Coupland, *Polaroids from the Dead* (London: Flamingo, 1996), 112.

5. *Achtung Baby*, Island Visual Arts, 1992, videocassette.

6. Joe Jackson, "In Search of Elvis," *Irish Times*, 1 November 1994.

7. C.S. Lewis, *Of This and Other Worlds* (Fount Paperback), 73.

8. David Fricke, "The Wizards of Pop," *Rolling Stone*, 29 May 1997.

9. Joe Jackson, "In Search of Elvis," *Irish Times*, 1 November 1994.

10. C.S. Lewis, *The Screwtape Letters* (London and Glasgow: Fontana Books, 1955), 7.

CHAPTER 11: MIDNIGHT IS WHERE THE DAY BEGINS

1. Niall Stokes, *Into the Heart* (London: Omnibus Press, 1996), 120.

2. Douglas Coupland, *Life After God* (London: Simon and Shuster, 1994), 359.

3. Bill Flanagan, *U2 at the End of the World* (London: Bantam Press, 1995), 202.

4. Ibid, 203.

CHAPTER 12: ... UNDER THE TRASH

1. Robert Hilburn, "Mysterious Ways," *Los Angeles Times*, 1 December 1996.

2. Ibid.

3. Stuart Bailie, "Pop Review," *Vox*, April 1997.

4. Joe Jackson, "Waiting for Beckett," *(Dublin) Hot Press*, 14 February 2001.

5. John Pareles, "Searching for a Sound to Bridge the Decades," *The New York Times*, 9 February 1997.

6. Jim Sullivan, "U2 Is Still U2 Even When Using the Tools of the Techno Trade," *The Boston Globe*, March 1997.

7. Mark Brown, "U2 Goes on a Successful Quest with Pop," *The Orange County (California) Register*, 2 March 1997.

CHAPTER 13: WAKE UP DEAD MAN

1. John Waters, *Race of Angels* (Belfast: The Blackstaff Press, 1994), 1.

2. Bono, Introduction to Pocket Canons Psalms (Edinburgh, Scotland: Canongate Books, 1999), xi.

3. Ibid.

4. Ibid.

5. Neil McCormick, "Growing Up with U2," *The Daily Telegraph*, 1 March 1997.

CHAPTER 14: LEAP OF FAITH

1. "The Million Dollar Hotel press pack" Interference Web page, 1999.

2. Sean O'Hagan, "Billion Dollar Dreams," *Guardian Weekend*, 4 March 2000.

3. Peter Murphy, "The Million Dollar Man," *(Dublin) Hot Press*, 29 March 2000.

4. Sean O'Hagan, "Billion Dollar Dreams," *The (London) Guardian Weekend*, 4 March 2000.

5. Chris Heath, "U2: Band of the Year," *Rolling Stone*, 15 January 2001.

CHAPTER 15: GRACE

1. Salman Rushdie, "Me Too," *(London) Sunday Times Culture*, 3 June 2001.
2. Aimee Mann, "4th of July," *Whatever*. Imago Recording Co., 1993.
3. Neil McCormick, "What Bob and Bono Did in Rome," *The (London) Daily Telegraph*, 1 October 1999.
4. John Leland, "Can Bono Save the Third World?" *Newsweek*, 1 February 2000.
5. Ibid.
6. Ibid.
7. Olaf Tyaransen, "U2: The Final Frontier," *(Dublin) Hot Press*, 8 November 2000.
8. Danny Eccleston, "The Elastic Bono Band," *Q*, November 2000.
9. Joe Jackson, "Waiting for Beckett," *(Dublin) Hot Press*, 14 February 2001.
10. Ibid.
11. Ibid.
12. Chris Heath, "U2: Band of the Year," *Rolling Stone*, 15 January 2001.
13. Chris Heath, "U2 Tour: From the Heart," *Rolling Stone*, 10 May 2001.

CHAPTER 16: THE GOAL IS SOUL

1. Watchman Nee, *The Breaking of the Outer Man and the Release of the Spirit* (Anaheim, California: Living Stream Ministry, 1997), 79.
2. Frederick Buechner, *Wishful Thinking* (New York: Harper Collins, 1973, 1993), 107.

CHAPTER 17: PROPHETS TURN PASTORS

1. Anthony Bozza, "People of the Year: Bono," *Rolling Stone*, 19 November 2001.
2. Niall Stokes, "Matter of Life and Death," *(Dublin) Hot Press Annual 2002*, December 2001.
3. Ibid.
4. Jonathan Ross, BBC One's *Friday Night with Jonathan Ross*, November 2004.
5. "500 Greatest Songs of All Time," *Rolling Stone* (*www.rollingstone.com/news/story/_/id/6596661/500songs*), November 2004.
6. Niall Stokes, "Matter of Life and Death," *(Dublin) Hot Press Annual 2002*, December 2001.

CHAPTER 18: TONIGHT THANK GOD IT'S THEM INSTEAD OF YOU

1. Alastair Campbell, *Alastair Campbell Meets Bono*, Channel 5 (UK), October 2004.

2. Chrissy Iley, "Group Therapy," *The Sunday Times Magazine*, November 2004.

3. Kelley Eskridge, "Promise Me You Will Tell Them," *www.U2.com*, October 2004.

4. Jonathan Ross, BBC One's *Friday Night with Jonathan Ross*, November 2004.

5. Ibid.

6. Stephen McGinty, "Bono Still Hasn't Found What He Is Looking For," *Debt Relief, The Scotsman*, 25 September 2004.

7. Bono, "Diaries from the Road" (*www.DATA.org*), December 2002.

8. Ibid.

9. Ibid.

10. Transcript of Bono's Speech at Labour Party Conference, *www.DATA.org*, September 2004.

11. Larrissa Nolan, "Ali Launches Own Fair Trade Clothing Brand," *(Dublin) Sunday Independent*, 7 November 2004.

12. Josh Tyrangiel, "Bono," *Time*, 4 March 2002.

13. Ben Okri, *A Way of Being Free* (London: Phoenix House, 1997), 112.

14. Bono, *How to Dismantle an Atomic Bomb* (book edition). Island Records, 2004.

15. John Masterson, "Ali's Other Eden," *(Dublin) Sunday Independent*, 6 March 2005.

16. Josh Tyrangiel, "Bono," *Time*, 4 March 2002.

CHAPTER 19: AMERICAN PRAYER

1. Cathleen Falsani, "Bono's American Prayer," *Christianity Today*, February 2003.

2. Cathleen Falsani, "Bono Issues Blunt Message to Christians," *Chicago Sun-Times*, December 2002.

3. Bono, "Diaries from the Road" (*www.DATA.org*), 2002.

4. Cathleen Falsani, "Bono's American Prayer," *Christianity Today*, February 2003.

5. Bono, "Diaries from the Road" (*www.DATA.org*), 2002.

6. Cathleen Falsani, "Bono's American Prayer," *Christianity Today*, February 2003.

7. Ibid.

8. Ibid.

9. Bono, *The aWAKE Project*, (Nashville: W Publishing Group, 2002), 80.

10. Angela Pancella, "The Nashville Summit: Behind the Scene with Bono, DATA and the

Christian Music Industry" (*www.U2.com*), July 2003.

11. Angela Pancella, Sidebar: "Jars of Clay's Dan Haseltine on the Nashville Summit" (*www.U2.com*), 2003.

12. Mark Allan Powell, Encyclopedia of Contemporary Christian Music, (Peabody, Massachusetts: Hendrickson Publishing, 2002), 838.

13. Roberta Croteau, "Ready for His Close Up," *CCM* magazine, 2004.

14. Eugene Peterson, *Get Up Off Your Knees* (Cambridge, Massachusetts: Cowley Publishing, 2003), xiv.

15. Ibid.

16. Cathleen Falsani, "Bono's American Prayer," *Christianity Today*, February 2003.

17. Editorial, "Bono's Thin Ecclesiology," *Christianity Today*, February 2003.

18. Ibid.

19. Chuck Klosterman, "Mysterious Days," *Spin*, November 2004.

CHAPTER 20: IT COULD BE ABOUT GOD

1. Adrian Deevoy, "It Could Be About God," *Blender*, October 2004.

2. Edna Gundersen, *USA Today*, November 2004.

3. Milan Kundura, *The Unbearable Lightness of Being* (New York: Perennial Classics, 1984, 1999).

4. *www.U2.com*.

5. Christopher Nolan, "I Learn to Bow," *Dam-Burst of Dreams*, (Weidenfeld & Nicolson, 1981).

6. Jim Wallis, *The Soul of Politics* (London: Fount Paperbacks, 1995), 258.

7. Stuart Clark, "On Your Marks, Get Set—Vertigo!," *(Dublin) Hot Press*, December 2004.

8. *www.U2.com*.

9. *How to Dismantle an Atomic Bomb* (book edition). Island Records, 2004.

10. Adam Block, "Pure Bono," *Mother Jones*, May 1989.

11. Eddie Rowley, "My Family Are My Rock," *Sunday World*, 26 December 2004.

12. Cathleen Falsani, "Bono's American Prayer," *Christianity Today*, February 2003.

13. *www.U2.com*.

14. Ibid.

15. "Meet the Bomb Squad," *Irish Times*, 23 December 2004.

16. Steve Turner, *King of Twist* (London: Hodder and Stoughton, 1992).

17. Chris Iley, "Group Therapy," *The Sunday Times Magazine*, November 2004.

CHAPTER 21: EVERYONE

1. Cathleen Falsani, "Bono Credits Church for Leading AIDS Fight," *Chicago Sun-Times*, 5 December 2003.

2. Michka Assayas, *Bono: In Conversation with Michka Assayas* (Riverhead Books, 2005), 64.

3. Martin Wroe, Vertigo Tour Program, 2005.

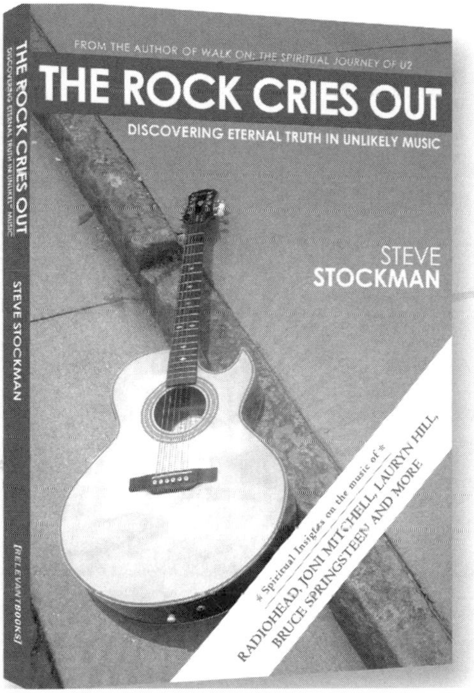

ALSO FROM STEVE STOCKMAN

AVAILABLE FROM RELEVANT BOOKS

ABOUT THE AUTHOR

Steve Stockman is a Presbyterian Chaplain at Queen's University in Belfast. He is a regular speaker at universities, colleges conferences, and festivals across the world, and he has his own radio show on BBC Radio Ulster. He has recently spent time at Regent College in Vancouver, Canada, as a writer-in-residence. His passion for social justice and Christian spirituality has attracted him to the music of U2, which he has been using in his sermons and writings for twenty years. He has also published six collections of poetry, an album, and *The Rock Cries Out: Discovering Eternal Truth in Unlikely Music* (Relevant Books). He is married to Janice, and they have two daughters, Caitlin and Jasmine.